THE CENTERED LIFE

THE CENTERED LIFE

AN INTRODUCTION TO

I CHING

BOOK OF CHANGES

THE UNIVERSAL PRINCIPLES OF LIVING
AND ITS AMAZING ORACLE

FRANKLIN HUM YUN

Pentland Press, Inc.
www.pentlandpressusa.com

Disclaimer/Warning

The divination directions and predictions described in this book are based on the author's interpretation for reader's information only, and their accuracy cannot be guaranteed in their specific applications by different individuals. The author and publisher are not responsible for any loss or harm that might result from the use of any prediction or divination method described in this book.

PUBLISHED BY PENTLAND PRESS, INC.
5122 Bur Oak Circle, Raleigh, North Carolina 27612
United States of America
919-782-0281

ISBN 1-57197-269-2
Library of Congress Control Number: 00-136204

Printed in the United States of America

To the late Dr. Elizabeth McBroom, my professor at the University of Southern California School of Social Work, who helped me learn and grow in the new culture without losing the strength of my old culture.

Table of Contents

The Lower Section

List of Figures

Acknowledgements

My fascination with *I Ching* began early in my life. It took me many years of study to understand this classic. The idea of writing a book on *I Ching* came to my mind a few years ago. In the process of studying *I Ching*, I felt that there was a need for an introductory book on *I Ching* that would help a reader gain a basic yet comprehensive understanding that reflects the meaning in the original *I Ching* texts without extensive research and references.

A chain of events guided me to write this book. Throughout my life, I read books on *I Ching* in Chinese and Korean. In the late 1960s, a social work colleague, Marion Mills, gave me James Legge's *The I Ching, The Book of Changes* as a gift. This book was my first introduction to an English text on *I Ching*. In the succeeding years, I read many other *I Ching* books written in English, and each provided me with different and unique perspectives.

In *I Ching,* "crossing the great river" represents undertaking a venture. The process of writing this book on *I Ching* is my venture into "crossing a great river." Hexagram #61, Central Sincerity, explains that a person with a sincere heart can overcome any difficulty in life, comparable to crossing a great river in an unsinkable boat with every advantage. The sincere efforts of friends who were with me in this crossing helped me keep the boat afloat during my journey and reach the other shore. They made my journey a friendly and beneficial undertaking, in spite of some arduous times.

In 1992, the late Dr. Elizabeth McBroom, who had been my professor at the University of Southern California and my mentor since I came to the United States in 1965, gave me useful advice and encouragement to write this book. Until she passed away in the spring of 1997, she continued to be most helpful in advising me and in editing the first section of the book.

The most heartwarming experience I had in this project was with a friend who journeyed with me during this crossing. Mrs. Barbara Uchida Mills, my professional colleague for many years, helped me with dedication and enthusiasm, spending many hours reading my manuscripts, asking questions, and raising points for discussion.

My sincere thanks to Dr. Hwa-Wei Lee, Dean Emeritus, University Libraries, Ohio University, for writing the validating foreword and for all the help he has given me.

Members of Saddleback Valley IBM-PC User Group helped me solve many computer problems I encountered as a novice computer user, especially Ms. Marka Quinn, who helped me with her versatile computer knowledge and skill.

Writing this book became a family project. Dr. Seung S. Yun of Ohio University has given me a great deal of help in writing this book for publication. It was his great-grandfather from whom I received my education in Chinese literature. My thanks to my daughter Ogyoun, for designing the cover of the book and work on illustrations, and her husband Young Lim for their encouragement and help whenever I needed it. In writing this book, I focused on my grandchildren, Eunice and Jason, and other English-speaking future generations of Asians, with my hope that this book will help them understand their root cultures. Most importantly, I want to thank my wife Grace for her sincere and enduring support all these years and for making this book a reality.

My *I Ching* Odyssey

My own *I Ching* journey began as a young child. I was born in a small farming hamlet surrounded by a high mountain on the east coast of South Korea, where a population of about five hundred of mostly the Yun clan lived. At the foot of this mountain, there was a small spring water pond, fresh and clean, which was the source of drinking water for the village people. It was called Infant Spring. On the hillside above this spring stood a small house set aside for the study of Chinese literature, and it was called Infant Spring Institute.

Later in my life, as I studied *I Ching,* I discovered that the Chinese character for "Infant Spring" was the same character as the name of *I Ching* Hexagram #4. I concluded that the spring and the institute were deliberately named "Infant Spring" to represent the theme of the hexagram, which is the inexperienced and the young. This hexagram is the natural sequence to Hexagram #3 Germination, and it emphasizes education of the young, which encompasses both intellectual and moral development.

My great uncle taught me Chinese literature in my early boyhood. He told me about our scholar ancestor who was renowned for his knowledge of Chinese literature and had written a book on *I Ching*, and in whose honor the Infant Spring Institute was built. Thus, the seed of my curiosity and interest in *I Ching* was planted in the early years of my life. Ever since, my fascination with *I Ching* has persisted.

During the turbulent years of World War II, the Korean War, and the ensuing period of political, social, and economic upheavals in Korea, I did not have much time to pursue my interest in *I Ching*. However, I continued to read related literature whenever I had the opportunity. I moved to the United States in 1965 and continued my career in social work. In the late 1960s, a colleague gave me the Dover edition of Legge's

The I Ching. It was my first exposure to *I Ching* written in English. I began reading other books on *I Ching* written in English.

It has taken many years of studying *I Ching* books in Chinese, Korean, and English for me to grasp the scope and depth of this classic, and my understanding of the classic is still evolving. Though arduous and time-consuming, the efforts have been very worthwhile and inspiring. *I Ching* teachings have served as my primary guide in my pursuit to gain a wider and deeper understanding of life and cultures. Its greatest influence on me has been the incorporation of the *I Ching* principle of the centered life in my approach to living. In examining a life situation, I deliberately look at the total picture and attempt to make a balanced decision or choice that will keep me centered and stable.

I have been convinced for many years that this classic should be read more widely to benefit both the individual and society. To this end, I came to the realization that an introductory book on *I Ching* teachings and divination will help a reader new to *I Ching* to understand the essence of *I Ching*.

My *I Ching* odyssey has now led me to write this book. It is a natural development of space, time, events, and myself, with much learning and "good fortune" along the way.

Foreword

About two years ago, I had the pleasure of reading the first draft of Mr. Franklin Hum Yun's writing on *I Ching (The Book of Changes).* It is widely known that *I Ching* is perhaps the oldest of the ancient Chinese classics written by a number of sages over a period of three thousand years. The ancestor-king *Fu Hsi* (c. 3000 B.C.), who invented the trigrams (the *pa kua*), began it and then it went through numerous editions and interpretations by Chinese scholars in the ensuing two thousand years. However, few of us, even among contemporary learned Chinese, have read it in its entirety or understand the essence of it. I was one of them until I had the opportunity of reading Mr. Yun's writing.

Throughout Mr. Yun's teaching and other professional careers in Korea and California, he has been very attracted to the *I Ching*, which is also highly regarded and respected in Korea, and he has devoted a great deal of time to studying it. This longtime devotion and love have enabled Mr. Yun to write this profound and scholarly book of *I Ching* in English, which is very easy to read and understand for those readers who may not be able to read the texts in Chinese or Korean.

I Ching is generally known as a book on the ancient Chinese method of divination that uses the symbols for the two opposing forces in the universe, *yin* and *yang*. Today, it remains a popular medium of divination for predicting the future and for obtaining direction for a future course of action. Some scholars also study it for clues to the development of the Chinese language. Dr. Everett Kleinjans, a contemporary scholar of East Asian philosophies, regards *I Ching* as a basis for reflective wisdom, theoretical understanding, and pragmatic application. He sees that *I Ching* can be used (1) for one's own spiritual growth regardless of the religion one adheres to; (2) for an understanding of medicine, management, communication, conflict, and other human thoughts and activities; and (3) for providing insight into everyday decisions.*

*Everett Kleinjans, *Living in Harmony with the 1 China.* (Singapore: The Institute of East Asian Philosophies, National University of Singapore, 1989), p. 12.

According to Mr. Yun, what makes *I Ching* a respected and enduring classic is its scope and depth beyond the realm of divination. It presents a philosophy of life based on *Tao* (nature's way), and it provides universal principles of human conduct to follow. These principles have greatly influenced Asian philosophies and religions (Taoism, Confucianism, Buddhism, etc.) as well as other aspects of Asian cultures.

The sages who developed *I Ching* present the conceptualization of the universe, from how the universe was created to how the universe operates through continual interaction of all its forces and elements. These interactions result in constant changes in recurring cycles.

In the midst of constant changes, it is essential to strive for the center to maintain equilibrium or balance. *I Ching* affirms maintaining the center as the integral force in the universe, and it emphasizes the importance of having human conduct follow that mode. The *I Ching* divination is based on the fundamental truths of the universe; thus, its predictions will be reliable, and one's conduct will be proper and propitious if the principle of being in the center is applied to everyday living.

Mr. Yun's book on *Centered Life* is an introductory book of *I Ching*. It presents the key aspects of *I Ching* within the context of their original meanings, including historical and cultural perspectives. These aspects are covered in sufficient depth so that the reader can gain basic but comprehensive understanding of this classic.

I Ching consists of sixty-four hexagrams representing the whole universe. Through the analysis of the individual lines and sets of lines and the interpretation of its symbols, images, and movements, one can obtain predictions of good or bad fortune and guidance in living a virtuous life. The teachings and divination of *I Ching* have relevance in today's world for those who seek wisdom and a virtuous life.

Mr. Yun's book is a significant contribution to the understanding of *I Ching*. It is also an important guide to our way of life and thinking in the rapidly changing world of the new millennium. I hope all readers of this great Chinese classic will find it to be intellectually and spiritually stimulating.

Hwa-Wei Lee, Ph.D.
Dean Emeritus, University Libraries
Ohio University
Athens, Ohio 45701, U.S.A.

January 29, 2000

Preface

The prevailing belief system in Asian cultures is based on two forces, yin and yang, contained in the unified primal energy called *Chi.* Yin and yang interact to produce all the phenomena in the universe. Heaven is the yang force that originates everything, but without form. Earth is the yin force that gives form to what it receives from Heaven.

Using two graphic symbols, a broken line (--) as yin and an unbroken line (—) as yang, to form sixty-four hexagrams that represent the total universe, *I Ching* provides the universal truth for man to follow. It explains nature's way (*Tao*[1*]) as the universal principle to help man find a way to resolve his predicaments through its method of divination and to provide moral standards to guide him in his pursuit of righteous living. *I Ching,* commonly translated as the *Book of Changes,*[2] explains the principles of *Tao* through its hexagrams. The way in which *I Ching* explains all the phenomena in the universe is both profound and mysterious. What *I Ching* teaches is profound because it encompasses all the phenomena in the universe. It is mysterious because it is full of symbolism and metaphors, and the divination is beyond the realm of human knowledge. The universe of *I Ching* unfolds the wonders and mysteries of nature's way, like the heaven that displays the splendors of stars in the summer skies and the earth that brings forth colorful flowers and harmonious songs of birds in the spring.

The origin of *I Ching* divination, which replaced the cumbersome turtle divination, can be traced back five thousand years in China. The book of *I Ching* was originally an ancient Chinese book on divination based on the principle of yin and yang to guide people out of their confusion and trouble. In the fifth century B.C., Confucius expanded upon *I Ching* to deal with the fundamental principles of human conduct. His *I Ching* commentaries have served as some of the most important

* Numbered notes are listed in the back of the book, beginning on page 347.

writings on statecraft and virtuous conduct in China and other Asian countries and have pervasively influenced the development of Asian cultures. Throughout Asia, *I Ching* has been studied as the source of wisdom in fields as varied as governance, philosophy, ethics, medicine, cosmology, astrology, numerology, and art.

Despite the importance of *I Ching* in understanding the Asian cultures, serious studies of this classic in the Western world have been limited to a small number of people, principally scholars, even though its divination methods are widely known. Western scholars began to study *I Ching* in the seventeenth century. The German philosopher G. W. Leibniz, the discoverer of the binary system, established that *I Ching* hexagrams were based on the binary system.[3] Since then, several Western scholars have successfully translated *I Ching* texts into Western languages. Although the scholars made efforts to preserve the original meanings of the text, deciphering its symbolisms and understanding the metaphors are difficult tasks, and these factors have resulted in different interpretations.

The study of *I Ching* can benefit anyone who aspires to attain self-realization, as well as those who want to have a greater understanding of Asian cultures. *I Ching* study contributes to the enlightenment of one's mind as it teaches the universal principles of righteous living. Its divination process activates a person's subconscious mind about problematic life situations to provide direction as to a course of action.

My purpose in writing this book is to help the readers meet their aspiration for self-realization and to gain more understanding of Asian cultures without an inordinate investment of time and effort. A plethora of *I Ching* books in English has been published, each with different emphasis and interpretation. This book is my humble undertaking to present *I Ching* from the perspective of "the centered life" as its main theme. This introductory book on *I Ching* offers a concise but comprehensive overview of *I Ching* and the analysis and interpretation of each of the sixty-four hexagrams, which include key attributes, essential teaching, structural analysis, interpretation, and divination direction for the hexagram as a whole and its individual lines.

The basic focus of books on *I Ching* is the interpretation of its hexagrams through the analysis of the hexagram structure and the hexagram images in the original judgment texts of King *Wan* and the Duke of *Chou*. Where relevant, this book also includes explanations to clarify the original texts from Confucius's *Ten Wings*, the most important commentary texts on *I Ching*. Confucius wrote the ten texts based on his interpretation of *I Ching*. They provide the philosophical basis for family and social interaction, governing, morality, and the centered life.

Although this book is intended for entry-level study, the reader who is interested in a deeper study of *I Ching* may find this book helpful because of its different perspective.

Current global economic and cultural interactions and the concurrent policies of Asian countries call upon everyone to develop a deeper understanding of the Asian cultures. The study of *I Ching* provides insights into the belief systems of Confucianism, Taoism, and Buddhism, as well as important traditional cultural features of Asia in such areas as reverence for nature, ancestral worship, filial piety, family relationships, social stratification, the governance of people, and the use of authority. These traditions and others can be traced back to the time of Confucius and before. Today, when Asian societies are experiencing rapid and sometimes tumultuous social and economic changes, the insights of *I Ching* are particularly valuable in understanding the tenets of Asian cultures.

I chose *The Centered Life* as the title of this book, instead of *I Ching* or The Book of Changes (see chapter X: *I Ching* and the Centered Life). The concept of the centered life is the essence of *I Ching* teachings and the spirit of *Tao*. *I Ching* teaches that man should follow *Tao*, the principles of yin and yang that operate in heaven and on the earth. Everything in the universe, including man, is in the state of constant change. For principled human conduct, *Tao* emphasizes the importance of being in the center or staying within the perimeters of the arena as the yin and yang forces constantly interplay, thereby maintaining a balanced state between the two opposing forces.

In writing this book, I am especially indebted to James Legge's translation of *I Ching*, first published in 1899 as Volume XVI of *The Sacred Books of the East* and later under the title *The I Ching.** Legge translated the Chinese texts word for word with painstaking efforts to reflect the original work as closely as possible. Although his transliteration of the judgment texts is difficult to read and understand, it most closely reflects the original Chinese texts. He discovered " . . . that the written characters of the Chinese are not representations of words, but symbols of ideas, and that the combination of them in composition is not a representation of what the writer would say, but of what he thinks."**

To convey this perspective in this book, the analysis and interpretation for each hexagram begin with Legge's hexagram judgment translation. In *I Ching* textbooks, the analysis of each hexagram is done

*James Legge, (The *I Ching*; *The Sacred Books of China*: New York, N.Y. 10014: Dover Publication, Inc. 1966).
**ibid., p. xv.

within the context of the hexagram theme. The interpretation consists of two parts: (1) the hexagram judgment, or the interpretation of the whole hexagram, and (2) the line statements, or the interpretation of each of the six lines of the hexagram. A different format was developed in this book to facilitate a beginning reader's understanding. This book contains a concise statement of what each hexagram teaches under the heading, "Essence of the Hexagram." To help guide readers who are interested in divination, a "Divination Direction" for the hexagram as a whole and for each line of the hexagram, based on the analysis and interpretation of the hexagram and its lines, provides a course of action for the seeker.

I Ching is a mysterious book based on the way of nature. Its extensive symbolism and metaphors have psychological, historical, and cultural meanings that make translating the texts extremely difficult. Historically, even among Chinese scholars, many different interpretations have been offered. In interpreting *I Ching* texts, I have attempted to reflect the spirit and the meaning of the original texts as closely as possible, in order to aid the reader in understanding this unique and important classic.

With uncluttered minds and discerning observations, the ancient Chinese sages[4] developed *I Ching*. Through the use of sixty-four hexagrams, *I Ching* explains universal phenomena multidimensionally in relation to time, space, event, and human psychology. This ancient classic is as relevant today as ever, and it presents continuous challenges to people who are in search of universal truth.

Part I: Overview of *I Ching*

Introduction to *I Ching*

1

Brief History

Originally, *I Ching* consisted of two ancient Chinese texts written by *King Wan* and his son, Duke of *Chou,* dating back to twelfth century B.C. The English translation of *I Ching* is "Book of Changes." The Chinese character "*I*" (pronounced ē) means "changes," and "*Ching*" refers to a canonical text. The character "*I*" is formed from the character "sun" placed above that of "moon" 易. It symbolizes the interaction between the two heavenly bodies, the sun and the moon, which influence changes in everything on the earth. Besides "changes," "*I*" has other meanings, including unchanging truth, simple and easy.

Most scholars acknowledge that the character "*I*" in the book title *I Ching* refers to interactive changes between earth and heaven (yin and yang). Some scholars postulate that the character "*I*" in the book title refers to the simple or easy divination process. The process is simple or easy because only two lines, one broken (— —) and the other unbroken (——), are used to conduct the divination, in contrast to the extremely complicated procedures in the tortoise divination prevalent thirty-three hundred years ago. Another theory promotes the idea that the Chinese character "*I*" was adopted because it resembles the shape of a lizard, which changes its color.

In the Neolithic period in China, three thousand to five thousand years ago, the Chinese rulers practiced turtle-shell divination for governance. In turtle divination, a hot iron rod was applied to a tortoise to produce cracks on its shell, which a diviner deciphered to tell the fortune. This was a very cumbersome and difficult procedure.

A new divination process gradually evolved with the conceptual development of yin and yang. The concept of yin and yang, which is the basis of *I Ching*, is generally attributed to *Fu Hsi,* one of the first five legendary emperors of China in the Neolithic period. The *I Ching* states that *Fu Hsi* studied the heaven and the earth and devised eight trigrams, a vertical alignment of three yin line (--) and/or yang line (—) symbols, to represent all things in nature and their qualities and characteristics. From his creation of the trigrams, a new divination process gradually evolved, with the trigrams replacing the turtle.

The next major development in *I Ching* was in 1143 B.C. The famous King *Wan*, one of the founders of the *Chou* dynasty who reigned from 1171 to 1122 B.C., created hexagrams from *Fu Hsi*'s eight trigrams by combining two trigrams, placing one on top of the other, a total of six lines. All the possible combinations of the eight trigrams totaled sixty-four hexagrams. King *Wan* wrote a text consisting of a judgment (prediction of fortune) for each of the sixty-four hexagrams. He based these judgments on his analysis and interpretation of each hexagram. A few decades later, his son, the equally famous Duke of *Chou,* wrote a text with a prediction for each of the six lines of each hexagram, which are referred to as line statements. The use of these hexagram texts simplified the divination process, although the hexagrams were still difficult for the diviners to interpret.

Confucius (571–479 B.C.) and his followers expounded on the *I Ching* judgments of King *Wan* and the line statements of the Duke *of Chou* to clarify their meaning and to develop a philosophy of life and governance based on *Tao*. These commentaries of Confucius are contained in ten books called *Shi I,* or *Ten Wings.*[5] The texts of *Ten Wings* provide commentaries that include the interpretation of the original judgments and line statements, the structural analysis of the hexagrams, the significance of the sequential arrangement of the sixty-four hexagrams, and the divination method and process.

From these developments came the two works most important to the *I Ching* legacy: *I Ching,* consisting of the two original texts written by Kang *Wan* and the Duke of *Chou*, and *Ten Wings*, which is one of the five Confucian classics[6] or canonical texts. *I Ching* is valued as the most important classic because of its profound influence over the belief systems and cultures in China and other Asian countries over many centuries. *Ten Wings*, especially the sections referred to as "Great Commentary," elevated *I Ching* from a book of divination to a classic text on proper human conduct, and it became the most revered of all the Confucian classics. In his later years, Confucius was said to have become so devoted to the study of *I Ching* that the leather strap on his *I Ching* text wore out three times. In the *Analects*, the collection of his commentaries, Confucius is quoted as saying, "If more years were added to my life, I would spend fifty years to the study of the book and might then be able to avoid falling into major faults."*

In its final form, *I Ching* consists of the sixty-four hexagrams (the two ancient texts of the judgment and the line statements of each hexagram), and *Ten Wings*.

I Ching Terms

Many *I Ching* terms are symbolic and metaphysical, and difficult to define. The following terms require some explanation. The terms are arranged roughly in the order of their significance. In this book, the capitalized terms "*Heaven*" or "*Earth*" describe the virtues embodied in those terms, and lowercased "*heaven*" or "*earth*" describes the physical aspects of each term.

I Ching (Yi King): Book of Changes.

Tao (Dao): Nature's way or the true way, which is above form. *Tao* is referred to as "constancy," the concept of one constant truth in the continually changing world. The operational principles of *Tao* are anchored to and represented by nature, and each operational principle is also referred to as *Tao* or "the way." "Correct *Tao*" means to follow the operational principles of *Tao*.

Tai Chi: The unified primal energy called *Chi* that contains the two opposing energies of yin and yang. *Tai Chi* is the prototype of all the energies in the universe from which everything was created. It is referred to as *Tao*, "the Supreme Ultimate."

Chi: The primal energy or the universal force that is represented in *Tai Chi* with the yin and yang energies, which are the cause and the foundation for all the phenomena in the universe.

Heaven (*Khien*): The originator of everything in the universe, as manifested by the yang force; heaven; the opposite of earth, and generally represented by the sun. Connotes creativity, leadership, power, and greatness.

Earth (*Khwan* or *K'un*): The receiver of what Heaven gives, which it transforms into myriad of patterns, as manifested by yin force. The place where human beings and other lives live. Connotes nourishing and compliance.

Virtue (*The*): The superior inner quality of a person that has the unadulterated mind-set with "an eye" that correctly sees things in order that the person will conduct himself in accordance with the way of nature.

*ibid., p. 1, (*Analects*, VII, xvi).

Judgment (*Tuan* or *Thwan*): The prediction of good or ill fortune that King *Wan* attached to each hexagram. Judgment is used to predict the fortune of the question that is posed in the divination. The order of the fortunes from best to worst is: "good fortune," "no error," "no blame," "regret," "remorse," and "bad or ill fortune."

Line statement (*Hsiao Tz'u*): The prediction of fortune for each line of the hexagram. The order of the fortunes is the same as for the hexagram judgment.

The Mean: The moral principle in both *I Ching* and Confucianism of capturing the center or the middle (on the balance), in compliance with *Tao*. The person who abides by the principles of the Mean is said to "practice (the virtues of) the Mean," or "observe the Mean."

Good fortune: Fortune that augurs well for the situation in question, as it complies with the principles of *Tao*. A prediction of "great good fortune" or "fundamental good fortune" refers to a gain because everything is in harmony with *Tao*.

No blame: Fortune in which the conduct will produce no gain but is acceptable despite some shortcomings found in the hexagram readings because one's mistake can be corrected and damage can be avoided. It is variously translated as "there will be no error," "he will incur no blame," or "there will be no blame."

No error: Fortune in which you are taking a correct course of action and should continue with it.

Regret: Fortune in which one's conduct has minor deviation from complying with the principles of *Tao*.

Remorse: "Regret" and "remorse" are interchangeable. If one's conduct is regrettable, the conduct is also remorseful. Fortune of remorse suggests that one should take corrective action.

Ill (bad) fortune: Fortune that augurs ill because the hexagram meanings are in disharmony with the principles of *Tao*. Refers to a loss.

Progress and success: The result of good fortune when a conduct or condition is in harmony with *Tao*. The Chinese character for "progress and success" is often translated as "to prevail."

Advantageous: Opportune time to make a move to receive favorable results. It is expressed as "fitting" to act.

Disadvantageous: The opposite of "advantageous," meaning that it is untimely to make a move. It is also expressed as "unfitting" to act to resolve a difficult situation.

Cross the great stream: To undertake an important or major task involving great risk in the pursuit of one's goal.

To be firm and correct: To strictly abide by the principles of *Tao*, persevering against all odds.

The great man (*Dai ren*): A person who practices the principles of *Tao*. A sage or a man of great influence.

The wise and noble (*chun tzu*): Often referred to as the "superior man" or the noble man; the man who actualizes the principles of *Tao*; the virtuous and wise man.

The small man (*Xiao ren*): The man who is lacking in the virtues of *Tao*. The ordinary man who has little interest in practicing *Tao*. The man of lower status or the petty man.

The Origin of Yin and Yang

2

Tai Chi

I Ching is the concept of two opposing universal forces, yin and yang, and the transformation that results from their interactions in time and space. These two opposite forces cannot exist independently of each other.

In the beginning there was a unified force called *Tai Chi*, the original being or "Supreme Ultimate," symbolized by a sphere. *Tai Chi* was made up of the primal energy called *Chi* as the unified force of the two opposing energies of yin and yang. When this unified force became separated into two distinct and opposing energies, yin and yang began to interact, creating the universe. *I Ching* refers to this phenomenon of the splitting of *Tai Chi* into yin and yang as "spiritual" or mysterious.

Ten Wings, Confucius's commentaries on *I Ching*, explains that one yin and one yang constitute *Tao,* and the coming or going of yin or yang creates changes (the "*I*" of *I Ching).* The coming or going of yin or yang refers not only to the mutual pushing of the yin and yang lines in a hexagram, but also to their movements in all nature, such as that of the moon (yin) and the sun (yang). When the moon rises, the sun sets, and vice versa; when cold (yin) arrives, heat (yang) dissipates or goes away, and vice versa.

This interaction of yin and yang is the basis of *I Ching* and its hexagram interpretations. *I Ching* is the study of nature's way or *Tao* as it is manifested in the interactions of yin and yang. *Tao* is so fundamental that nothing in the universe exists outside of *Tao*. The Chinese philosopher *Lao Tzu*[7], the father of Taoism, advocated that man should strictly follow the *Tao* of nature and not create any man-made rules that do not conform with the natural laws.

The *Tai Chi* Symbol

Although the unified energy of *Tai Chi* developed into two separate energies of yin and yang, each carries within itself a prototype of *Tai Chi*. Thus, yin contains yang, its opposite energy, and yang contains yin, its opposite energy.

When the entire sphere of *Tai Chi* is white, the symbol denotes a totally spiritual state and represents the attribute of Heaven. When the entire sphere is black, it denotes the material state and represents the attribute of Earth. Different *Tai Chi* emblems represent the state of the yin and yang energies in *Tai Chi*.

Figure 1—*Tai Chi* Symbol

This emblem is the fundamental *Tai Chi* symbol. It represents the static yin (black) and yang (white) forces.

  ◐   This is another representation of Tai Chi. This emblem illustrates the dynamism of the yin and yang forces. The yang energy is light and therefore goes upward, while the yin energy is heavy and goes downward.

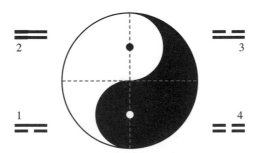

Figure 2—*Tai Chi* in motion

(The dotted lines, four symbols of elements, and numbers are added for the reader's reference.)

This emblem, with the black spot in the yang (white) area and the white spot in the yin (black) area, is another representation of *Tai Chi*, indicating that each force contains its opposite force within itself. The white area of the *Tai Chi* sphere is called *major yang*,[8] and the black area *major yin*. The yang force in the yin area (white spot) is called *minor yang*, and the yin force in the yang area (black spot) is called *minor yin*.

In contrast to the fundamental *Tai Chi* emblem that symbolizes the static yin and yang forces, this emblem represents the forces in motion, with the energies of yin and yang moving clockwise. The first quarter of the circle (1) is minor yang (represented by the white spot) and symbolizes Wood ☳. The second quarter of the circle (2) is major yang and symbolizes Fire ☲. The third quarter of the circle (3) is minor yin (represented by the black spot) and symbolizes Metal ☱. The fourth quarter of the circle (4) is major yin and symbolizes Water ☵.

Attributes of Yin and Yang

The two forces, yin and yang, that resulted from the separation of the force in *Tai Chi* have distinct individual attributes. In *I Ching,* yang, the masculine force, is symbolized by an unbroken line ▬, and yin, the feminine force, by a broken line ▬▬. The major attributes of yang are: heaven, light, life, male, strong, competent, aggressive, sunshine, south, above, anterior, hard, light (in weight) and initiator. The major attributes of yin are: earth, darkness, death, female, weak, gentle, incompetent, submissive, shadow, north, below, posterior, soft, heavy, and receptor.

Attributes of the Five Elements

When the yin line and the yang line were placed on top of each other, four different symbols resulted, and they represented all the phenomena in the universe. These four symbols were called four *Hsiang* (images).

☵ Water   ☲ Fire
☱ Metal   ☳ Wood

Earth is a basic integral part of each of these four images and works as the stabilizing force. Water, Fire, Wood, Metal, and Earth were later called collectively *Wu Hsing,* or the five elements. The concept of the five elements is firmly embedded in the Asian cultures and has many applications that utilize the dynamism of this energy cycle or movement. As an example, a theorem in Oriental medicine is based on the concept of the five elements, relating each element to each of five main organs, five senses, five major tastes, and five complexions. (The health condition of each main organ is reflected in the person's complexion.) Knowing the attributes of each of the five elements is important in understanding *I Ching* and how the concept of the five elements is applied in Asian cultures. Along with other symbols, the symbolic representations of these elements serve as interpretative devices for *I Ching* divination. Some of the major attributes of each of the five elements are listed below.

Water: Formless, penetrating, shaped in the form of its container, nourishing, sustaining life, moving downward, letting things happen naturally, dangerous (deep water), moon, kidney, bladder, fear, black,. salty.

Fire: Bright, clear, intelligent, civilized, starts slowly and spreads quickly, transforms things, destroys things, moving upward, sun, light, heart, small intestine, joy, red, bitter.

Wood: Crooked, slow in movement, embracing care and protection, covering, persevering, genetic or spiritual roots, moving and spreading in all directions, boat, liver, gallbladder, anger, blue, sour.

Metal: Static, cutting, moldable or needing to be shaped, hard and firm, inflexible, lungs, large intestine, sorrow, white, hot in taste.

Earth: The most stable foundation for the other four elements. Spleen and stomach, worries and thoughts, yellow, sweet.

The five images that represent the dynamism of *Tai Chi* also portray the cyclical energy movement, which is expressed in the workings of nature. In Figure 2 above, the emblem has been divided into four quarters to illustrate the cyclical movement of energy. In the daily cycle, the first quarter represents morning until noon, in which yin energy is gradually being taken over by yang energy; the second quarter represents the afternoon, the third quarter the evening, and the fourth quarter the night. In the yearly cycle, the first quarter represents spring, the second quarter summer, the third quarter autumn, and the fourth quarter winter. When each quarter is further divided into three parts, each section represents one month of the year. Quarters can also refer to portions of the life cycle. When each quarter is divided into fifteen parts, each part represents one year; it takes sixty years to complete one life cycle. In the Chinese lunar calendar, sixty years represent one cycle. For this reason, a person's sixtieth birthday has special meaning in Asian cultures.

Trigrams

3

Through his observation of natural phenomena, Emperor *Fu Hsi* is reputed to have devised the eight trigrams to explain the work of yin and yang energies in the universe. These eight trigrams provide the structural basis and the images of the sixty-four hexagrams that constitute the main component in *I Ching* and the conceptual basis for understanding the universe.

A trigram consists of three yin and/or yang symbols arranged vertically, one on top of the other. Utilizing all the possible combinations of the yin and yang line symbols, the result is eight discrete trigrams, which symbolically represent everything in the universe.

The bottom line of the trigram symbolizes Earth, representing the objective category of things on the earth (i.e., ruled by laws of nature), with the attribute of "firm" for yang and "compliant" for yin. The middle line symbolizes Man, representing the subjective category of man (i.e., ruled by man-made laws), with the attribute of "love" for yang and "morality" for yin. The top line symbolizes Heaven, representing the capacity of Heaven as creator and provider of eternal and spiritual principles, with the attribute of "light" for yang and "dark" for yin. Each trigram has various attributes and symbols that are the basis for divination and the universal principles of living.

The trigrams constitute the basis for the sixty-four hexagrams of *I Ching*, which are used as the medium in *I Ching* divination and to interpret the unceasingly changing phenomena in the universe. There are two ways to create a hexagram. To correspond with the principle of duality in the universe, each line in a trigram is doubled, creating a hexagram. In a hexagram the odd number positions (lines 1, 3, and 5, counting from the bottom) are the yang line positions and the even number positions (lines 2, 4, and 6) are the yin line positions. Another way to create a hexagram is to use two trigrams, putting one on the top of the other.

In formulating trigrams, *I Ching* expresses the creative design of *Tai Chi* in three incremental stages of separation of yin and yang energies. Each yin or yang symbol from each of the three stages is placed on top of the other in order to make a trigram. The result is eight trigrams that symbolically represent everything in the universe. The configuration of each trigram in these eight trigrams is referred to as a "minor conformation," in contrast with that of each hexagram in the sixty-four hexagrams of *I Ching*, which is referred to as a "major conformation."

Tai Chi consists of the yin and yang forces, as depicted in its symbol of the sphere, with one half of the area yin (black) and one half yang (white).

Tai Chi

1st stage of separation: *Tai Chi* separates into one yang and one yin.

—   – –

2nd stage of separation: Each line in the first stage contains its opposite force within itself as in *Tai Chi,* and each line separates into two lines of one yang and one yin for a total of four lines.

—   – –   —   – –

3rd stage of separation: Each line in the second stage is further depicted as containing its own and its opposite force and separates into two lines of one yang and one yin for a total of eight lines:

—   – –   —   – –   —   – –   —   – –

When a line from each stage is placed on top of the other, the following eight trigrams are obtained. The first stage line becomes the bottom line of the trigram and the third the top line. The eight trigrams and their names are:

(Khien)	*(Tui)*	*(Li)*	*(Ch'en)*	*(Son)*	*(Khan)*	*(Ken)*	*(K'un)*
Heaven	**Lake**	**Fire**	**Thunder**	**Wind**	**Water**	**Mountain**	**Earth**

Figure 3—Eight Trigrams

Sequence of Early Heaven

After *Fu Hsi* constructed the eight trigrams, he made a circular arrangement of the trigrams. *Fu Hsi*'s trigram arrangement is known as the "Sequence of Early Heaven," and it is referred to as the primal or Early Heaven arrangement. Until the hexagram was created, this arrangement of trigrams was the most important device for understanding the work of the yin and yang energies in the universe.

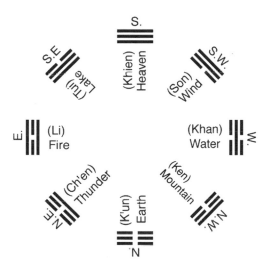

Figure 4—*Fu Hsi's* Trigram Arrangement (Early Heaven Arrangement)

The trigrams are arranged in the entrenched order that generates no interaction among the trigrams. This arrangement pairs Heaven and Earth, Mountain and Lake, Thunder and Wind, and Fire and Water. The paired trigrams with mutually opposing energies represented in the Early Heaven arrangement do not interact with each other, and each carries out its function independently. The opposite trigrams exist merely as the counterforce without mutual infringement. As an example, when Fire (Light) and Water work as a pair, their opposite attributes do not neutralize each other, and each trigram carries out its function independently. The singlular line of a trigram is the dominant energy for each trigram as a whole, and the dominant energies of opposing trigrams are mutually complementary; Mountain and Lake are paired, complementing each other with yang as the dominant energy in Mountain and yin as the dominant energy in Lake.

When this arrangement is viewed from the perspective of the flow of yin and yang energies, the positions of the eight trigrams in the circular arrangement indicate the increase or decrease of the energies in a cyclical fashion. The pure yang energy of Heaven is weakened when yin energy enters at the bottom in trigram Wind. The yang energy is further weakened when it is surrounded by the yin energy in Water and then pushed to the outer position by the yin energy in Mountain. Finally, the yang energy is taken over completely by the pure yin energy in Earth.

At this point, the reverse phase of the energy cycle begins with successive decreases in the yin energy. The pure yin energy of Earth is weakened when the yang energy enters at the bottom in trigram Thunder. The yin energy is then surrounded by the yang energy in Fire and then pushed to the outer position by the yang energy in Lake. The yin energy is then taken over completely by the pure yang energy in Heaven.

The Early Heaven arrangement orients the trigrams with the cardinal points in the universe. In addition, the trigram positions serve as the reference points to indicate the passage of time—the past, present, and future. To understand what constitutes the past (the backward movement of time), one must have the knowledge of what is happening now and in the future (the forward movement or future orientation). To understand what is to come (the forward movement of time), one must have the knowledge of what happened in the past (the backward movement or past orientation). The divinatory aspect of *I Ching* relies on the backward movement or the contracting phase in a time cycle in order to divine what is to come.

The forward movement represents the expanding phase in a time cycle, and the backward movement the contracting phase. For example, in the life cycle of a flowering plant, the process of germinating, budding, and flowering is the forward movement or the expanding phase. The process of bearing fruits, withering leaves, and forming seeds is the backward movement or the contracting phase. In the sixty-year human life cycle in the Chinese calendar, the first thirty years constitute forward movement or the expanding phase, and the latter thirty years backward movement or the contracting phase.

In the Sequence of Early Heaven, the forward and backward movements in the passage of time are represented in the following diagram.

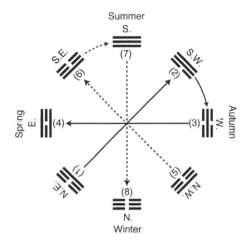

Figure 5—*Fu Hsi*'s Trigram Arrangement and Passage of Time

An energy activity in a trigram brings about changes in nature, and the change is used as the vehicle for measuring the passage of time. In the Early Heaven arrangement, the movement or an activity begins with trigram Thunder (1) that symbolizes movement. The forward movement in the passage of time that began with the Thunder trigram activates energy to flow toward Wind (2) that disperses the energy, toward Water (3) that moisturizes the energy, and toward Fire (sun) (4) that warms it. The backward movement or the contracting phase begins with the trigram Mountain (5), which is the symbol of keeping still. The energy in the first phase that ended in trigram Fire (the east) shifts its course abruptly back to the trigram Mountain (the northwest) to start the new phase or the contracting phase, and the passage of time in this course of energy movement is called the backward movement phase.

In the backward movement phase, Mountain (5), which represents Keeping Still (Resting), brings time to a standstill before changing in direction; Lake (6) or the Joyous brings pleasure; Heaven (7) or the Creative brings sovereignty; and Earth (8) or the Receptive brings shelter.

The attributes of these eight primary trigrams depict how the energy in each trigram is manifested in nature. The first four trigrams, Thunder, Wind, Water, and Fire that comprise the forward movement phase, represent generative forces. The latter four, Mountain, Lake, Heaven, and Earth, that comprise the backward movement phase, refer to potent preservative forces.

The Early Heaven arrangement of the eight elements places each cardinal point to relate to each seasonal period, coordinating the orientations of space and time naturally. For instance, the east is where the sun (Fire trigram) rises and the season of spring arrives. This harmonious arrangement of the eight trigrams is considered as an ideal representation of the human mind that is in harmony with nature, and to which the energy of one's mind should be directed in order to live in peace. For example, one should be warm and positive in relating to other people, like the spring warmth that helps the seeds to germinate and plants to grow. One should be intense with enthusiasm, like the summer heat, in his pursuit of self-improvement; joyful in appreciating nature, like the pleasant, invigorating fall; strict and severe in self-discipline like the winter elements. A good fortune or a bad fortune in *I Ching* divination indicates the degree to which one's mind is in harmony with this ideal state.

Sequence of Late Heaven

King *Wan* developed his own trigram arrangement, referred to as the "Sequence of Late Heaven." The Late Heaven arrangement of trigrams represents the interaction of the energies on Earth, of which Fire and Water are the governing energies. All life on earth is created and sustained through the interactions of these two energies. King *Wan* arranged the trigrams in a circle to obtain an uninterrupted energy flow and correlated them with the cardinal points and seasons.

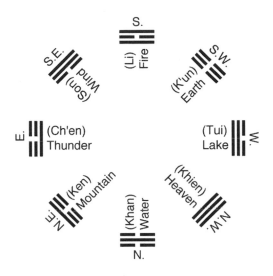

Figure 6—King *Wan*'s Trigram Arrangement
(Late Heaven Arrangement)

Activities of nature flow from the left side of the circle to the right in the clockwise direction without interruption. The movement begins with trigram Thunder (movement, arousing), which is east in direction and spring in season and spring is the season when seeds germinate and trees and plants produce buds. Next to trigram Thunder is trigram Wind (purity, gentle), southeast in direction and late spring to early summer in season. At this time of year, creatures attain appropriate size in growth and development and in their forms.

Trigram Fire (bright, clinging) is south in direction and summer in season. In summer, abundant light brightens the world, enabling all creatures to perceive one another. The sages turned their faces to the south, the source of light, to govern with clarity and wisdom. Trigram Earth (receptive, nourishing) is southwest in direction and late summer to early autumn in season. This is the season of nourishment, and the earth is receptive in carrying out its productive role to nourish all creatures. Trigram Lake (joy, pleasure) is west in direction and autumn in season. Autumn is the season of harvest and abundance, which brings joy to all.

The trigrams Wind, Fire, Earth, and Lake are yin trigrams (a single line in a trigram determines the yin or yang characteristic of a trigram). Yang trigrams begin with trigram Heaven (power, masculine), which is northwest in direction and late autumn to early winter in season. With the arrival of the yang force, the yang force battles the yin force in order to become the controlling energy force.

Trigram Water (the gorge, abysmal) is north in direction and winter in season. Like water that flows downward and collects in the lowest point, at this time of the year the harvested crops are stored in the barns. It is the time for respite. Trigram Mountain (keeping still, gates) is northeast in direction and later winter to early spring in season. At this time stirrings begin from the winter dormancy, like the seeds in the ground preparing to sprout in the spring, renewing a new cycle beginning with the trigram Thunder. The yin and yang energies have completed the yearly cycle. Therefore, this trigram represents completion.

Differing from the Early Heaven arrangement, Late Heaven arrangement pairs the opposite energies to interact with each other. Fire and Water are opposite energies as well as governing energies. Therefore, Fire was positioned at the top of the circle and Water at the bottom. Thunder (wood) and Lake (metal) are paired, and Wind (wood) with Heaven (metal). Mountain (earth) and Earth are paired as the harmonizing and stabilizing forces.

In contrast to the Early Heaven arrangement of trigrams, which generates no interactions, the Late Heaven arrangement depicts the conflicts that the interacting forces of the trigrams generate, which bring about creation and changes. Likewise, in the daily interactions of living, conflicts occur in the psychic energy of the human mind. This arrangement points the way, through *I Ching* divination, to the course one should take in order to avoid or minimize the harm that can come from conflict.

Attributes and Symbols of Trigrams

The eight trigrams provide the attributes and symbols that are used in interpreting *I Ching* hexagrams. Each trigram has a number of characteristic attributes and also serves as a symbol that represents a family member, a part of the body, and an animal.

In designating trigrams to represent members of the family, King *Wan* assigned "Heaven" for father, "Earth" the mother, and the remaining six trigrams the sons and daughters and their birth rankings. A single yang line in a trigram indicates a son, and a single yin line in a trigram a daughter. The position of the line in a trigram indicates the birth ranking of the child, with the bottom line the oldest, the middle line the middle child, and the top line the youngest.

The following chart presents King *Wan*'s trigram arrangement in table form and indicates the family member represented by each trigram.

1	2	3	4	5	6	7	8
☲ Fire	☴ Wind	☳ Thunder	☶ Mountain	☵ Water	☰ Heaven	☱ Lake	☷ Earth
Middle daughter	Oldest daughter	Oldest son	Youngest son	Middle son	Father	Youngest daughter	Mother
S.	S.E.	E.	N.E.	N.	N.W.	W.	S.W.

Figure 7—King *Wan*'s Trigram Arrangement in Table Form

Trigram	Name	Nature	Body	Major Qualities	Animal
☰	Khien	Heaven	Head	Strength & Power; Creativity; Masculine; Wise	Horse
☱	Tui	Lake; Marsh	Mouth	Pleasure; Harmony; Dancer; Joy	Sheep
☲	Li	Light; Fire	Eye	Bright; Elegant; Sun; Civilized; Hollow	Pheasant
☳	Ch'en	Thunder	Foot	Moving; Noise; Exciting; Power; Immortal; Road	Dragon
☴	Son	Wind;Wood	Leg	Penetration; Modesty; Purity; Flexibility; Rope; Profit; Bird	Rooster
☵	Khan	Water	Ear	Peril; Difficulty; Suspicion; Clouds; Moon; Worry	Pig
☶	Ken	Mountain	Hand	Resting; Stopping; Gate; Fruits; Lazy; Virtuous	Dog
☷	K'un	Earth	Stomach	Receptive; Submissive; Multitude; Puzzled	Cow

Figure 8—Trigram Chart of Key Attributes, Qualities, and Symbols

This chart summarizes other key attributes, qualities, and symbols that the eight trigrams represent, according to *Fu Hsi*'s trigram arrangement.

Hexagrams

4

The hexagram is the oracle in the *I Ching* divination process. There are sixty-four hexagrams in all, and they comprise the universe in *I Ching,* representing everything that exists and manifests itself in the entire universe. The first thirty hexagrams deal primarily with the sequence of natural forces, and the remaining thirty-four deal primarily with human and social forces.

Each hexagram is comprised of two trigrams, one placed on top of the other, a total of six lines. Only when the two trigrams come together in a hexagram do dynamic interactions occur. The interrelationships between the two trigrams and the individual lines of the hexagram form the basis for hexagram interpretations. The hexagram as a whole describes images unique to its composition, and each of the six lines represents changes, timing, social status, developmental stages, physical body parts, and other attributes.

Fu Hsi, who devised the eight trigrams, is also credited with devising the hexagram. However, many scholars believe that King *Wan* developed the system of sixty-four hexagrams. In the beginning, the hexagrams served exclusively as the medium in divination. Later, with Confucius's writings in *Ten Wings*, *I Ching* was studied to understand universal laws and human conduct in order for people to live in harmony with nature's way or *Tao*. This elevation of *I Ching* to a book of philosophy has not diminished its value as the authoritative book on divination.

In a hexagram, the trigram placed below is called the *lower trigram* or *inner trigram,* and the one above is the *upper trigram* or *outer trigram.* Another concept related to the composition of the six lines in a hexagram is based on the principle that each force (yin and yang) contains its opposite force within itself. Each line possesses the universal forces of yin and yang. In a hexagram, this concept of the yin and yang is reflected by adding another line to each line of the trigram, producing a hexagram.

In a trigram, the bottom line represents "Earth," the middle line "man" and the top line "Heaven." In the hexagram, the bottom two lines represent "Earth," the middle two lines "man," and the top two lines "Heaven."

Hexagram Sequence

In *I Ching*, the sixty-four hexagrams are sequentially arranged, based on their basic theme that relates to either a natural force or a social force. The first thirty hexagrams deal primarily with the sequence of natural forces, and the remaining thirty-four deal primarily with human and social forces. The sixty-four-hexagram sequence begins with Heaven as the first hexagram because Heaven originates everything. The hexagram Earth follows as the receiver of what Heaven originates. The third hexagram is the hexagram Germination, representing the beginning of everything on earth, a logical sequence to the creative activities of Heaven and the developmental activities of Earth. The sequential arrangement of the sixty-four hexagrams is complex, and one text of *Ten Wings* is devoted exclusively to the sequence.

The logical sequence to the last or the sixty-fourth hexagram Incomplete is Hexagram #1 Heaven. They demonstrate the basic principle of the perpetual cycle or the state of continual change in *I Ching*. The theme of the last hexagram is Incomplete, as the energy returns to Hexagram #1 Heaven to begin the universal cycle again.

I Ching teaches that when anything attains perfection, what naturally follows is decline. The concept of completion is recognized as a hexagram, but it precedes Hexagram #64 Incomplete.

63. The Completion 既濟 (Ki Zi) Hexagram

Hexagram #63 has the most perfect structural composition of all the hexagrams. The main theme of this hexagram is appropriately "Completion." In Legge's *The I Ching*, he translates as follows: "There has been good fortune in the beginning; there may be disorder in the end,"* indicating the beginning of a decline from perfection and leading to the last Hexagram #64 Incomplete.

*ibid., pp 204-205.

Major Hexagram Principles

- Yin or yang by itself is only a static energy and cannot bring about any change. Change occurs when yin and yang interact.

- Everything changes constantly, as the name of the book *I Ching* (*The Book of Changes*) indicates.

- Changes occur in cycles. The bottom line of a hexagram represents the beginning of the cycle, and the top line, the end. What happens at a particular point in the cycle is the fortune for that time.

- The sixty-four hexagrams are an integrated whole representing the total universe, even though each hexagram and its lines represent different roles and functions. The integration of the sixty-four hexagrams occurs through interactive relationships of cause and effect within the cyclical principle of *I Ching*.

- The centerline of a trigram is valued as the ideal. When applied to man, it symbolizes a person of moral integrity who practices the Mean. In a hexagram, the second and fifth lines are the two centerlines, as each is the centerline of a trigram.

- The odd number lines represent the yang lines (first, third, and fifth lines), and the even number lines (second, fourth, and sixth lines) represent the yin lines. Improper positioning of a line occurs when a yang line is in the even number line position, or when a yin line is in the odd number line position. Being in the improper position tempers its strength.

The *I Ching* Maps
and Numbers

5

I Ching hexagrams are based on the binary system with 0 representing the yin line and 1 representing the yang line of each hexagram. Numbers play a central role in *I Ching* because they translate the symbols to a measurable form. In the divination process, the numbers are obtained by counting the yarrow sticks which are used to construct the hexagram. (For detailed information on yarrow stick, see chapter VII under "The Orthodox Method.") An odd number represents Heaven or yang, and an even number Earth or yin. Thus, *I Ching* is a system of numbers as well as a system of yin and yang. In the constantly changing universe of *I Ching,* a system of numbers can translate future events in a calculable way in the *I Ching* divination.

The Yellow River Map

The framers of *I Ching* used two major maps, the *Yellow River Map* and the *Writing from River Lo*, to explain the universe in numbers. Ancient writings indicate that the legendary Emperor *Fu Hsi* received his inspirations from a map called *Ho Tu* or the *Yellow River Map*, an arrangement of marks on the back of a dragon-horse rising from the Yellow River. In the numerical principles of *I Ching*, 0 and 1 constitute the basic unit, with 0 representing the established force and 1 the engendering force. The map below provides the numerical principles of *I Ching* in relation to the five elements of Water, Fire, Wood, Metal, and Earth.

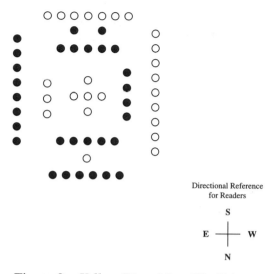

Directional Reference
for Readers

S

E ─┼─ W

N

Figure 9—*Yellow River Map (Ho Tu)*

In this map, the odd numbers—1, 3, 5, 7, and 9—represent yang and are shown as light circles. The even numbers—2, 4, 6, 8, and 10—represent yin and are shown as dark circles.

The arrangement on the map corresponds to that of the Late Heaven and is based on the principle of pairing the yin and yang numbers. The following are the pairings on the *Yellow River Map* (See "Directional Reference"):

One yang and six yin numbers pair to produce Water in the north.

Two yin and seven yang numbers pair to produce Fire in the south.

Three yang and eight yin numbers pair to produce Wood in the east.

Four yin and nine yang numbers pair to produce Metal in the west.

Five yang and ten yin numbers (the five yang numbers in the center with five yin numbers on top and five yin numbers below it) pair to produce Earth in the center.

When the larger number in the pair is subtracted from the other, the result is always five. The number five symbolizes both the neutralizing and stabilizing force. The number 5 is located in the center of the *Yellow River Map*. In *I Ching* divination, fifty sticks are used. The number 50 is the sum of 1, which represents *Tai Chi*, and 49, the number that represents Heaven (7x7 for Heaven and 8x8 for Earth).

One of the treatises in Confucius's *Ten Wings* deals with the meaning of numbers. On the *Yellow River Map*, the odd numbers—1, 3, 5, 7, and 9—are the numbers of Heaven (yang), and the even numbers—2, 4, 6, 8, and 10—are those of Earth (yin). The sum of all the Heaven numbers is 25, and the sum of all Earth numbers is 30, a total of 55. This number, 55, represents everything that exists in the heaven and on the earth.

Centuries later, King *Wan* replaced the circles in the *Yellow River Map* with line symbols, —— as the yang symbol and —— as the yin symbol. The lines were convenient and practical in devising the trigrams and hexagrams. In *I Ching*, the odd numbers belong to yang and the even numbers to yin.

The Writing from River Lo

The second major map in *I Ching* is *Lo Shu, Writing from River Lo*. Ascertaining the true source of *Lo Shu* is difficult. According to the *Book of History*, one of the five Confucian classics, China experienced a great deluge about five thousand years ago. It was believed that such a catastrophe was the result of man not following *Tao*. In order to avoid future catastrophes, the emperor and his officials carried out a ritual to invoke the spirit. Failure to conduct the ritual would bring about a misalignment in the interplay of the five elements of Earth, Fire, Wood, Metal, and Water.

Seven years of governmental efforts to control and drain off the floodwater did not succeed. Finally, King *Yu*[9] (prior to becoming an emperor) had the land partitioned into nine parts and successfully drained off the water. For his achievement, Heaven rewarded him with the Great Plan and the Nine Classifications, which were recorded on the back of a great tortoise rising from the River Lo. This schematic arrangement of marks is called *Writing from River Lo*—some call it the "Magic Square"—and it corresponds to the Early Heaven trigram arrangement. The eight trigrams in the Early Heaven arrangement can be expressed in numbers of the Magic Square: Heaven for 9, Lake for 4, Fire for 3, Thunder for 8, Wind for 2, Water for 7, Mountain for 6, and Earth for 1.

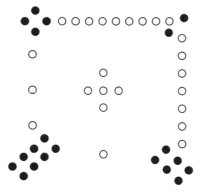

Figure 10—*Writing from River Lo (Lo Shu)*

Counting the light and dark marks in the *Writing* produces the following numerical scheme:

4	9	2
3	5	7
8	1	6

In this scheme, the numbers from 1 to 9 are arranged in such a way that in whichever direction the numbers are added, the sum is 15, with 5 in the center as the stabilizing force, as in the *Ho Tu* map. The number 15 symbolizes the perfect balance of *Tao* as the universal truth. Taoists and Confucian scholars with a mystic veneration uphold 15 as the number of *Tao*. *Tao*, the central belief system in Asian cultures, advocates naturalism as the way of Heaven. When man fails to follow *Tao*, his world becomes disorderly, and chaos will ensue.

The *I Ching* Maps and Time Orientation

Ho Tu and *Lo Shu* represent not only the numerical principles of *I Ching*, but they also symbolize the passage of time. In *I Ching*, it is not time that passes; it is the "*I*" or the "change" that makes time pass. The universe of *I Ching* encompasses both space and time, which are represented in the numbers of the *Ho Tu* and *Lo Shu* maps. The concept of time in *I Ching* can be stated as follows: there is no beginning without an ending, indicating continuity of "change." In this continuity of "change," the concept of the present represents both the past and the future simultaneously. *Ho Tu* is past-oriented, beginning with 10 and ending with 1, at which point it becomes future-oriented. *Lo Shu* is future-oriented, beginning with 1 and ending with 9, at which point it becomes past-oriented. The concept of time represented in the two maps provides a structure for human understanding of time and its passage.

Numerical Principles and the Time Orientation of Hexagrams

The numerical principles of *Lo Shu* and *Ho Tu* are represented in the hexagram. *Lo Shu* represents the lower trigram with a future orientation, beginning with 1 for the first line, 5 for the second line, and 9 for the third line. *Ho Tu* represents the upper trigram with a past orientation, beginning with 10 for the fourth line, 5 for the fifth line, and 2 for the sixth line. The number 5 represents both the second and fifth lines, and 5 is the number that is revered to symbolize the most stable in *I Ching* interpretation, representing the wise and noble or the sage ruler who will bring peace to the domain.

In a hexagram, the bottom line is the beginning line, and the force moves progressively upward to the sixth (top) line. In interpreting the passage of time in a hexagram, the numerical principles of *Lo Shu* and *Ho Tu* are applied. The beginning is 1, the *Lo Shu* number applied to the first line. Future time orientation moves from the beginning to the future, or from 1 to 5 to 9 (the lower trigram numbers). The past time orientation moves from the farthest past to the present, or from 10 to 5 to 1, the *Ho Tu* numbers for the upper trigram. (Note: The *Ho Tu* number for the sixth line is 2, but it becomes the number 1 as the hexagram begins its cycle again.)

I Ching Divination

6

I Ching has two major components that make it unique and important in its application to human living. Both aspects are modeled after *Tao* or nature's way, as represented in the hexagrams. The first component is divination, as *I Ching* was originally written in a book. The second component is moral status of human conduct. *I Ching* explains moral standards that are based on the principles of Tao.

Chinese rulers, and later, the rulers in other Asian countries, utilized *I Ching* for divination to obtain guidance in resolving a predicament or a crisis. They also sought guidance through *I Ching* divination before making an important decision. Later, this practice became popular among the general populace in Asian countries. Among all the methods of divination in Asian countries, *I Ching* divination was respected as the most reliable.

The hexagram images and the judgments are thought to be "magical" because its predictions are reputed to have uncanny accuracy. In *Ten Wings*, Confucius exalts *I Ching* divination because it explores what is complex, searches out what is hidden, connects with what lies deep, reaches out to what is distant, and determines the issues of good or ill for all events under the "sky."

Opinions diverge regarding the propriety of *I Ching* divination. One view is that because *I Ching* preaches righteous living, when one understands *I Ching* and lives righteously, one does not need to practice divination in order to obtain a correct course of action. *Szema Kiku,* an eminent *I Ching* diviner in the *Ming* dynasty (15th century A.D.), has been frequently quoted in this regard. To a prominent client who sought his help, he said: "Ah! Is it the way of Heaven to love any (partially)? Heaven loves only the virtuous. What intelligence is possessed by spirits? They are intelligent (only) by their connection with men. The divining stalks are so much withered grasses; the tortoise-shell is a withered bone. They are but things, and man is more intelligent than things. Why not listen to yourself instead of seeking (to learn) from things?"*

What can be implied in his observation is that *I Ching* teaches *Tao*, the universal principles for righteous living; therefore, one who practices these principles does not need to resort to divination. Hardly anyone, however, can claim to have achieved that level of righteous living, since people usually come up short in their practice of the principles of *Tao*. Therefore, they have a strong desire to know what is in their future, and they seek guidance for a proper course of action to achieve their goals and objectives.

The next four chapters cover the five steps in *I Ching* divination: constructing the hexagram, analyzing the hexagram, developing images of the hexagram, interpreting the images of the hexagram, and providing the answer to the divination question.

Basic Divination Guidelines

People who seek consultation through *I Ching* divination need to keep a few points in mind.

It matters little which method is used to receive (construct) the hexagram. What is important is that during the divination the seeker maintains an unprejudiced and balanced mind-set, as well as a sincere attitude.

The most propitious time to seek an answer through *I Ching* divination is when one is in a predicament and feels an earnest desire for guidance.

The question one poses in divination should be clear and specific. A good approach is to first write down the situation that is causing one dilemna, and formulate a question one would like answered or for a course of action to take, starting with"What if I did . . . ?" "What will be the consequence if I did . . . ?" "What is happening in this situation?" "How should I approach this situation?" No wicked intention should contaminate the question, especially if it might cause harm to others.

No repeat divination of the same question is allowed. To repeat the same question is to question the validity of the answer that was given the first time.

The divination answer is a symbolic one, representing the person's situation and the unseen force that is working at that moment. It will give

*ibid., p. 41.

guidance as to the forces at work, how or what is the most effective way to handle the situation, and whether it augurs well or ill.

Throughout the many centuries of *I Ching* divination practice, professional divination practitioners developed elaborate divination analyses to deal with specific topics such as personal fortune, family matters, business or trade, finance, health, marriage, employment, childbirth, travel, and weather. Part II of this book provides a "Divination Direction" for each hexagram and for each of its lines. The directions are general, offering the most representative, overriding predictions, except for a few conspicuous hexagram predictions.

Hexagram Construction

7

The hexagram is the oracle through which the diviner obtains an answer to a question that is being posed. Hexagram making is the process to receive (construct) the hexagram. Before constructing the hexagram, the person seeking divination needs to examine his mind in order to formulate a well-defined question. After the hexagram is constructed, he consults the hexagram identification chart or the sixty-four-hexagram chart to identify the hexagram number. The trigrams, the individual lines and the attributes of each hexagram serve as the interpretive tools of the hexagram.

Throughout the centuries of *I Ching* divination practice, different methods were used to construct a hexagram or, to describe it more accurately, to receive a hexagram. Two of the methods for receiving a hexagram are explained below: the orthodox or the yarrow (milfoil) stalk method and the coin method. The orthodox method is commonly referred to as the eighteen-step method. The simplified method, called the coin method, was first used in the thirteenth century in the *Sung* dynasty (1127-1279 A.D.).

The Orthodox Method

The orthodox method of hexagram making that is described in *Ten Wings* is cumbersome and time-consuming. Over the years, simplified versions have been devised. In ancient times, the orthodox method utilized yarrow stalks to receive a hexagram. The yarrow stalks were used out of the folklore belief that this plant has a longevity of over one hundred years and produces more than one hundred sprigs. In more recent times, bamboo or other dried wood sticks have been in common use, replacing the yarrow stalks. The dried wood sticks were made slender and rounded to about one-sixteenth of an inch in diameter and twelve to eighteen inches in length. (The five- to six-inch-long round bamboo skewers for cooking can be used.)

Fifty sticks are needed to receive a hexagram. The kind or the size of the sticks, or even another method that uses a medium other than the sticks, is not an essential factor. What is significant is the state of the practitioner's mind, which should be sincere and earnest and prepared to receive the answer with an attitude of respect and reverence.

In the orthodox method, it takes three cycles consisting of six steps each (a total of eighteen steps) to receive one hexagram line. Therefore, the eighteen steps are completed six times to obtain the six lines of the hexagram. The following is the procedure for constructing a hexagram under the orthodox method.

1. Hold the fifty sticks in your left hand. Randomly pick out one stick. Place this stick on the table or on the floor in front of you. This stick represents *Tai Chi*, the Supreme Ultimate.

2. There are forty-nine sticks remaining in your left hand. Randomly grab about half of the sticks with your right hand. The sticks in your right hand represent Earth (yin), and the sticks in your left hand, Heaven (yang).

3. Place the sticks that are in your right hand on a table or floor in front of you, separate from the first stick. Pick one stick from this pile to represent Man in the Heaven-Man-Earth triad. Hold this stick between the ring and small fingers of your left hand. (This is the method practiced in *I Ching* divination. It is practical and convenient because it prevents the practitioner from making mistakes in following the repetitive procedures in counting the sticks.)

4. Count off every four sticks (represents the four seasons) from the sticks in the left hand, and set aside all except the last count, (represents the intercalary month) which will be four or less. Hold the sticks between the middle and ring fingers of your left hand.

5. Repeat the same procedure in step #4 with the other pile of sticks that you placed in front of you in step #3. Again, the last count will be four or less. Hold the sticks from the last count between the index and middle fingers of your left hand.

6. Count all the sticks that you are holding in your left hand. The total will be 5 or 9. This total is the first line numerical total. This step completes the first cycle.

Remove the value represented in the first line numerical total from the whole pile, and repeat steps #1 through #6 with the remaining pile of sticks. The second line numerical total in this cycle will be four or eight. Remove the first and second line numerical totals from the remaining pile of sticks, and repeat #1 through #6 for the third time. The line numerical total in this cycle will be four or eight.

Count the first, second, and third line numerals. The sum of the three line numerical totals determines the line of a hexagram, which is the bottom line. A hexagram always starts with the bottom line and works upward.

If the sum of the three numerical totals is thirteen, this value represents "major yang."

If the sum is seventeen, it represents "minor yin."

If the sum is twenty-one, it represents "minor yang."

If the sum is twenty-five, it represents "major yin."

The major yang or minor yang produces a yang line ▬▬ . The major yin or minor yin produces a yin line ▬ ▬ .

Each of the four numbers described above represents one line of the hexagram, and a total of six lines are needed to complete a hexagram, which is obtained by going through step #1 through step #6 six times. If the resulting number of a line is a major yin or a major yang, it becomes a changing line and is changed to its opposite, creating a new hexagram. (See "Changing Lines" below.)

The Coin (Simplified) Method

The simplified method discussed here is called the "coin method." It uses three coins. The numerical value of 2 (representing yin) is assigned to the tail and 3 (representing yang) to the head of the coin.

Throw the coins randomly on a flat surface in front of you, or shake the three coins in your hands formed in the shape of a ball and throw them onto a level surface. The sum of the three coins will be one of the following: 6, 7, 8, or 9. The numerical value of 6 is "major yin" and the value of 9, "major yang." These are changing lines. The numerical value of 7 is "minor yang," and 8, "minor yin." (For discussion of the major and minor lines, refer to the section on the *Tai Chi* Symbol in chapter II.) The numerical value obtained with the first toss of the coins determines the first line, which is the bottom line of the hexagram. Repeat the same procedure five times until all six lines of the hexagram are obtained.

Changing Lines

The major yang and major yin lines are called *changing lines*. These lines are characterized by placing an "0" mark on the yang line and an "X" mark on the yin line: ▬0▬   ▬X▬

The changing lines perform two functions. First, depending on how many changing lines one receives in a hexagram, there is a rule to follow as to which changing line(s) should be used to obtain the answer to the posed question from the judgment. (For a detailed explanation, refer to the chapter on Hexagram Interpretation.) Second, each changing line is changed to its opposite line, i.e., the yang line to yin line and vice versa, to form a new hexagram, which is called a *changed hexagram* (also called *transformed hexagram* or *branch hexagram*). The original hexagram symbolizes the current situation. The changed hexagram symbolizes the future and the actions that you should take or not take in order to handle the situation to your advantage.

Example: you have completed the procedures and received the numbers 13, 17, 21, 21, 21, and 25 as the sum of each of line numerals of the hexagram. It will look like this:

By referring to the Hexagram Identification Chart, you will identify this as Hexagram #49 Revolution. The first and sixth lines are the changing lines. (Note: Some hexagrams obtained from a divination method will not have changing lines.) In this example, when these two lines are changed, the changed hexagram will be:

Again, by referring to the Hexagram Identification Chart, you will identify this as Hexagram #33 Retreat.

After the original and the changed hexagrams are received, the applicable hexagram must be determined to obtain the judgment, based on the rules on changing lines (see chapter 9, Hexagram Interpretation).

Hexagram Images and Analysis

8

Upon receiving the hexagram, the process of analysis begins. The hexagram is analyzed to obtain the images of the hexagram and the line attributes that constitute the basis of the judgment and the line statements of the hexagram.

Hexagram Analysis

Hexagram analysis involves the examination of the structure of the hexagram. The hexagram is composed of two trigrams, one placed above the other. In the analysis, one looks at the position of the trigrams and the individual lines of the hexagram, the images they create together and separately, and the role of each line and its relationship with the other lines. Through this analysis, the diviner obtains the necessary information for the hexagram judgment and line statements.

The hexagram analysis of the individual hexagrams in Part II of this book has general application. A practitioner may refine this analysis using insight in the analysis process to obtain an answer that is more specific to the question that is being posed in the divination.

Hexagram Images

The framers of *I Ching* devised hexagrams as the most convenient and appropriate means to represent and understand universal phenomena, by which each hexagram and its lines are interpreted. An overall image of a hexagram is obtained from the images and positions of its lower and upper trigrams. In addition, each line of the hexagram presents changing aspects of the hexagram interpretation from its position and interrelationships with the other lines of the hexagram.

The diviner first obtains the images of the hexagram by studying the hexagram within the context of its main theme and the posed question. He then analyzes the hexagram judgment and the line statements from the book of *I Ching* to arrive at the answer. For changing lines, the rules on changing lines should be complied with, which are discussed in the following chapter under "Changing Lines and the Judgments."

Hexagram Composition and Numerical Identification of the Lines

Each trigram has attributes and qualities from which its image(s) is determined, and the combined images of the two trigrams create the overall image(s) of the hexagram.

The bottom trigram of a hexagram is referred to as the *lower* or *inner trigram*, and the trigram on top, the *upper* or *outer trigram*. Besides the meanings of the individual trigram, the lower trigram symbolizes "in the past," "in the rear," "below," and "the general public." The upper trigram symbolizes "in the future," "in the front," "above," and "the high echelons of government."

For the purposes of brevity and convenience, when the lines of a hexagram are referenced for analysis and interpretation, numerals are used in *I Ching* to indicate a specific line and its nature (yin or yang).

A hexagram starts at the bottom line and works upward. The bottom line is referred to as the first line, and the top line is the sixth line or the last line. Each of the six lines is either a yin or a yang line. The numeral "9" indicates a yang line, ⸻ or the unbroken line. Thus, "1-9" indicates that the first line (bottom line) of a hexagram is a yang line. The numeral "6" indicates a yin line, ⸺ or the broken line. Line "2-6" indicates that the second line (second from the bottom) of a hexagram is a yin line.

Correlative, Contiguous, and Lead Lines

Depending on how a line is positioned in relation to the other lines, each line of a hexagram may have added meaning.

Correlative lines exist when two lines holding the same position in the lower and upper trigrams of a hexagram are opposite lines (one is yin and the other yang). A *proper correlation* exists when these two are "properly" positioned, with the yang line on an odd number line and the yin on an even number line, and it will generally receive favorable interpretations. When the two lines holding the same position in the lower and upper trigrams of a hexagram are the same (yin and yin or yang and yang), the lines are considered antagonistic to each other and produce unfavorable interpretations.

Contiguous lines are two lines next to each other. Although this contiguous relationship is not as strongly resonating as the correlative relationship, a close relationship exists between two contiguous lines, especially when a yang line rides atop a yin line.

Both correlative and contiguous relationships play special roles in hexagram interpretations, as will be further explained in the chapter on Hexagram Interpretation.

The following hexagram demonstrates the concepts of correlative and contiguous lines.

Figure 11—Correlative, Contiguous and Lead Lines

Of the six lines of the hexagram, one or more lines exert controlling influence over the other lines in interpreting the hexagram. These are called *lead lines*. Some hexagrams have only one lead line, while others have as many as four. In a trigram, the line that is different from the other two lines is the lead line of the trigram. When the three lines are all yin or yang (the Heaven and Earth trigrams), the whole trigram is interpreted as one lead line.

Lead lines have two categories, the *structural lead line* and the *directive lead line*. The structural lead line is always the centerline of a trigram that makes up the hexagram; most often, it is the centerline of the upper trigram (the fifth line). The directive lead line can be any line or lines of the hexagram that exert the most influence in interpreting the hexagram. In this book, the structural and directive lead lines are included in the Hexagram Analysis section for each hexagram.

Nuclear Hexagrams

The original hexagram (the hexagram that is originally received) is called the *primary hexagram*. As stated in the previous chapter, a hexagram changed by changing the yin or yang line to its opposite is referred to as a *changed hexagram*. Another way to create a different hexagram is to use any four adjoining lines of the primary hexagram (see example below). The hexagram obtained in this manner is called a *nuclear hexagram* and is formed when the diviner needs further clarification.

A hexagram, whether primary, changed, or nuclear, presents its own hexagram image that represents the universal force at work. The practitioner must choose the hexagram image that is most congruent with the judgment to enhance the validity of the interpretation.

A nuclear hexagram indicates causative factors in relation to the timing or the condition of the primary hexagram. If the answer received from the primary hexagram is clear, a nuclear hexagram is not necessary. If the answer is not clear, use a primary nuclear hexagram to clarify it.

Among the nuclear hexagrams, the most important is the *primary nuclear hexagram.* The primary nuclear hexagram is formed by making lines 2, 3, and 4 of the primary hexagram the lower trigram, and lines 3, 4, and 5 of the primary hexagram the upper trigram. The secondary and tertiary nuclear hexagrams can also be formed. Using the bottom four lines of the primary hexagram, with the lines 1, 2, and 3 as the lower trigram and lines 2, 3, and 4 as the upper trigram, a secondary nuclear hexagram is formed. Using the top four lines of the primary hexagram, with lines 3, 4, and 5 as the lower trigram and lines 4, 5, and 6 as the upper trigram, a *tertiary nuclear hexagram* is formed. The secondary and tertiary nuclear hexagrams are less useful, as they are not considered as relevant as the primary nuclear hexagram in hexagram interpretation. A divination practitioner may want to use the secondary or tertiary nuclear hexagram to obtain further clarification on a hexagram interpretation.

To illustrate the creation and use of a primary nuclear hexagram, Hexagram #41 Decrease is the primary hexagram. To make its primary nuclear hexagram, lines 2, 3, and 4 of the primary hexagram become the lower trigram of the primary nuclear hexagram, and lines 3, 4, and 5 the upper trigram of the primary nuclear hexagram. The resulting primary nuclear hexagram is Hexagram #24 Return.

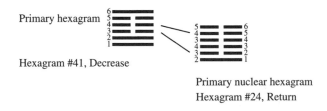

Primary hexagram

Hexagram #41, Decrease

Primary nuclear hexagram
Hexagram #24, Return

Figure 12—Nuclear Hexagrams

In the above illustration, we first look at the image of Hexagram #41 Decrease and then attempt to obtain further clarification on the image and time factor of the hexagram through the primary nuclear hexagram. Hexagram #41 consists of the Lake (lower) trigram and the Mountain (upper) trigram. It presents the image of the Lake at the foot of the Mountain, with the lake water evaporating to form rain that will help to add vegetation to the Mountain, making the Lake level lower by losing lake water and the Mountain higher by gaining vegetation. When the distribution of yin and yang energies in these trigrams is considered, the trigram Lake is formed from the trigram Heaven. When the trigram Heaven with its three yang lines relinquishes its top yang line to a yin line, it becomes the Lake trigram. The loss of the yang line presents the image of diminution of the Heaven trigram. The upper trigram Mountain is obtained when the trigram Earth with three yin lines replaces its top yin line with the stronger yang line, also presenting the image of Earth's diminution.

With the image of the primary Hexagram #41 Decrease in mind, its primary nuclear Hexagram #24 Return is examined to find out if it provides some clarification of the situation and the timing (developmental stages) of the situation.

The primary nuclear Hexagram #24 Return consists of Thunder as the lower trigram and Earth as the upper trigram. Earth symbolizes obedience, and Thunder movement. The hexagram presents an image of the Thunder hiding in Earth, unable to perform its functions in the sky. One yang line has returned at the bottom of the hexagram to begin its upward push. The Return hexagram suggests that the process of Decrease is phasing out, since the new yang energy has just taken hold under the pressure of the predominant yin force that has served as the force in the Decrease phase. There will be little opposition to the upward movement of the yang line, which reflects the beginning of the Increase phase (Hexagram #42).

The above discussion of nuclear hexagrams should make clear, among other things, that each hexagram is interrelated with the other sixty-three hexagrams, making all sixty-four hexagrams a functional unit.

Hexagram Interpretation

9

A hexagram is a symbol with images. *Ten Wings* explains the reason the symbol is used in *I Ching*: "No writing can exhaust what one wants to say, and no speech can exhaust what one intends to say." With a symbol, one is not limited by words to explore a truth. The use of symbols enables one to interpret the hexagram image(s) to fit individual situations. The analysis of the hexagram and its line interaction brings forth the images that are used as the material for interpretation.

Interpretation follows the analysis of the hexagram. Interpreting is the process of applying the images and the interactions of the trigrams and lines and their attributes to the appropriate judgment and line statements from the original *I Ching* texts to answer the question at hand.

Hexagram interpretations are versatile and intricate. In interpreting the hexagram, the diviner retraces the thought process that the framers of *I Ching* must have undergone to arrive at the judgment and the line statements, which are concise and conclusive. In order to apply the judgment or a line statement to a specific situation effectively, the interpretation of a hexagram must be based on a thorough and appropriate analysis. The analysis provides the underlying dynamics and reasons behind the judgment and line statements and gives the practitioner a perspective on how they can be applied to answer the specific question.

The Judgment (Divinatory Statement)

The judgment is the answer to the question posed in the divination. The framers of *I Ching* wrote the judgments and line statements based on their analysis and interpretation of the sixty-four hexagrams. Every *I Ching* judgment has two levels of meaning: (1) the universal truth, or *Tao*, for man to model his life after; and (2) the source of wisdom for man to solve a problem or to seek guidance for the future. The concept of the universe in *I Ching* encompasses event, space, and time. A specific divination provides the seeker the answer or prediction within the context of the event, space, and time.

The judgment and line statements of the original *I Ching* texts must be applied to the specific divination question at hand. This application is accomplished by interpreting the hexagram by connecting the image(s) and line dynamics from the analysis with the theme and the judgment of the hexagram. The line dynamics refer to changes that are represented in each line.

When the judgments and commentaries of *I Ching* were written in ancient China, they were based on observations of human and social conditions that were vastly different from the conditions in modern times. Therefore, one must keep this fact in mind in interpreting the hexagram and applying it to the appropriate *I Ching* judgment and line statements. The fables and legends cited in the original writings increase the difficulties in understanding the judgments.

For example, in ancient times, men, with their greater physical capabilities, had to hunt and work in the fields to provide food for their families, and the women stayed at home to care for children and prepare food for the family members. In modern times, the man is not always the sole provider for the family. This change in social condition needs to be considered in interpreting *I Ching* texts.

To give another example, the trigram Water is often interpreted as facing a perilous situation. In ancient China, crossing a river always posed a great risk because of the lack of bridges, or the perilousness of existing bridges. Historical references also illumine the interpretations. The army of King *Wu* (King *Wan*'s second son) had to risk the perils of crossing the Yellow River to rebel against the tyrant king of the *Yin* dynasty. You need to digest the meaning of water as a symbol of peril within the historical and cultural contexts and reflect upon them to determine how they apply to the divination question.

Hexagram Themes and Attributes

Each hexagram has a basic theme and attributes. The theme is the overriding attribute and is the name of the hexagram. The theme in Hexagram #1 is Heaven, which has such attributes as the physical heaven, king, father, being firm, and originator. Hexagram #2 Earth symbolizes the physical earth as well as other attributes, such as the common people, mother, being submissive, and the receiver. Attributes are the characteristics that have been applied to the hexagram and its trigrams.

The hexagram theme determines its position in the sequence of the sixty-four hexagrams. Theme also determines the way in which the hexagram is analyzed and interpreted. One must select the right attribute(s) of the hexagram in order to interpret a hexagram correctly and answer the divination question or to explain the moral principle.

The following is an example of interpreting from the attributes. Legge's translation of the line statement of the first line (1-6) of the Earth hexagram reads: "The yin energy sets in as hoarfrost and the day of ice will come soon." This statement of the natural truth is based on human observation that when frost comes, winter will soon arrive. This universal truth provides insights into the process of the natural phenomenon of the four seasons.

In *I Ching*, this example of nature's way is expanded to other natural and human phenomena. Since the framers of *I Ching* had human welfare in mind in developing the system, every principle contained in a judgment or line statement has a human application. Thus, *Ten Wings* expands the interpretation of the first line judgment of the Earth hexagram, giving yin the attribute of "cold" or evil. It states, " . . . a stirring of the evil. Unless one can tame and control it, it has the potential of developing into something more serious." Applying this concept to human affairs, the seventh book of *Ten Wings* interprets: "The family that accumulates goodness is sure to have superabundant happiness, and the family that accumulates evil is sure to have superabundant misery. The murder of a ruler by his minister, or of his father by a son, is not the result of the events of one morning or one evening. The causes of it have gradually accumulated, through the absence of early discrimination."*

Hexagram #37 Family illustrates the application of the right attribute of a hexagram to explain a moral principle.

37. The Members of a Family 家人 (Kia Zan or Jiaren) Hexagram

This hexagram is composed of the lower trigram Fire and the upper trigram Wind. Fire burns upward, creating the wind that is represented by the upper trigram. The hexagram presents the image of wind blowing over fire and reflects the natural and harmonious interaction between fire and wind.

In examining the lines in each trigram, the lower trigram Fire has a yin line (line 2) in the middle, and the upper trigram has a yin line (line 4) at the bottom. Based on King *Wan*'s trigram arrangement, the lower

*ibid., pp. 419-420.

trigram also represents the middle daughter and the upper trigram the oldest daughter, presenting the image of the younger daughter in the home being obedient to the older one. Thus, the image of fire and wind in natural harmony and the proper relationship of the oldest and middle daughters reflect the hexagram theme of family.

Attributes of the Hexagram Lines

Each line of a hexagram represents changes and possesses distinct characteristics or attributes relative to its position and its relationship with the other lines in the hexagram. In addition to the inherent attributes of yin and yang, the position of each line plays an important role in interpreting the hexagram. In the hexagram, the first, third, and fifth lines, or the odd number lines, are yang line positions, and the second, fourth, and sixth, or the even number lines, are yin line positions.

A yang line in the yang position or a yin line in the yin position is judged to be "properly" positioned and carries some relatively preferential leverage in interpreting the hexagram. A yin line in the yang position or a yang line in the yin position is judged to be "improperly" positioned. For example, when the first line of a hexagram is a yin line, it is "improperly" positioned, and the line lacks the corresponding yang characteristics of initiative, strength, and aggressive nature.

The position of each line in a hexagram also indicates the stage of an event or a situation in progress. In a hexagram, the event or situation starts at the bottom line and reaches a climax at the sixth line. The first position represents the beginning stage and the sixth line the final stage or apex. The second through the fifth lines represent the progressive stages of the event or the status of the situation in progress.

The third line (the top line of the lower trigram) is considered vulnerable because it is in a transitory position to the upper trigram. Even when this third line is yang and "properly" positioned, it usually carries a negative leverage with an unfavorable interpretation because it lacks the stability of being in the center position of a trigram, and, as yang, has a surplus of energy. Similarly, when the third line is yin and "improperly" positioned, it connotes an unfavorable interpretation of being weak and incompetent because it is in the wrong position in the hexagram. If one receives the divination judgment on this line, it behooves the person to be especially prudent and deliberate in undertaking an important action.

In contrast to the third line, the middle line of each trigram (the second line of the lower trigram and especially the second line of the upper trigram) carries a special leverage of favorable values and forces. In a hexagram, the centerlines of the trigram are in harmony with the principles of the Mean and receive prestigious interpretations. When the second and fifth lines of a hexagram are opposite forces (one yang and the other yin), they correlate and mutually reinforce its merits.

Another attribute of each line position is the social status of a person.

Line 6: the retired (a high official, such as the ruler's advisor)
Line 5: the ruler or a commander-in-chief
Line 4: a prime minister; nobility
Line 3: high official
Line 2: a scholar; an army officer
Line 1: the general public; a soldier

When a hexagram represents the human body, the first and second lines that symbolize Earth represent the lower limbs; more specifically, the first line represents the toes and the second line the calves. The third and fourth lines that symbolize Man represent the trunk portion of body—namely, the hips and the heart. The fifth and sixth lines that symbolize Heaven represent the head.

Interpreting the Hexagram Images and the Line Interactions

Five major areas are examined for hexagram interpretation: (1) the image(s) of the whole hexagram, (2) the image(s) of each trigram that is paired in the hexagram, (3) the interactions among the lines of the hexagram, (4) the sequential positioning within the sixty-four hexagrams, and (5) the yin and yang interactions. The following are representative examples of the five major areas that are examined in interpreting hexagrams. (Note: These examples describe only partial characteristics of the hexagram.)

Interpreting the hexagram as a whole

There are eight hexagrams constructed from two identical trigrams. Their image is derived from the whole. Hexagram #1 ☰ Heaven 乾 with all yang lines and Hexagram #2 ☷ Earth 坤 with all yin lines are the best examples, emphasizing their respective functions of Heaven as the creator and Earth as the receiver.

Interpreting the image(s) of the trigrams

Hexagram #22 ☶ Ornamental 賁 consists of the lower trigram Light and the upper trigram Mountain. The combined image of the two trigrams, light illuminating the mountain or the sun setting below the mountain, presents the ornamental or decorative theme of the hexagram.

Hexagram #11 ☷ Peace ❋ consists of the lower trigram Heaven and the upper trigram Earth. The proper position of Heaven is above the Earth, but in this hexagram, the trigram Heaven places itself below the trigram Earth, symbolizing modesty in its attitude and its interactions with Earth. When the stronger one is modest and cooperates with the weaker, the overall theme is peace.

Interpreting line interactions

Hexagram #46 ☷ Rising and Advancing 升 consists of the lower trigram Wind (tree) and the upper trigram Earth. The bottom line (1-6) of the hexagram symbolizes the root of a tree and the following two yang lines (2-9 and 3-9) the tree trunk. This tree will grow above the earth, giving this hexagram its name, "Rising and Advancing."

Hexagram #61 ☴ Central Sincerity 孚 consists of the lower trigram Lake that denotes joy, and the upper trigram Wind, compliance. The Chinese character for sincerity in the hexagram name is the ideogram that depicts a bird protecting a hatching egg with maternal care and devotion. The yin lines at the center of the hexagram symbolize the egg yolk; the two yang lines of 2-9 and 5-9, the egg white; and the two yang lines of 1-9 and 6-9, the eggshell. Furthermore, the image of sincerity is derived from the two yin lines at the center and represents the emptied mind (devoid of sordid thoughts). The two yang lines from the center of each trigram represent the integrity of the heart. The combined image of the lines depicts love, care, and purity of the mind that constitute the ingredients of Central Sincerity, the hexagram theme.

Interpreting the Sequential Position of a Hexagram

The 64 hexagrams are arranged in their logical or natural sequence of cause and effect. (See the section on Hexagram Sequence in chapter IV.) Each hexagram has its own cycle (micro cycle), starting at the bottom line and moving upward, completing a cycle at its sixth line. It then begins a new cycle beginning at the bottom line of the following hexagram.

The sixty-four hexagrams also represent a macro cycle. This cycle starts with Hexagram #1 Heaven as the creator or the originator of the universe, and the last hexagram of the cycle is Hexagram #64 Incomplete, which follows Hexagram #63 Completion. Hexagram #63 Completion applies to the theme of completion of the individual hexagram, not the completion of the macro cycle of the sixty-four hexagrams. Hexagram #64 Incomplete indicates that a new sixty-four hexagram cycle will begin with Hexagram #1 Heaven, repeating the perpetual cyclical movement of the sixty-four hexagrams.

Another example of hexagram sequence is the sequence of Hexagram #14 The Great Possession, Hexagram #15 Modesty, and Hexagram #16 The Harmonious Joy. When a state is governed well with great statesmanship that suppresses evil and promotes good, great wealth is produced, and the people of the state are enriched both morally and materially. This is represented by Hexagram #14 The Great Possession.

However, both the ruler and the people must guard against overextending themselves in their efforts to attain more and more possessions, as such insatiability is the beginning of a decline. For this reason, Hexagram #15 Modesty follows Hexagram #14 The Great Possession, as there is the realization that the true sense of fulfillment is not derived from attaining fullness, but from the virtue of modesty, which is one of the highest virtues that *I Ching* teaches.

When the ruler and the ruled are modest without being greedy, they care for the less fortunate and understand the value of equitable distribution of wealth. Hexagram #16 The Harmonious Joy follows Hexagram #15 Modesty, as the people in the state are joyful when the state is well-governed and all the people participate in sharing the wealth that they produce without greed, but with caring.

Interpreting Yin and Yang Interactions

The main principle in *I Ching* is change, based on yin and yang interaction. This interaction between yin (Earth) and yang (Heaven) produces the dynamism for the transformation of all natural and human phenomena. In *I Ching,* changes occur through the exchange of energies.

This principle is well demonstrated in hexagrams #11 Peace and #12 Stagnation.

Hexagram #11 Peace

This hexagram is made up of the lower trigram Heaven and the upper trigram Earth, which have exchanged their natural positions. It presents the image of Heaven interplaying with Earth. This interplay between the energies of Heaven and Earth is the fundamental interaction in the universe, and it produces changes that are in harmony with nature's way or at peace with nature. It produces the ideal state.

Hexagram #12, Stagnation

This hexagram is made up of the lower trigram Earth and the upper trigram Heaven in their natural positions. When Heaven and Earth maintain their own natural positions, there is no interplay of energies between them, and no dynamic changes can take place. Therefore, this hexagram symbolizes stagnation.

In the totality of the sixty-four hexagrams, yin and yang have equal strength and status in their interactions. Yang reaches its apex or fullness when all six lines are yang lines. At this stage, yang begins its decline, as yin takes over the first line and the yang line is pushed away from the sixth (top) line. Yin begins its own ascendancy, reaching its apex or fullness when all six lines are yin lines. When yang takes over the first line (bottom position), the sixth (top) yin line is pushed away, yang begins its ascendancy again, and the cycle repeats.

This principle of equal standing of yin and yang can be seen through the interaction of yin and yang in the twelve months of the year.

Hexagram #1 ☰ 乾 Heaven (*Khien*) represents April, the month when yang attains its fullness.

In May, the yang at the top of the hexagram is pushed away by the return of yin at the bottom of Hexagram #44 ☰ 姤 Meeting (*Kau*).

The yin energy continues its upward push in the ensuing months.

June: Hexagram #33 ☴ 遯 Retreat (*Thun*)

July: Hexagram #12 ☷ 否 Stagnation (*Phi*)

August: Hexagram #20 ☶ 觀 Observation (*Kwan*)

September: Hexagram #23 ☶ 剝 Splitting-Apart (*Po*)

In October yin attains its fullness in Hexagram #2 ☷ 坤 Earth (*K'un*).

In November yang returns at the bottom of the hexagram, pushing off yin at the top.

November: Hexagram #24 ☳ 復 Returning (*Fu*)

December: Hexagram #19 ☱ 臨 Advance (*Lin*)

January: Hexagram #11 ☰ 泰 Peace (*Thai*)

February: Hexagram #34 ☳ 大壯 Great Strength (*Ta Kwang*)

March: Hexagram #43 ☱ 夬 Breakthrough(*Kwai*)

Changing Lines and the Judgments

A major yin or yang line in the construction of a hexagram becomes a changing line in the primary hexagram and creates a changed hexagram with the line that is the opposite of the original line in the primary hexagram. The constructed hexagram may not have any changing line or have as many as six. The following explains how changing line(s) affect the interpretation of the judgment.

When there is a changing line(s) (see "Changing Lines" section in chapter VII), the primary hexagram and its judgment describe the current situation of the inquirer. The changing line or the changed hexagram describes what is to come in the future. The following guidelines apply in obtaining the answer to the posed question if one or more changing lines are received when the hexagram is constructed.

When there is no changing line, the judgment of the primary hexagram will be the answer.

When there is one changing line, the judgment of the changing line of the primary hexagram will be the answer.

When one receives two changing lines, the judgment of the upper changing line of the primary hexagram will be the answer.

When one receives three changing lines, the judgment of the primary hexagram is the answer for the current situation, and the judgment of the changed hexagram is the answer for the future.

When one receives four changing lines, there will be two unchanging lines in the changed hexagram. The judgment of the lower unchanged line in the changed hexagram will be the answer.

When one receives five changing lines, the judgment of the one unchanging line of the changed hexagram will be the answer.

When one receives all six lines as changing lines, the judgment of the primary hexagram is the answer for the current situation, and the judgment of the changed hexagram is the answer for the future.

❋   ❋   ❋

In concluding the chapters on the process of *I Ching* divination, I present below an example of my *I Ching* divination.

In the course of preparing my manuscript for publication, the slow progress due to inadequacies in my computer knowledge and skills made me feel frustrated and concerned. I was not certain if I would ever be able to put the manuscript in an acceptable format to send to a publisher. I decided to seek advice through *I Ching* divination. I wrote down, "I am frustrated over the slow progress in completing the manuscript for publication. How should I handle this situation?"

I used the coin method and received 8, 6, 7, 8, 7, 7, which formed the hexagram #53, "Progressive Advance" with the second line as a changing line. According to the changing-lines guidelines, when there is one changing line, the judgment of the changing line of the primary hexagram is the answer to the posed question. I looked up Line 2-6 text of Hexagram #53. It stated: "This yin line is properly positioned at the center of trigram, contiguous to 3-9 and correlating with 5-9. The images signify that the wild goose has gradually advanced to the crag and enjoys eating and drinking, for it feels safe and content. Likewise, the noble man who practices the virtues of the Mean (2-6) is content with what he is doing, as he is certain that the ruler (5-9) will summon him to serve the state when the need arises." Furthermore, in the Divination Direction for this line, I read, "You are not yet ready for a leadership position. Make continuous efforts to accumulate experience and to prepare for the opportunity that will come to you before long."

Examining the images of the hexagram, I interpreted that it suggested that I stay on the present course firmly, like a mountain, and to proceed gradually, like the tree on the mountain soaking water. The images also suggested that my undertaking was sound and the process should be a source of joy and satisfaction like a planned wedding, instead of being in a hurry to get to the end. Line 2-6, with its contiguous Line 3-9 and the correlating Line 5-9, has strong allies that would help if in need.

I was reassured by the divination results and felt more relaxed and optimistic about the outcome of my efforts. I found many friends willing to help me when I needed them, and my continuous and gradual efforts have resulted favorably not only in improving my manuscript but in increasing my computer knowledge.

I Ching and the Centered Life

10

Ancient Chinese sages developed and wrote *I Ching* as a guide for man in his pursuit of the righteous or virtuous life. *I Ching* is based on the principles of nature that operate in the universe or nature's way. In nature, everything is continually undergoing change in established cycles, and each thing or being must maintain balance or equilibrium to function in this ever-changing universe. The sages believed that man is an integral part of nature and should conform to nature's way.

Nature's way is called *Tao*. The generic definition of *Tao* is "a way" or "a path." *Tao* is also a Chinese philosophy based on nature. In this context, it is a metaphysical concept relating to the creation and functioning of the universe, and a precise definition is not possible.* *Tao* is translated as "nature's way," "the true way," "the path of virtuous conduct," and "the constancy." Constancy is the concept of *Tao* as the one constant truth, and each operational principle of *Tao is* represented in nature also referred to as *Tao*.

The sages taught different ways for man to follow nature's way or to practice *Tao*. Taoism and Confucianism represent two of the most significant of these teachings. Taoism, originated by *Lao Tzu* in the sixth century B.C., emphasizes going along with nature (letting nature take its course). According to *Lao Tzu*, the way to conform to *Tao* is *Wu Wei*, which translates as "doing nothing" that will interfere with nature's way. It deemphasizes human and social development, in order to preserve human nature in its pure or unadulterated state. Confucianism emphasizes

*Tao Teh Ching, I. *Lao Tzu*, the author, explains the metaphysical concept of *Tao* as follows: "What is called *Tao* is not necessarily the true *Tao,* and what is called name is not necessarily the true name. The nameless is the beginning of the universe, and the naming is the mother of everything." He goes on to say, "*Tao* is the gate through which everything in the universe, both the seen (the material) and the unseen (the spiritual), is produced but each with a different name. Without desire, one will be able to see the unseen but with desire, only the manifesting."

development of human potentialities and harmony in human relationships by following a moral code of conduct that Confucius developed in his classics and *Ten Wings*, an exposition on *I Ching* that became one of the basic *I Ching* texts. Both Taoism and Confucianism place emphasis on maintaining balance and harmony by taking the middle path or the centered life, which is to follow the principles of *Tao*.

I Ching is the "change" aspect of *Tao* and deals with the fundamental principles in nature as expressed through yin and yang. In *I Ching*, the universe consists of Heaven and Earth, which are represented by yin (Earth) and yang (Heaven), the two opposing natural energies that create and operate in the universe. The constant interactions of yin and yang govern all of nature. The universe expands and contracts; the four seasons repeat their cycles; living things perpetuate their life cycles through birth and death. In the universe of perpetual changes, a central force must undergird and stabilize each element in nature, including man. *I Ching* emphasizes this paradigm of *Tao*.

I Ching manifests the universe in graphic terms through its sixty-four hexagrams. The concept of centrality is built into the structure of the hexagrams. The hexagram is composed of two trigrams (three horizontal lines), each with a centerline. The two centerlines of a hexagram are the second and fifth lines, which correspond to the centerlines of its upper and lower trigrams. In the structural interpretation of the hexagram, the centerline of each trigram commands a privileged status. The centerline generally symbolizes a person of moral integrity who practices the Mean or the centered life. Two maps, the *Yellow River Map (Ho Tu)* and *The Writing from River Lo (Lo Shu)*, lay out the numerical structure of *I Ching*. The numerical principles of *I Ching* on the maps explain the universe in numbers. In both maps, the number "5" is the middle number and occupies the center position, symbolizing the stabilizing force.

In *Ten Wings* Confucius explains how the mechanism of the hexagrams operates to reveal *Tao* for man to pursue in his living. The interpretations of the hexagrams convey the material and spiritual aspects of the universal phenomena within the context of time, space, and event. The basic concept that runs throughout *I Ching* is the centered life; it is the essence of *I Ching* and the spirit of *Tao*. The centered life in human living is comparable to the gravitational force that keeps circling heavenly bodies in their orbits.

I Ching teaches that for principled conduct, man should follow *Tao*, the principle of yin and yang that operates in the universe. *I Ching* emphasizes the need to stay within the boundaries of the arena as the yin and yang forces interplay, maintaining a centered position (*Tao*).

Confucius warns that an extreme position creates imbalance, blocking progress and inevitably producing its opposite. One should not resort to an extreme measure to fulfill one's greed. In the book *Doctrine of the Mean (Chung Yung)* compiled by *Tsu Ssu,* the grandson of Confucius, it is explained that when expressed emotions are timely and bring about harmony among the people, the conduct has attained the center.

Man is a microcosm of the universe with spiritual, emotional, intellectual, and physical attributes. Throughout life, each person has a wide range of choices as to how to live one's life. One individual may choose to live life as naturally as possible with childlike purity of mind and heart; another may choose to devote one's life to developing intellect; many pursue a way of life that falls somewhere in between the two. Each is in pursuit of *Tao* in one's own way, and the outcomes may differ in the way that one's life and those of others are affected.

To live the centered life, the yin force of one's physical and materialistic desires must be balanced with the yang force of purity in one's heart and mind. By maintaining the center in daily living, man will have an underlying unity and stability that conforms to *Tao.* To center one's life is to balance one's mental, emotional, spiritual, and physical energies and needs. Greed and ignorance create confusion in the mind, impairing man's ability to follow *Tao.* What is paramount is how one journeys through life. When the path that one pursues in life's journey is in harmony with the principles of *Tao,* that person is said to "practice correct *Tao*" or live the centered life.

The decision making process in everyday living involves an element of prediction. *I Ching* offers man the wisdom of its divination. Man can seek the guidance of *I Ching* divination to help resolve a predicament or crisis. Because the divination predictions of *I Ching* are based on the universal principles of righteous living, the seeker will receive a prediction and a direction that is in harmony with the principles of the centered life. Hence the one who lives the centered life or the enlightened person need not to resort to divination.

The centered life comes from one's heart and mind. Hexagram #31 Influence deals with human interactions and relationships. The fourth line, the seat of the heart and mind, points out how important it is for man to follow *Tao.* The line statement reads, "Influence has reached one's heart. If he stays on the practice of the correct *Tao,* he will be able to influence others and have no cause for remorse. Love and affection grow in the heart but should affect relationship naturally without manipulation." *Ten Wings* expanded on the interpretation of this line by explaining that when a thought enters the mind, it activates the mind for action. When that action is in accord with *Tao,* one will have peace and serenity. This unity of mind and nature transcends man's consciousness and can transform not only one's own life but also influence the lives of others.

Hexagram #61 The Central Sincerity represents love and kindness in the heart and moral integrity in conduct. It advocates sincerity as the way to conform to the *Tao* of centered living. The two yin lines that occupy the center of this hexagram represent the emptied mind or unadulterated human nature, devoid of any sordid thought or greed; the two yang lines, one from the center of each trigram, represent the moral integrity of the heart. For man, his moral sense is his core.

Early Chinese sages recognized how challenging it is for man to take the middle path. In one of his five classics titled *Shu Ching (Book of History)*, Confucius quoted from the sayings of earlier Chinese sages: "The human state of mind is precarious and its determination to follow *Tao* weak, and with all the sincerity in efforts one should concentrate on maintaining the center." Through the sixty-four hexagrams that graphically portray the universe, *I Ching* provides man the principles of moral conduct and its divination to guide him in his pursuit of the centered life.

The following paragraphs convey the concept of the centered life with more specificity.

Some words used to describe a person living the centered life are disciplined, sincere, modest, reliable, compliant, loyal, faithful, firm, harmonious, humble. Some words that are applied to a person who deviates from the centered life are disobedient, unreliable, impudent, impatient, stubborn, rigid, greedy, self-righteous, overly aggressive, selfish, arrogant.

Cited below from Part II of this book are a sampling of images, analyses, and interpretations from individual hexagrams providing suggestions for living the centered life.

The images signify that the dragon keeps speeding upward and is exceeding the proper limits. He is using too much of his energy in a single direction and will soon face difficulties because he will not be able to turn around. (Hexagram #1 Heaven, Line 6-9)

The images signify that he is chasing a deer without a gamekeeper to guide him, and he finds himself lost in the forest. A person of wisdom will refrain from the pursuit, in order to save himself from further regret. If he presses on, his dilemma will be aggravated. (Hexagram #3 Germination, Line 3-6)

The images signify that this teacher or the government employs overly harsh discipline to dispel ignorance or disobedience, resulting in negative effects. If modest methods are employed, a more effective collaboration will be established with the students or the governed. (Hexagram #4 Inexperience, Line 6-9)

The images signify that this competent and virtuous man waits in the countryside in the face of danger that is still distant. He is strong and prepared, but it is not appropriate for him to take premature action when the danger is still far removed. By waiting, he preserves his strength without violating his integrity. (Hexagram #5 Delaying, Line 1-9)

The images signify that 1-9 reaches a decision not to use force but to return to his own position and stay within his boundary of *Tao* (maintaining the virtues of *Tao*), and avoid committing an error. (Hexagram #9 Minor Restraint, Line 1-9)

It is the time of prosperity and contentment. However, you must live up to the spirit that this hexagram teaches, which is to maintain the attitude of humility and modesty in the midst of prosperity and abundance. (Hexagram #14 Great Possession, Divination Direction for hexagram)

Modesty is making lower what is high and making higher what is low. It brings both ends of the extreme to meet at the center to bring about transformation. (Hexagram #15 Modesty, Interpretation of Judgment)

The images signify that in the era of Darkening of the Light, this strong and wise man goes hunting in the south; this is the metaphor for the powerful and wise man going on an expedition to subdue the enemies in order to restore the era of brightness. He captures their great chief, resulting in victory. Although his intention is commendable, he should not undertake such a drastic corrective action hastily unless there is a pressing need. He must first dispel the darkness within himself. (Hexagram #36 Darkening of Light, Line 3-9)

The principle represented by the Decrease hexagram is to obtain a balance in benefits by reducing what is in excess and adding to what is lacking. (Hexagram #41 Decrease, Interpretation of Judgment)

The images signify that this competent man responds quickly to help his friend, the sick prime minister. He must provide help without bragging or calculating the benefit, once his own emergency is taken care of; in return, his friend in the higher status should carefully assess how much help he should accept without causing the helper undue harm. There should be a meeting of the mind. (Hexagram #41 Decrease, Interpretation of Judgment, Line 1-9)

His insistence on the extreme practice of the correct virtues of humility and compliance will lead him to misfortune. (Hexagram #57 Mildness, Line 6-9)

❀ ❀ ❀

Part I of this book presented a historical perspective of *I Ching*, its philosophy of the centered life, the principles of the yin and yang and how they operate in trigrams and hexagrams, hexagram construction, analysis and interpretation, and the divination process.

The following section presents the sixty-four hexagrams in the original sequence, with their Chinese names and the English translation of the names by James Legge.

This chart is a reference point to study themes, sequence, and identification of the constructed hexagrams.

Notes: The Chinese characters of the hexagram names are in the beginning of each hexagram. Where another widely used transliteration differs markedly from Legge's, this Chinese name has been included in the individual hexagram in Part II and in the Table of Contents. The phonetic signs for Chinese pronunciation of hexagram names from Legge's *The I Ching* are omitted. Though the Chinese name of each hexagram is unique and different from the others, some of the translated names are the same.

HEXAGRAM IDENTIFICATION CHART

Each trigram in the first column makes the lower trigram and each trigram in the first row makes the upper trigram of a hexagram

Upper & Lower Triagrams	1 Heaven Trigram	2 Lake Trigram	3 Fire Trigram	4 Thunder Trigram	5 Wind Trigram	6 Water Trigram	7 Mountain Trigram	8 Earth Trigram
1 Heaven Trigram	1 Heaven Hexagram	43 Break through Hexagram	14 Great Possession Hexagram	34 Great Strength Hexagram	9 Minor Restraint Hexagram	5 Delaying Hexagram	26 Major Restraint Hexagrm	11 Peace Hexagram
2 Lake Trigram	10 Treading Hexagram	58 Joy Hexagram	38 Division & Disunion Hexagram	54 Marrying Maiden Hexagram	61 Central Sincerity Hexagram	60 Regulation Hexagram	41 Decrease Hexagram	19 Advance Hexagram
3 Fire Trigram	13 Companionship Hexagram	49 Revolution Hexagram	30 Clinging Hexagram	55 Abundance Hexagram	37 Member of a Family Hexagram	63 Completion Hexagram	22 Ornamental Hexagram	36 Darkening of the Light Hexagram
4 Thunder Trigram	25 Freedom from Error Hexagram	17 Following Hexagram	21 Biting through Hexagram	51 Shock Hexagram	42 Increase Hexagram	3 Germination Hexagram	27 Nourishment Hexagram	24 Returning Hexagram
5 Wind Trigram	44 Meeting Hexagram	28 Large Excess Hexagram	50 Cauldron Hexagram	32 Constancy Hexagram	57 Mildness Hexagram	48 Well Hexagram	18 Decaying Hexagram	46 Rising & Advancing Hexagram
6 Water Trigram	6 Conflict Hexagram	47 Oppression Hexagram	64 Incomplete Hexagram	40 Loosening Hexagram	59 Dissolution Hexagram	29 Abysmal Hexagram	4 Inexperience Hexagram	7 Host Hexagram
7 Mountain Trigram	33 Retreat Hexagram	31 Influence Hexagram	56 Wanderer Hexagram	62 Small Excess Hexagram	53 Progressive Advance Hexagram	39 Inhibition Hexagram	52 Checking Hexagram	15 Modesty Hexagram
8 Earth Trigram	12 Stagnation Hexagram	45 Gathering together Hexagram	35 Advance Hexagram	16 Harmonious Joy Hexagram	20 Observation Hexagram	8 Union Hexagram	23 Splitting Apart Hexagram	2 Earth Hexagram

Figure 13—Hexagram Identification Chart

THE 64 HEXAGRAMS (CHART)

The hexagrams, in the order in which they appear in *I Ching*

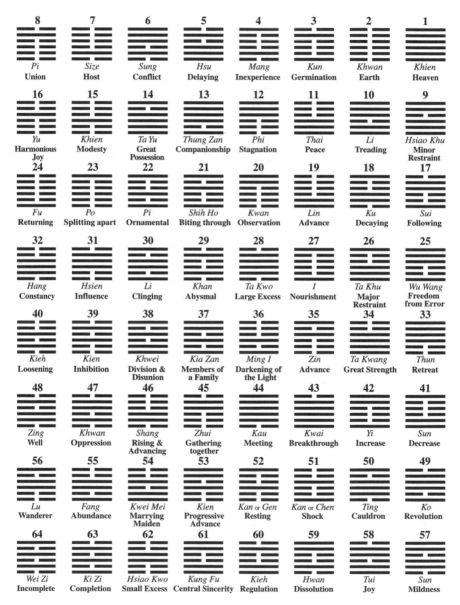

8	7	6	5	4	3	2	1
Pi Union	*Size* Host	*Sung* Conflict	*Hsu* Delaying	*Mang* Inexperience	*Kun* Germination	*Khwan* Earth	*Khien* Heaven
16	**15**	**14**	**13**	**12**	**11**	**10**	**9**
Yu Harmonious Joy	*Khien* Modesty	*Ta Yu* Great Possession	*Thung Zan* Companionship	*Phi* Stagnation	*Thai* Peace	*Li* Treading	*Hsiao Khu* Minor Restraint
24	**23**	**22**	**21**	**20**	**19**	**18**	**17**
Fu Returning	*Po* Splitting apart	*Pi* Ornamental	*Shih Ho* Biting through	*Kwan* Observation	*Lin* Advance	*Ku* Decaying	*Sui* Following
32	**31**	**30**	**29**	**28**	**27**	**26**	**25**
Hang Constancy	*Hsien* Influence	*Li* Clinging	*Khan* Abysmal	*Ta Kwo* Large Excess	*I* Nourishment	*Ta Khu* Major Restraint	*Wu Wang* Freedom from Error
40	**39**	**38**	**37**	**36**	**35**	**34**	**33**
Kieh Loosening	*Kien* Inhibition	*Khwei* Division & Disunion	*Kia Zan* Members of a Family	*Ming I* Darkening of the Light	*Zin* Advance	*Ta Kwang* Great Strength	*Thun* Retreat
48	**47**	**46**	**45**	**44**	**43**	**42**	**41**
Zing Well	*Khwan* Oppression	*Shang* Rising & Advancing	*Zhui* Gathering together	*Kau* Meeting	*Kwai* Breakthrough	*Yi* Increase	*Sun* Decrease
56	**55**	**54**	**53**	**52**	**51**	**50**	**49**
Lu Wanderer	*Fang* Abundance	*Kwei Mei* Marrying Maiden	*Kien* Progressive Advance	*Kan or Gen* Resting	*Kan or Chen* Shock	*Ting* Cauldron	*Ko* Revolution
64	**63**	**62**	**61**	**60**	**59**	**58**	**57**
Wei Zi Incomplete	*Ki Zi* Completion	*Hsiao Kwo* Small Excess	*Kung Fu* Central Sincerity	*Kieh* Regulation	*Hwan* Dissolution	*Tui* Joy	*Sun* Mildness

Figure 14—The 64 Hexagrams Chart

Part II: The Sixty-Four Hexagrams

Analysis, Interpretation and Divination

1. The Heaven 乾 (Khien) Hexagram

Key attributes: Heaven, king, father, creativity, firmness, *Tao*

Judgment

"*Khien* (represents) what is great and originating, penetrating, advantageous, correct, and firm." (James Legge, *The I Ching,* 57.)

Essence of Hexagram

This hexagram explains the *Tao* of Heaven as the paradigm of creativity and leadership.

Hexagram Image(s)

The two trigrams of all yang lines that make up the Heaven hexagram symbolize the unceasing functions of Heaven. The six yang lines represent the strong and steadfast functions of Heaven. The wise and noble uses the images as his guide to make unceasing efforts to excel in his virtues.

Hexagram Analysis

This is the first of the sixty-four *I Ching* hexagrams. Its position as the first in the hexagram sequence indicates the fundamental beginning of the universe. The Heaven hexagram consists of two trigrams of Heaven. Together, they represent Heaven as a single, unified embodiment of yang and inseparable. The repeated Heaven trigram emphasizes the unceasing nature of Heaven.

The Heaven hexagram consists of all yang lines for both the lower and upper trigrams. With all six lines as yang, Heaven is pure yang energy and symbolizes being great (powerful, encompassing both time and space), originating, and fundamentally correct. The lines represent the progressive movement of the yang energy, beginning at the bottom line and culminating at the sixth or top line.

Since the Heaven and Earth hexagrams represent the pure energies of yang and yin respectively, each line is properly positioned. Heaven culminates its functions with the yang line, and a next hexagram begins with yin as the bottom line.

5-9 is the only lead line of this hexagram.

Interpretation of Judgment

Four Chinese characters constitute the judgment in the Heaven hexagram. The basic theme in all four is to comply with *Tao*.

"Great and originating": Heaven's fundamental force or *Chi* of creation and the beginning.

"Fundamental goodness": For man, it is the highest level of attainment and functioning.

"Penetrating and prevailing": In order to prevail, man must achieve excellence in all aspects of his life.

"Advantageous": Good and beneficial. For man, it is to be in harmony with nature.

"Correct and firm": Just and persistent in conduct and action. For man, it is to be fair and objective and persevere.

Heaven is great, as all things originate from Heaven. It is in full command. All things in the universe, including earth and the element of time and the nature of things, were conceptualized in Heaven. It makes clouds move to bring rain in order that things grow. The sage ruler on earth is compared to Heaven, with its attributes of greatness, originator, correctness, and conceptualizer. The sage ruler rides (rules) in a carriage drawn by six dragons (the six yang lines represent six dragons, symbolizing Heaven), and he attains the high position above all things on earth. He commands his domain through correct leadership to bring about peace among all nations and harmony in nature, with everything realizing its true potential.

Divination Direction

It augurs well in practically every aspect of your life: family life, business, trading, and employment. Pursue with persistence your virtuous objectives; you will reap excellent results. This augury is especially auspicious for prevailing in a competitive situation and profiting in trading. You have reached the top, and you should be careful not to overextend your goal because a declining trend will start before long.

Individual Lines: Analysis, Interpretation, and Divination Direction

Note: The dragon symbolizes Heaven or sage on the earth and is used as the metaphor for each line of this hexagram.

Line 1-9: This yang line is properly positioned at the beginning of the hexagram.

The images signify that the dragon (the great person) is hidden deep in the earth. He is not yet ready to engage in his rainmaking function in the sky. The metaphor suggests that he is not yet recognized for his abilities and it is not an opportune time for taking action.

Divination Direction

With your creative ability, you have a potential for a great achievement, but time is not ripe for you to make a move. Refrain from rushing into an activity. Be patient and prepare for an opportunity that is sure to come.

Line 2-9: This yang line is positioned at the center of the lower trigram. Even though 2-9 is normally a yin position, for this hexagram, it correlates with 5-9 to produce favorable interpretations. Since both are the centerlines of the lower and upper trigrams, they have the virtues of the Mean.

The images signify that the dragon comes out of hiding and appears in the field in order to bring benefits to the world. Likewise, this virtuous person is ready to serve the world, and it will be propitious for him to meet with the great man (5-9)[10] who will recognize his virtues and use his services.

Divination Direction

You see different opportunities open before you. It is the time to decide which route you will choose and set up your goal. It will be to your advantage to seek help from the person who has the resources so that you can advance to achieve your goal.

Line 3-9: This yang line is properly positioned but lacks the merits of the center position. Though strong and competent, it is still in a precarious situation, especially because it is the transitory last line of the lower trigram. (It is transitory because it borders the lower and upper trigrams.)

The images signify that the dragon prudently prepares for his next move. Likewise, the man of virtue puts in his efforts all day and in the evening reflects as to whether his efforts were virtuous. Even if he is in a vulnerable position, he will seldom make a mistake in conduct because he is careful and reflective and follows the correct principles of *Tao*.

Divination Direction

You feel confident and ready to tackle any task creatively. But reflect carefully on your activities and avoid taking any precipitous, impulsive action.

Line 4-9: This yang is strong, but it lacks stability because the fourth line is the beginning of a new trigram and it has to decide which way to turn.

The images signify that the dragon is still deep in the lake and in a position to either remain in the lake or leap forward. Likewise, the man (4-9) can choose between moving or not moving from his present situation. A man who follows the principles of *Tao* will avoid a mistake if he seizes the right opportunity to act.

Divination Direction

The more resourceful you become, the better it will be for you to take advantage of an opportunity when it comes your way. Prepare more thoroughly while waiting, and watch for an opportunity. Be decisive in your action when the right time comes.

Line 5-9: This yang line occupies the center of the upper trigram, the most prestigious position of the ruler.

The images signify that the dragon is flying in the sky. Metaphorically, the sage king will govern the state well because the dragon brings beneficent rain to the world. It will be a good omen for the ruler to find a great man to assist him.

Divination Direction

It augurs well. The time is ripe for you to act. This is the most favorable fortune. It will be to your advantage to find an able assistant or advisor to help you achieve your goal.

Line 6-9: This yang line is at the apogee of this hexagram, signifying that this dragon observes no limit in its flight upward.

The images signify that the dragon keeps speeding upward[11] and is exceeding the proper limits. He is using too much of his energy in a single direction and will soon face difficulties because he will not be able to turn around.

Divination Direction

It is as important to maintain what you have already achieved as trying to keep achieving more. Slow down and reassess your activities, or you will face difficulties.

The Interpretation on the Use of Yang Lines

The hexagram of all yang lines will change to the hexagram of all yin lines when it reaches its sixth line. Therefore, in interpreting yang of all yang lines, its strength and greatness are accompanied by tenderness and modesty, like the group of flying dragons whose heads are hidden above the clouds. The *I Ching* text says that the use of yang lines will bring good fortune if the dragons in flight are seen without their heads. It is the metaphor for modesty (the attribute of yin) to mean that, although one may be the head of other people, he should not be vain because of his position, but should be humble. Such a disciplined exercise of one's power and authority will result in good fortune.

2. The Earth 坤 (Khwan or K'un) Hexagram

Key attributes: Earth, people, mother, substance, the symbol of submission

Judgment

"*Khwan* (represents) what is great and originating, penetrating, advantageous, correct and having the firmness of a mare. When the superior man (here intended) has to make any movement, if he take the initiative, he will go astray; if he follow, he will find his (proper) lord. The advantageousness will be seen in his getting friends in the southwest, and losing friends in the northeast. If he rest in correctness and firmness, there will be good fortune." (James Legge, *The I Ching*,. 59.)

Essence of Hexagram

This hexagram explains the *Tao* of Earth as the paradigm of productivity and compliance.

Hexagram Image(s)

The *I Ching* texts explain that the basic nature of earth is embodied in the Earth hexagram, which is to comply with the leadership of Heaven. The two trigrams with all yin lines represent the image of the mare that has the qualities of strength and gentleness. The wise and noble with his magnanimous virtues uses the images as his guide in accommodating all things.

Hexagram Analysis

This is the second in the hexagram sequence and logically follows the Heaven hexagram. Earth receives what Heaven originates and transforms them. The Earth hexagram consists of two trigrams of Earth, emphasizing the expansiveness of earth to accommodate and transform all that it receives from Heaven.

All six lines of this hexagram are yin lines, symbolizing the pure yin attributes of earth. The Chinese character for the Earth hexagram is composed of dirt (earth) and expansion (of the energy that Earth receives from Heaven). The trigram of three yin lines resembles the Chinese character for "river" (川); the river follows the topography of the land, which is the concept of obedience.

2-6 is the sole lead line of this hexagram.

Interpretation of Judgment

The first two Chinese characters of the Earth hexagram judgment are the same as the first two characters of the Heaven hexagram judgment. The two characters of the Earth hexagram judgment are paraphrased below.

"Great and originating": Earth's fundamental force of yin energy as the creator and the beginning of all the forms on the earth.

"Penetrating": Receptive and maternal force that prevails at all times for all things on the earth.

Great is the fundamental nature of Earth, which gives birth to all things on the earth. It is the way Earth complies with Heaven. It is the generous virtue of Earth that it bears and nourishes all things that exist on the earth. The combined effect of all its virtues is limitless, and its vast capacity to accommodate all things and allow each to follow its own nature is gloriously great.

The attribute of pure yin is comparable to that of a mare (as a dragon is that of Heaven), which is steadfast and obedient. Yin receives what yang originates. Therefore, the fundamental attribute of this hexagram is not to take the leadership role, but to follow a strong, principled leader.

The mare belongs to Earth as the dragon to Heaven, and it travels on the earth without limits.

It is the virtue of compliance, or the correct way of *Tao*, that the wise and noble should follow. If he takes the lead, he will be confused and violate the *Tao*, but if he follows compliantly, he will secure his proper place. In *I Ching,* southwest is the direction of yin on the earth, and northeast, the direction of yang on the earth. The wise and noble finds friends in the southwest to travel with him. However, he will lose friends if he travels in the northeast direction. The one who follows the principled leader will have blessings in the end. By following the principles of *Tao*, one will receive the fortune of peace and stability, which the limitless capacity of Earth provides.

Divination Direction

It augurs well for a person who is modest in character and cooperative with other people and for people engaged in philanthropic endeavors. If you have a rebellious personality, make special efforts to be prudent in your activities. It is not a good time to start a new business or expand the present business except in the real estate business. Try not to carry out an activity alone, but find a good friend or helper for cooperative efforts. It is favorable to conclude a marital arrangement. An expectant mother will have an easy delivery to a daughter. Guard against stress-related health problems.

Individual Lines: Analysis, Interpretation, and Divination Direction

Line 1-6: As the beginning line of the Earth hexagram, yin energy sets in as hoarfrost, and the day of ice will soon come. Yang represents warm energy, while yin, cold energy; yang, life, yin, death; yang, good, yin, evil.

The images signify that evil is stirring. Unless one can tame and control it, it has the potential for developing into something more serious.

Divination Direction

It is not the good time for you to start a new venture. Instead, devote yourself to guard against any personal or family problem. A small problem may develop into a more serious problem. You should make every effort to confine the problem or loss to forestall a more serious consequence.

Line 2-6: This yin line is at the center of the lower trigram and properly positioned.

The images signify that the line has the qualities of being straight, square and great. Earth is obedient (correct) and straight (honest) in carrying out its functions, square in its directions and shape, and great in its expansiveness and performance.

Divination Direction

It augurs well. It is one of the most favorable auguries. Make sure everything is in order to help you achieve your goal. Set your goal high, and maintain your steady efforts to achieve your goal.

Line 3-6: This yin line is at the yang position as the top line of the lower trigram, representing a high official.

The images signify that the person has special talents and fine virtues, but he is not yet in a position to use them to his favor. It is to his advantage to keep his superior qualities under restraint and firmly maintain correct *Tao*. Should he have an occasion to engage in the king's service, he will carry out his duties successfully without claiming his services for his own benefit, for he is wise and talented.

Divination Direction

Be decisive, yet be prudent and deliberate in utilizing your resources. Assess your resources accurately and carry out your plans without being ostentatious.

Line 4-6: This line is properly positioned but lacks advantages because it fails to correlate with any other line below or above it.

The images signify that a sack is tied up to safeguard its contents. There will be no reason for blame or praise if he acts with humility and prudence.

Divination Direction

The time is not yet ripe for you to act to achieve your goal. Patiently safeguard what you have in both talent and resources, and act discreetly in taking care of your daily tasks.

Line 5-6: This yin line is positioned at the center of the upper trigram, thus occupying the most honored position, that of the sovereign. The color yellow represents the centerline of a trigram and the centrality of life. The lower trigram symbolizes the garment that adorns the lower part of the body.

The combined image of the yellow color and the lower garment signifies modest conduct on the part of the ruler and the ruled with the virtues of loyalty, faithfulness, and goodness. There is fundamental good fortune for all that practice the Mean.

Divination Direction

It augurs well. It is one of the most favorable auguries. You will be able to get help from an unexpected friend. Carry out your plans with confidence, and you will be successful.

Line 6-6: This yin line is the last line of the Earth hexagram and represents the apogee of yin forces. It is at the stage of confronting the yang forces.

Yin energy has been accelerating its dominance in the hexagram, and the sixth line has exceeded its boundary into yang territory, as if it were a yang force or a dragon of Heaven. The result is a bloody fight between two equally powerful yin and yang forces. The images signify that two dragons, the fake yin dragon of Earth and the genuine yang dragon of Heaven, are fighting in the wild, covered with the yellow color of Earth and the black color of Heaven's blood.

Divination Direction

It augurs ill. Do not be obstinate but look around and listen to what other people say about you. Be flexible in your attitude and extremely discreet in your activities, as it is an ominous augury.

The Interpretation on the Use of Yin

Since yin and yang are the fundamental and most powerful forces that formulate the sixty-four hexagrams of *I Ching*, a special paragraph is added for the Heaven and Earth hexagrams (hexagrams of pure yang and pure yin energies) to explain how to apply these forces in interpreting each force.

The *I Ching* texts explain that with the yin lines, it is advantageous to always practice the yin principle of compliance to attain greatness. The sixth line of the Earth hexagram is an example of a disadvantageous result when the yin line does not conform to this principle. In the Earth hexagram, the bottom yin line turns more aggressive as it advances upward, culminating at the sixth line. There, the yin line invades yang, and a bloody fight takes place between the two fundamental forces of yin and yang, and greatness cannot be accomplished. The correct *Tao* for yin is to be obedient and comply with the leadership of the yang force.

3. The Germination 屯 (Kun or Chun) Hexagram

Key attributes: Difficulties of beginning, symbol of bursting force

Judgment

"*Kun* (indicates that in the case which it presupposes) there will be great progress and success, and the advantage will come from being correct and firm. (But) any movement in advance should not be (lightly) undertaken. There will be advantage in appointing feudal princes." (James Legge, *The I Ching,* 62.)

Essence of Hexagram

This hexagram explains the *Tao* of beginning as the paradigm for planning, priority-setting, and orderly process in governing and in other areas of life.

Hexagram Image(s)

Thunder is below the clouds (Water) and forebodes rain, though not yet certain. In governing the nation, it is the time for a sage ruler to establish the principles of good governing as the priority before he begins to govern, in order to help the people overcome the difficulties and confusion in living with the government policies.

Hexagram Analysis

This hexagram follows the Heaven and Earth hexagrams as a natural sequence to fill and populate the earth. It symbolizes the difficulties of beginnings, such as a blade of grass (1-9)[12] breaking out of the earth and gradually pushing above the surface with the vigor that it possesses at this stage. This hexagram is composed of the upper trigram Water, symbolizing peril, and the lower trigram of Thunder, the symbol of mobility, and it presents the image of action or movement with a perilous element.

1-9 and 5-9 are the lead lines of this hexagram.

Interpretation of Judgment

The Germination hexagram stands for the beginning interactions of yin and yang and the accompanying difficulties of germination or birth. The movement occurs with potential perils. (Whenever there is movement, there is a possibility of peril because of the change from the known to the unknown.) However, germination is a natural phenomenon and results in great progress and success. The movement of thunder and rain in the sky fills the earth for the primordial creativity of Heaven for all things to come, in order that things that germinate on earth will be nurtured. The great beginning must be correct and firm.

In human affairs, it is the time to appoint the feudal chiefs to rule the states in an orderly way. However, to expect peace and stability at this stage is premature.

Divination Direction

At present, you are under great distress, like a blade of grass that may experience hardship in breaking out of the ground. Do not despair, for great opportunities lie ahead for successful enterprises. Prepare for the future, proceeding cautiously without haste and with good motivation. It is unfavorable to undertake any business or financial dealings at present. Guard against health problems.

Individual Lines: Analysis, Interpretation, and Divination Direction

<u>Line 1-9:</u> This yang line is the first line of this hexagram and properly positioned, with a proper correlation with 4-6. Usually this line can move ahead, but 4-6 with which it correlates is the first line of the upper trigram Water that symbolizes peril, and there is a hesitation to move in the beginning. 1-9, being the yang line, possesses capabilities for advancement, but its low status (the lowest line of the hexagram) presents difficulties in making its move to advance decisively.

The images signify that the virtuous man is hesitant to make a move because of the perils that can occur in the beginning process. He maintains the correct practice of *Tao* with good motivation and right conduct (properly positioned) and treats the humble and inferior with respect and honor. It is the time to seek help in overcoming the difficulties and advance to achieve his goals. Because he has great popularity among the people, it will be the opportune time for him to become a feudal chief.

Divination Direction

A new environment calls for new ideas. If you take the initiative with a well-prepared and deliberate move, along with proper motivation and attitude, your ideas will eventually result in a great achievement.

Line 2-6: This yin line is properly positioned at the center of the lower trigram Thunder (movement) and correlates with 5-9; there is a loving relationship between the two. A young man who resides in the same village (1-9) is a spoiler because he wants to marry 2-6 and stands in the way to prevent her from marrying 5-9, as if the horses are unhitched from the carriage.

The images signify that she (2-6) is at an impasse and does not know which way to turn. This difficult situation is due to the fact that she is riding atop the yang line (yin above yang symbolizes difficulties). She chooses to stay on the correct course of *Tao* without giving in to the pressures of 1-9 and wait. During the natural time cycle of ten years, she becomes betrothed to the man she truly loves (5-9).

Divination Direction

It augurs a sign of impasse. In the beginning, your plans will not progress as you hope. But your patience and persistent efforts to achieve your original goal will bring about successful results. You will find a good friend who will be of great help toward your success.

Line 3-6: This yin line is improperly positioned and is in an antagonistic relationship with 6-6, indicating improper ambition with no friend to back him up.

The images signify that he is chasing a deer without a gamekeeper who can guide him, and he finds himself lost in the forest. A person of wisdom will refrain from pursuing it in order to save himself from further regret. If he presses on, his dilemma will be aggravated.

Divination Direction

Examine yourself as to whether your attitude and conduct are proper to bring changes and improvements to you. Beware of an action coming from one's greed and improper ambition. Be conscientious, honest, and sincere to maintain good friendships.

Line 4-6: This yin line is contiguous to 5-9 and properly correlates with 1-9.

The images signify that her predicament is likened to the horse, which is pulling at odds with the wagon she is riding, creating an impasse. 4-6 finds some merit in getting married to 5-9, but she is more in love with 1-9. In order to overcome this impasse, she should seek marriage with 1-9, for this is the correct and wise decision.

Divination Direction

The time of impasse is about to end. The time has come for you to move cautiously, and find a person in a modest position but with great potential to help you achieve your goal.

Line 5-9: This yang line is properly positioned in the ruler's position at the time of impasse and peril (upper trigram Water), and it correlates with 2-6.

The images signify that it is not a proper time for the ruler to extend himself on a grand scale, as such efforts will fall short of benefiting the ruled. In order for the ruler to overcome the difficulties created by the impasse, he needs to make correct and firm decisions, beginning with small but important matters, such as strengthening his relationship with 2-6. This will result in good fortune.

Divination Direction

You are at a difficult time of impasse. Do not be immobilized, but keep your eyes open widely to find resources and friends to help you make the move. Set a small but definitive goal for each step of the way, and work on it diligently to succeed.

Line 6-6: This yin line is positioned at the top of the hexagram of impasse and peril. There is no one he can ask for help because he has an antagonistic relationship with 3-6, and there is no line above him.

The images signify that he has fallen into a dire predicament with no one from whom he can get help, as though his yoked horses are pulling at odds with the wagon. He weeps profusely with tears of blood running down his face. In this situation, he cannot last long and will have to give up his efforts.

Divination Direction

It augurs dire predicament and misfortune. Take whatever actions necessary to minimize the misfortune. Do not despair; a better time will come in time.

4. The Inexperience 蒙 (Mang) Hexagram

Key attributes: The young and inexperienced, enlightenment, education

Judgment

"*Mang* (indicates that in the case which it presupposes) there will be progress and success. I do not (go and) seek the youthful and inexperienced, but he comes and seeks me. When he shows (the sincerity that marks) the first recourse to divination, I instruct him. If he apply a second and third time, that is troublesome; and I do not instruct the troublesome. There will be advantage in being firm and correct." (James Legge, *The I Ching,* 64.)

Essence of Hexagram

This hexagram explains the *Tao* of education[13] as the paradigm for growth and development.

Hexagram Image(s)

The spring below the Mountain stands for the image of the Inexperience hexagram. The wise and noble uses the image as his guide to educate himself continually and cultivate his virtues deeply. This process of initially educating the young and continuing one's development as an adult is like the spring water that reaches the ocean as a deep and great river.

Hexagram Analysis

This hexagram is composed of the inner trigram Water symbolizing danger, peril, or pitfall, and the outer trigram Mountain, halt. A person who is insecure in his mind is being stopped from advancing because he is still young, inexperienced, and hesitant, and he fears the unknown. "I" in the judgment above refers to 2-9, the teacher, who correlates with 5-6, the young and inexperienced. It is not for the teacher to seek the inexperienced pupil to educate; the inexperienced should seek a teacher to be educated. The teacher must provide clear answers to the pupil's questions, like a person seeking an answer from divination. If the pupil repeats the question after he receives an answer, it indicates distrust, and the teacher will refrain from answering.

2-9 and 5-6 are the lead lines of this hexagram.

Interpretation of Judgment

The Inexperience Hexagram presents the image of a spring (Water), the symbol of danger, at the foot of the Mountain, the symbol of halt. Like the spring that has begun a long and perilous journey, a young person who perseveres to obtain a full education will make great progress and succeed in the long run. However, at this stage, he is still inexperienced and finds many obstacles (Mountain) to overcome in his explorations. He (5-6) needs a good teacher (2-9) for his education and for guidance in cultivating good moral character and judgment. Successful education depends on how motivated the young person is; he should seek out the teacher to teach him, not vice versa. The teacher's approach is to develop the potential of the young and inexperienced with correctness and firmness and to nourish his pupil's virtues. The youth's bright and successful future will be like a spring that develops into a great river.

Divination Direction

At present you are groping for a direction, but good fortune lies ahead. This is the time for you to educate yourself as much as you can on the subject you are interested in to prepare yourself for your future. You may not become successful immediately, but if you are well motivated and continue with sincere efforts, you will become increasingly confident and successful. Guard against ill health, financial loss, and difficulties related to travel or a move.

Individual Lines: Analysis, Interpretation, and Divination Direction

Line 1-6: This yin line is improperly positioned at the beginning of this hexagram, symbolizing the most inexperienced. It is in a contiguous relationship with 2-9, who will educate 1-6 if the inexperienced is motivated to learn from him.

The images signify that the young and inexperienced has begun his educational development with his teacher (2-9), who uses discipline to teach him restraints and rid him of fetters and shackles, and then relaxes the discipline to teach him self-control. Otherwise, the young will be undisciplined, and this will bring about regrettable consequences.

Divination Direction

Your beginning must be modest and sure-footed in your efforts to achieve your goal. To deal with the changing realities, you must examine your attitude and mind-set for the right motivation and not be motivated by greed or selfish desires. Sincere efforts will result in good fortune.

Line 2-9: This yang line is positioned at the center of the lower trigram, contiguous to 1-6, and it correlates with 5-6. 2-9 represents a man with inner strength in three different roles. One is the teacher who educates all the young and inexperienced (all yin lines of the hexagram). In its correlative relationship with 5-6, it represents the husband with 5-6 as his wife, and the third representation is a son in the family, with 5-6 as his father. In this last context, 5-6 is a weak father (yin line), and 2-9 is a strong, capable son (yang line).

The first image signifies that this teacher educates all the young and inexperienced, leading them to good fortune. In the second image, the husband has the good fortune of being married to a virtuous lady (5-6) and treats her with proper respect (the wife is represented in the upper trigram and the husband in the lower trigram). In the third image, a son (2-9) manages the family affairs well and is competent to take charge of the family affairs, as the new generation (2-9) succeeds the old generation (5-6).

Divination Direction

A leader has to keep his mind open to listen to and understand the followers and to lead wisely. If you are in a leadership position, you will have great good fortune, since people will support your efforts. For the ordinary person, your efforts will result in good fortune.

Line 3-6: This yin line is improperly positioned and precarious. It is transitional in its move, because it is the top line of the lower trigram away from the center.

The images signify a woman who chases after a wealthy man (6-9). It will be a mistake for the man to marry her, as she will be unreliable and disobedient.

Divination Direction

It augurs ill. You have talents, but they can be wasted if they are misapplied. Be wary of sexual enticement and your greedy motivation.

Line 4-6: This yin line is far from 2-9, the positive force for leading others out of ignorance. It is surrounded by weak negative forces above and below it with no correlative line.

The images signify that the pupil persists in his ignorance and suffering and is far removed from the teacher.

Divination Direction

You are in a state of confusion and helplessness. Take time to conserve your energy and resources before you start an enterprise. Find someone who can guide you out of this dilemma. Maintain your sincere and persistent efforts to succeed.

Line 5-6: This yin line carries the merits of being at the center of the upper trigram in the high status position, and it correlates with 2-9.

The images signify that, although this person is young and inexperienced, he is modest and compliant in his attitude toward his teacher (2-9).

Divination Direction

It augurs well. In order to overcome the obstacles that you may face in your efforts to achieve your goal, cooperate closely with others who have the knowledge and experience, and you will succeed.

Line 6-9: This yang line is at the top of the hexagram and improperly positioned. He has the strength and ability to teach or govern people and dispel their ignorance and inexperience, but he is too aggressive, resorting to harassment and force.

The images signify that this teacher or the government employs overly harsh discipline to dispel ignorance or disobedience, resulting in negative effects. If modest methods are employed, a more effective collaboration will be established with the students or the governed.

Divination Direction

Before you utilize your resources, you must assess what and how to use and why. Avoid taking extreme measures. Guard against ill effects coming from extreme and harsh actions.

5. The Delaying 需 (Hsu) Hexagram

Key attributes: Delaying, waiting

Judgment

"*Hsu* intimates that, with the sincerity which is declared in it, there will be brilliant success. With firmness there will be good fortune; and it will be advantageous to cross the great stream." (James Legge, *The I Ching,* 67.)

Essence of Hexagram

This hexagram explains the *Tao* of preparation as the paradigm for waiting for opportunities to act.

Hexagram Image(s)

Clouds above Heaven stand for the image of the Delaying (Waiting) hexagram. The wise and noble follows the image to delay an action (wait for the rain). He is prepared, and he enjoys himself, eating, drinking, and relaxing as he waits confidently for the right time, or for the clouds to bring rain in due time.

Hexagram Analysis

This hexagram is made up of the lower trigram Heaven, the metaphor for great power, and the upper trigram Water, symbol for danger or peril. The movement of great power has to be deliberate in the face of a danger, which gives this hexagram the name Delaying. 5-9 is the lead line of this hexagram and occupies the center of the trigram Water, symbolizing the strength and integrity of the ruler in the midst of peril.

5-9 is the sole lead line of this hexagram.

Interpretation of Judgment

The Delaying hexagram means waiting, prepared and confident, for the right time to take action in the face of lurking danger so as to assure success. The ruler (5-9), who has the virtues of the Mean and practices the rectitude of *Tao,* will wait with sincerity and faith to cross the great river or proceed with an important enterprise. He will attain success.

Divination Direction

Your augury is like a cloud-covered sky with no rainfall in sight. Refrain from any hasty or premature undertaking. Study and prepare for an opportune time to act that is to come before long.

Individual Lines: Analysis, Interpretation, and Divination Direction

Line 1-9: This yang line is properly positioned and is farthest away from the danger (upper trigram Water). An attribute of the Heaven trigram is to move ahead (three yang lines), but waiting in the face of approaching danger does not diminish the significance of its attribute of strength, as it only conserves its energy.

The images signify that this competent and virtuous man waits in the countryside in the face of danger that is still distant. He is strong and prepared, but it is not appropriate for him to take premature action when the danger is still far removed. By waiting, he preserves his strength without violating his integrity. There will be no blame for his conduct.

Divination Direction

There is no need to hurry to take action. Relax and continue to carry out your routine duties, as it is still premature for any new undertaking.

Line 2-9: This yang line is at the center of the lower trigram, symbolizing both strength and the virtues of the Mean. He is one step closer to the danger (the upper trigram Water) and is depicted here as waiting on the sand.[14]

The images signify that this competent and virtuous man waits on the sand with confidence for the right time. In the beginning, there may be some rebuke by others because of delaying, but he will have good fortune in the end.

Divination Direction

Your patience will pay off, as a good opportunity for you to act is approaching fast. Maintain your good motive and wait for the opportune time to act. You will have good fortune.

Line 3-9: This yang line is at the top of the lower trigram, closest to the upper trigram Water (danger). The person is depicted here as waiting in the mud (wet soil). This yang line is the metaphor for the strong and aggressive who lacks the virtues of the Mean.

The images signify that this strong and aggressive person has moved close to the water. In his haste, he ends up impatiently waiting in the mud in the face of the danger. His premature move attracts his enemies to him. He must exercise extreme restraints in order not to suffer harm.

Divination Direction

You must cultivate your ability to control your aggressive urge for action. Impatient actions will invite calamities. Be alert and take extreme precautions and restraints.

Line 4-6: This yin line is properly positioned as the entry line of the upper trigram Water (peril), and it properly correlates with 1-9.

The images signify that he is in the middle of danger, as if in a bloody pit. In this desperate situation, he has to be able to maintain his calm, hoping for the best. Fortunately, he has a friend (1-9) who gives him wise advice that he listens to and with which he complies. He will be able to get out of this calamitous situation.

Divination Direction

This is the time you need to act decisively. You are in a desperate situation, and it is the time for you to maintain your calm and seek the advice of those who have more knowledge and experience.

Line 5-9: This yang line is properly positioned at the center of the upper trigram Water (peril). It does not correlate with any line, and it has an antagonistic correlation with 2-9. This competent ruler practices the Mean and confidently waits for his subject (2-9) to develop loyalty to

THE SIXTY-FOUR HEXAGRAMS ❀ 87

him. When the subject develops this loyalty, he (2-9) and his friends (the three yang lines of the lower trigram) will come to serve him.

The images signify that the ruler waits for his loyal subjects to come to serve him. While he waits, he prepares and shares a feast of food and wine, which is likened to strengthening one's inner resources while waiting. If the ruler continues to practice the Mean and stays on the correct course of *Tao*, there will be good fortune, as this is the way to overcome the perilous situation of the time.

Divination Direction

Everything seems to be going favorably. If you become relaxed and lazy, you will invite misfortune. On the other hand, if you take advantage of this favorable time to redouble your sincere efforts, your good fortune will multiply. You should refrain from undertaking any contentious matters. Make efforts to develop friends who can help you.

Line 6-6: This yin line is properly positioned at the top of the hexagram and correlates with 3-9. This line indicates a person at the height of a perilous situation (upper trigram Water). He will be able to get the help of 3-9 who brings two of his friends (1-9 and 2-9) to rescue him from the perilous situation.

The images signify that he is falling into the perilous pit. At this moment of desperation, an unexpected event or fate can rescue him, as if three unexpected guests arrive, and he treats them with respect. Though his position is perilous and he is incompetent for the high position (yin line) that he holds, he has a competent friend who brings his two friends to rescue him. In the end, he will not have a major problem, but good fortune.

Divination Direction

You may be experiencing some difficulties in your life or starting an undertaking. Your persistent and sincere efforts will be rewarded with unexpected help from others, which will lead you to good fortune. Always be sincere and friendly with other people.

6. The Conflict 訟 (Sung) Hexagram

Key attributes: Conflict, litigation, symbol of contention

Judgment

"*Sung* intimates how, though there is sincerity in one's contention, he will yet meet with opposition and obstruction; but if he cherish an apprehensive caution, there will be good fortune, while, if he must prosecute the contention to the (bitter) end, there will be evil. It will be advantageous to see the great man; it will not be advantageous to cross the great stream." (James Legge, *The I Ching,* 69.)

Essence of Hexagram

This hexagram explains the *Tao* of conflict resolutions as the paradigm for managing civil litigation, and taking preventive measures[15] to avoid conflict.

Hexagram Image(s)

The mutually opposing directional attributes of Heaven (upward) and Water (downward) stand for the image of Conflict (Contention) hexagram. The wise and noble uses this image as his guide to take preventive measures from the beginning against a contentious outcome in his conduct.

Hexagram Analysis

This hexagram is composed of the strength of the upper trigram Heaven and the peril of the lower trigram Water. The two trigrams possess mutually opposing attributes; Heaven takes its bearings upward, and Water flows downward. This creates a conflict, symbolizing disharmonious interpersonal relationships.

Line 2-9 is a yang line and represents a man who possesses both the virtues of the Mean (the middle line of the lower trigram) and the positive strength of yang, but without a correlative relationship with 5-9 for support. He has a contentious relationship with 6-9. Under the circumstances, it is favorable for 2-9 to maintain his virtues of sincerity with the Mean and resolve the conflict without resorting to litigation as quickly as possible by coming together halfway with 6-9. Protracted litigation will exacerbate the situation to the extreme; the overly energized 6-9 portends this point, suggesting that protracted litigation will not be advantageous to anyone. If a mutual understanding cannot be reached, one must seek the help of a virtuous and fair judge. 5-9 is a judge who possesses the virtues of the Mean. If 2-9 goes to him seeking a judgment to end the litigation, he will understand the need to end the conflict as quickly as possible and will exercise the authority of his high position and render a decision that is fair to both parties.

5-9 is the sole lead line of this hexagram.

Interpretation of Judgment

"Might" above and "peril" below stand for litigation or contention. The hexagram contains the element of peril in strength, symbolizing conflict in interpersonal relationships, or self-conflict from disharmony between mind and body. At times, even the virtuous one (2-9) with his sincerity will not be able to prevent the difficulties arising from a litigious situation. If a person, fearing damaging results, brings an end to conflict, there will be good fortune because the yang line that represents integrity occupies the center of the lower trigram. Protracting the litigation to the end will result in ill fortune because it goes against the principle of resolving conflicts inherent in this hexagram. Instead, it will be advantageous to seek the help of the great man (5-9), who will exercise the virtues of the Mean to resolve the contention. The contentious time is analogous to the danger in crossing a turbulent big stream; it is not a favorable time for 2-9 to venture aggressively (one is too self-righteous) to cross such a stream, as he could drown in the deep water.

Divination Direction

Your activities will cause conflicts, and you will face many hindrances in achieving your goal. You will experience difficulties in your relationship with your superior or your friend. Be friendly and cooperative and take special care to refrain from engaging in an argument with anyone, including family members. Pay attention to your health problems. Listen to friendly advice, and be modest in your attitude. To help you while waiting for a better time, cultivate your interest in and enjoy your hobbies. This will help you survive this difficult period.

Individual Lines: Analysis, Interpretation, and Divination Direction

Line 1-6: This improperly positioned yin line is weak and incompetent at the lowest position of the hexagram. It correlates with 4-9 and is contiguous to 2-9. Initially, 1-6 collaborates with its contiguous and powerful 2-9, creating a contentious situation with 4-9, with whom he has a correlative relationship. When 4-9 brings litigation against 1-6, he decides to cooperate with 4-9, and the matter is dropped.

The images signify that the litigation proceedings will be settled at the start. Although 1-6 will not escape rebuke for starting the conflict (yin in yang position), he did not initiate the litigation, and this fact will be clarified. Because the litigation was settled in the beginning, this will result in good fortune.

Divination Direction

Do not be expedient in your actions. Take a conservative approach when you have an advantage, and refrain from a matter that has a potential for contention. A better situation will be forthcoming that you can act upon.

Line 2-9: This yang line representing a community leader is improperly positioned and correlates antagonistically with 5-9 which represents the ruler of a whole nation.

The images signify that one must not be self-righteous, but instead yield to the greater good. It is disadvantageous for 2-9 to pursue to the end the litigation against 5-9 in the superior position. Fortunately, 2-9 possesses the virtues of the Mean and understands the situation and consequently withdraws from the litigation. He returns to his small town of no more than three hundred households and escapes potential calamity to himself and his town, since a conflict could tear a small community apart.

Divination Direction

You must not be self-centered and need to keep your mind open to accommodate opinions of other people. You are in a favorable situation at present, but you need to exercise appropriate self-restraint against pursuing too ambitious an outcome. Otherwise, hard times will come to you and yours.

Line 3-6: This yin line is improperly positioned and correlates with 6-9, sandwiched between two yang lines.

The images signify that one has to persevere with what one already has, like 3-6 who subsists on bequests (old virtues)[16] and is obedient to the powerful 6-9, with whom he has a correlative relationship. Due to its weak and improper positioning (weak, because it is not the position he earned but bequested), a litigious situation may develop, requiring a judgment from the ruler (5-9), who finds little to substantiate the reason for the litigation.

Divination Direction

Because of your weak and unsettling position, other people may take advantage of you. Strengthen your inner fortitude and avoid creating any contentious relationship with other people. Make your moves with due discretion and judiciousness. Seek the advice of those who are trustworthy, and be alert against any enticement.

Line 4-9: This yang line is improperly positioned, correlating with 1-6.

The images signify that one must be cautious not to take advantage of one's superior position that may cause needless suffering to the one in an inferior position. When 1-6 collaborated with its contiguous 2-9, 4-9 brought litigation against 1-6, with whom he has a correlative relationship. When 1-6 reverses his move and begins to collaborate with 4-9, he (4-9) withdraws his litigation against 1-6. It would have been better if he (4-9) had reached a mutual understanding without resorting to litigation in the first place. By not pursuing the litigation with timely restraint, 4-9 gets rid of his contentious (unsettled) mind, and by staying in the proper course of *Tao,* he regains serenity. Good fortune will follow.

Divination Direction

Be careful not to be single-minded and stubborn and take precipitous action. Instead, be deliberate and take the advice and opinions of other people. Reflect upon yourself to detect your doubts, weaknesses, or errors that need to be remedied.

Line 5-9: This yang line is properly positioned in the middle of the upper trigram.

The images signify that this great judge who is endowed with both the authority and a refined sense of justice decides on the cases; his rulings will result in great good fortune.

Divination Direction

It augurs well. If you have a plan to act on, now is the time to move decisively. The matters of your concern will work out in your favor from now on. However, if your intentions are wicked and inhumane, your activities will turn out adversely, bringing you great harm.

Line 6-9: This yang line is the topmost line of the Conflict hexagram. He is a litigant who has been victorious in every conflict and has been awarded an official decoration of the garment leather belt by the ruler. However, such illustrious victories do not earn him the respect of many people because carrying conflicts to the end is not virtuous. His contentious mind finally leads to difficult situations that make him unable to safeguard his honor.

The images signify that a lasting award lies in one's virtuous, peaceful mind, not in one's contentious mind. Although he receives the award of the official garment leather belt, he ends up being deprived of his honor (belt) three times in the short span of one day,[17] as his honor is attacked time and again. The honor that is derived from contentious matters does not deserve to last for long.

Divination Direction

Stay on the course of being honest and fair with others. One's peace of mind is what counts, not the temporary gratification of being honored. Guard against aggressive pursuit of contentious matters, which might result in unexpected harm to you.

7. The Host 師 (Sze or Shih) Hexagram

Key attributes: Army, group action, symbol of multitude

Judgment

"*Sze* indicates how, in the case, which it supposes, with firmness and correctness, and (a leader of) age and experience, there will be good fortune and no error." (James Legge, *The I Ching,* 71.)

Essence of Hexagram

This hexagram explains the *Tao* of safeguarding as the paradigm for military leadership and national defense.

Hexagram Image(s)

The image of this hexagram, Water in the Earth and therefore invisible, represents the invisible military power found in the masses of farmers who are called upon to fight in times of war. The wise and noble uses this image as his guide to increase the strength of his masses through his understanding and generosity.

Hexagram Analysis

The Host hexagram is composed of the inner trigram Water (peril) and the outer trigram Earth (obedience), which symbolize the attributes of army with internal "gravity" toward peril and "external" demand for obedience. The upper trigram symbolizes a mass of farming people who serve as reserve military strength; they are called into military service in a time of national peril (war). There is only one yang line (2-9) in this hexagram; 2-9 is the great general who leads the army. This line correlates with 5-6, which occupies the high position of ruler who delegates military matters to 2-9 to lead the mass into war with appropriate restraint to uphold a just cause.

2-9 and 5-6 are the lead lines of this hexagram.

Interpretation of Judgment

The host[18] means the army or a mass of people. If the general (2-9) carries out Heaven's commands correctly, he is a great man who will be victorious in the war and will not be blamed for the suffering of the nation that accompanies a war. The competent great general and the virtuous supportive sovereign are handling the situation with mutual resonance, one by risking himself against the peril, and the other by supporting the campaign, treating the national calamity of war as a bitter but necessary medicine.

Divination Direction

You will attain a leadership position with accompanying demands to make correct decisions and foster loyalty among followers. In business, put your emphasis on the harmonious relationships among the people with whom you must deal. The financial market will fluctuate. You will have strong competition in your job-seeking efforts. It is not a good time to move to a new house or to conclude a marital arrangement.

Individual Lines: Analysis, Interpretation, and Divination Direction

Line 1-6: This yin line is improperly positioned away from the center of the lower trigram.

The images signify the beginning of a move by the army headed by 2-9. The initial move is a crucial factor in a military campaign, along with the observation of military rules and military command. If 1-6 (improperly positioned) fails to observe the rules and command, misfortune will result, and the war will be lost.

Divination Direction

Your efforts to begin correctly will be rewarded with many folds of good results. Consult with others to see if your plan of action is justifiable and proper for implementation.

Line 2-9: This is the only yang line in the hexagram, positioned at the center of the lower trigram.

The images signify that the great general is well informed about his masses and leads them into a victorious war. He practices the virtues of the Mean (the middle line of the lower trigram) and enjoys good fortune, suffering no blame. He receives strong support from his sovereign (5-6) that confers a threefold commendation on him, denoting the sovereign's level of confidence in the general. The general supports the sovereign's vision to win the support of different nations to bring peace to the whole world.

Divination Direction

It augurs well. As a leader, you need to listen to your followers and accept new and good ideas from them. Everyone will be willing to help you succeed, and your problem will be resolved.

Line 3-6: This yin line inappropriately occupies the yang position at the top of the lower trigram.

The images signify that discordant commands or the weak and incompetent in the command position will bring misfortune. The army under such a command will face a great defeat, and the wagons will be used to transport the bodies.

Divination Direction

It argurs ill. It is not the time to act, but to conserve your energy and resources for a future opportunity. Refrain from undertaking any action that is beyond your qualifications or capability. Guard against any greedy or overambitious action.

Line 4-6: This yin line represents a weak commander, but it is properly positioned and will not commit the folly of making aggressive movements against the enemies.

The images signify that he observes the tactical military movement of retreat by pitching his camp to the left, thereby escaping a disastrous defeat. He will suffer no blame.

Divination Direction

You are in a rough situation and need to be flexible to deal with different problems that might emerge in the course of your actions. Remain inactive for awhile, and wait patiently for an opportunity to seize upon.

Line 5-6: This yin line occupies the position of the ruler at the center of the upper trigram.

The images signify that this ruler is gentle in nature and possesses the virtues of the Mean. He does not initiate aggression but responds appropriately when his nation is invaded (game birds in the fields), like trapping crop-destroying birds in the field when it becomes necessary. (The capture of the birds is comparable to the spoils of the war.)

Facing such an invasion, he must first make a declaration condemning the invasion. No one will blame him for such action. He will delegate military leadership to his eldest son, an experienced general (2-9), who is most trustworthy and competent. It is not suitable for him to appoint his younger weak sons (3-6, 4-6) to high-ranking positions in the military, as such appointments will bring confusion and disarray in the chain of command, leading to battle losses and to war casualties who will be transported by wagons. In the circumstance of appointing the weak to high command, the initial correct motive of a defensive military action cannot prevail over the error that results from misguided appointments in the chain of command; misfortune will be the sure result.

Divination Direction

You need to be decisive in your action in face of a danger, but be wary of being overconfident in your action plans. Be alert to any possibilities of unexpected hindrances that may occur in the course of your actions. Stay on the course of rectitude and befriend honest people.

Line 6-6: This yin line is properly positioned at the top of the Host hexagram.

The images signify that the war is over with a victorious outcome, and the sovereign gives orders to reward his subjects for their meritorious achievements.[19] To some he grants feudal lands to rule, and to others he bestows marquisettes. However, he should not reward the little man who lacks the virtues of *Tao* with land or a high governing position, or it will contribute to abuse of their power and will result in disorder in the state.

Divination Direction

You will be rewarded as much as you deserve, depending on the sincere efforts you made to achieve your goal. What is most important is your mind-set and ability. Make constant efforts to improve yourself.

8. The Union 比 (Pi) Hexagram

Key attributes: Union, closeness, concord, the symbol of collaboration

Judgment

"*Pi* indicates that (under the conditions, which it supposes) there is good fortune. But let (the principal party intended in it) re-examine himself, (as if) by divination, whether his virtue be great, unintermitting, and firm. If it be so, there will be no error. Those who have not rest will then come to him; and with those who are (too) late in coming it will be ill." (James Legge, *The I Ching*, 73.)

Essence of Hexagram

This hexagram explains the *Tao* of relationship as the paradigm for effective governing.

Hexagram Image(s)

Water above Earth stands for the images of the Union hexagram. It refers to the ancient kings who established feudal states within their kingdoms and developed good relations with the feudal lords, successfully bringing the states closely together.

Hexagram Analysis

This hexagram presents the images of water flowing on the earth and filling up the space in the earth, symbolizing the closeness of the two elements. 5-9 of this hexagram is the only yang line and represents the ruler who is properly positioned and possesses the virtues of the Mean. It properly correlates with 2-6 and has positive relationships with others in the hexagram. Everyone is willing to give him support and loyalty.

5-9 is the sole lead line of this hexagram.

Interpretation of Judgment

The Union (Closeness) hexagram means good fortune, as it represents the fundamental principle of support and obedience that brings the ruler and the ruled close together. Being a sage ruler, he (5-9) reflects upon himself to be sure that he is abiding by the virtues of *Tao* so that he will not make an error that may become the cause of blame. The ruler, 5-9, above, and the ruled, 2-6, below, resonate with each other. Even those who have not had a close relationship with such a ruler are now eager to become close to him. However, those who come too late (represented by 6-6) will suffer misfortune, as the opportunities to establish close relationships will eventually completely disappear.

Divination Direction

It augurs well, especially for marriage, employment, and any business endeavor that can be done harmoniously. There will be strong competition in your business dealings, and you might end up losing some good opportunities if you are indecisive and vacillate too much. It is not in your favor to do your business all by yourself. Cultivate cooperation with other people who are friendly, and have faith in the people who are willing to cooperate with you. Financial market will decline gradually.

Individual Lines: Analysis, Interpretation, and Divination Direction

Line 1-6: This yin line is the beginning of the Union (Closeness) hexagram.

The images signify that the spirit of this hexagram is for one to start with full sincerity, like earthenware that is always kept filled. (Earthenware is compared to the mind, which should be filled with sincerity at all times.) These attitudes of sincerity and cordiality will not only keep him from being blamed, but it will eventually attract other pcople to follow him. There will be good fortune.

Divination Direction

You do not have to stand ahead of others to succeed; what is more important is how well you are prepared for a task. You are faced with some difficult situations. You must maintain your good efforts with a sincere attitude and goodwill toward other people. In the meantime, you will receive help from unexpected sources.

Line 2-6: This yin line is properly positioned at the center of the lower trigram and correlates with the similarly properly positioned middle line of the upper trigram, 5-9.

The images signify that the mutual closeness between the two lines (2-6 and 5-9) emanates from the inner strength of 2-6. He practices the virtues of the Mean, resonating harmoniously with 5-9 who possesses the same attributes in the higher position. This line represents the principle that one who follows *Tao* with fortitude will not fail and will have good fortune.

Divination Direction

Have faith in what you are doing and keep up your good efforts, and you will be successful.

Line 3-6: This yin line is improperly positioned and has no friendly line with which it can maintain a close relationship, since 2-6 is befriended to 5-9. Both 4-6 and 6-6 are yin lines, which are antagonistic; therefore, they cannot form a collaborative relationship with 3-6.

The images signify that he cannot find the right person with whom he can establish a close relationship for mutual benefits.

Divination Direction

Although you are eager to have a close friend, you may end up with someone who lacks the virtues of genuine friendship. Pay careful attention and be discriminating in choosing your friends.

Line 4-6: This yin line of the outer trigram (upper trigram) is properly positioned, but it does not correlate with 1-6. Instead, it is in a contiguous relationship with 5-9, which occupies the higher status and possesses the virtues of the Mean.

The images signify that this person establishes a close relationship with one who has a higher status (5-9) in the same trigram. In this relationship, if 4-6 can maintain the correct course of *Tao*, the result will be good fortune.

Divination Direction

The time has come for you to review your associates in order to terminate improper relationships and strengthen relationships with those who are virtuous and reliable.

Line 5-9: It is the only yang line of this hexagram. It is properly positioned at the center of the upper trigram in the high status of ruler who practices the virtues of the Mean. It correlates with 2-6.

The images signify the closeness of the ruler and his subjects. His virtuous nature can be compared to that of a sage ruler who, in hunting game, always provided an escape route for the game.[20] The game was driven toward the penned area from three sides, but the fourth side was set aside to provide the game with a means of escape. The king shot only the animals that came into the penned area. Likewise, in his governance, he practices the virtues of the Mean and fairness. He allows his subjects leeway or free will, and they do not have to be on guard against him but have peace of mind. There will be good fortune.

Divination Direction

It augurs well. Be generous and understanding toward other people, and you will be rewarded with good fortune.

Line 6-6: This yin line is the top line of the Union hexagram. As yin, it is weak, and it does not correlate with 3-6.

The images signify that a good beginning is important in order to have a good ending. This one comes late with weak determination and cannot find anyone with whom he can establish a genuine close relationship. He is shunned and will not be able to bring anything to a fruitful conclusion. There will be misfortune.

Divination Direction

It augurs ill. Do not try to find faults with other people but yourself. You are losing your friends and supporters. You will not be able to succeed in your endeavor.

9. The Minor Restraint 小畜 (Hsiao Khu or Hsiao Ch'u) Hexagram

Key attributes: Minor (small) restraint, symbol of taming force

Judgment

"*Hsiao Khu* indicates that (under its conditions) there will be progress and success. (We see) dense clouds, but no rain coming from our borders in the west." (James Legge, *The I Ching*, 76.)

Essence of Hexagram

This hexagram explains the *Tao* of moral cultivation as the paradigm for using the inner strength of virtues to prevail over physical strength or tyranny.

Hexagram Image(s)

Wind blowing above Heaven stands for the images of the Minor Restraint hexagram. The wise and noble uses the images as his guide to cultivate his literary and artistic skills along with his virtues.

Hexagram Analysis

The overall image of this hexagram is the wind blowing above the sky. The only yin line in the hexagram represents inner strength, and the yang lines represent tyranny. 1-9 correlates with 4-6 in its efforts to mobilize other yang forces to turn the clouds into rain. The soft or weak yin line 4-6 collaborates with the strong and high status line of 5-9, making it possible to successfully restrain 1-9 from its rainmaking activities.

The inner trigram of the primary nuclear hexagram is "Lake" (*Tui*), which symbolizes both clouds and west in direction. Because of 4-6's restraining force, the clouds are still gathered in the western region, not yet able to produce rain. However, the effect of 4-6's restraining efforts in the midst of the overwhelming yang forces that surround it is temporary and limited. Therefore, the hexagram is named Minor Restraint. It is the time for the ruler to encourage nonmilitary activities, such as art and literature, to promote progress in the state.

4-6, the directive, and 5-9, the structural, are the lead lines of this hexagram.

Interpretation of Judgment

The soft (yin) gaining a high position (4-6) with the resonating lower line (1-9) stands for the Minor Restraint hexagram. It represents the virtues of being strong but modest in attitude. The strong (2-9, 5-9) that practice the Mean successfully help the soft (4-6) restrain the strong (1-9) in his activities. It presents a good omen. "Dense clouds but no rain" in the judgment means that an activity is still in progress toward the ultimate goal. The clouds starting in the western region[21] means that the benefit of rain (it rains when yin and yang, 4-6 and 5-9, come together) has yet to be realized.

Divination Direction

It augurs ill. At present, you are experiencing many minor hitches in your endeavor, slowing or stalling your progress. Watch yourself for marital problems. Special caution is warranted for an expectant mother against a miscarriage. It is time for you to rest and conserve your energy in order to prepare yourself for the next opportunity that is coming in the near future.

Individual Lines: Analysis, Interpretation, and Divination Direction

Line 1-9: This yang line is properly positioned and correlates with 4-6, which is also properly positioned. Nonetheless, 1-9 realizes that 4-6 is getting the support of the powerful 5-9 to place some restraint on him from advancing forcefully.

The images signify that 1-9 reaches a decision not to use force but to return to his own position and stay within his boundary of *Tao* (maintaining the virtues of *Tao*), and avoids committing an error. He incurs no blame for his actions. His conduct is exceptionally correct, and others will have difficulty following his example. It will result in good fortune.

Divination Direction

Accurately grasp the reality you are faced with, and be fair and quick in your decisions. Carry out your honest and sincere course of actions with courage.

Line 2-9: This yang line is improperly positioned but occupies the center of the lower trigram. All three yang lines of the lower trigram want to advance. 2-9, with the virtues of the Mean, realizes that 4-6 with the support of 5-9 has checked the advance of 1-9.

The images signify that 2-9, like others of his kind (the other two yang lines of the lower trigram), is forced by 4-6 to return to his own position, and he restrains himself from further attempts to advance. His virtue of restraint will result in good fortune, as 2-9 has not lost the practice of self-discipline.

Divination Direction

You have a strong urge to move ahead with your plans, but you will come across hindrances and barriers that will provide you with reasons to reassess the situation, calling for some restraint in your movements. Go ahead with your plans but only within the comfortable range of your resources and capabilities.

Line 3-9: This top yang line of the lower trigram has an antagonistic correlation with 6-9, the top line of this hexagram.

The images signify that its aggressive movement will encounter obstacles against his move, like the carriage that separates from its binding strap (axle housing), or like the husband (3-9) and wife (4-6) looking at each other with averted eyes and not being able to reconcile.

Divination Direction

It augurs ill. Beware. You may feel too confident and act against the sensible advice of your friend, and you will experience failures in your endeavor. You will often engage in altercations with other people. Understand your weakness and act discreetly.

Line 4-6: This is the only yin line of the hexagram and is properly positioned, making it one of the lead lines of the Minor Restraint hexagram.

The images signify that he is soft (weak) but sincere. This sincerity helps him to secure the confidence of the powerful ruler (5-9) who supports his efforts to restrain the aggressive advance of the three yang lines that make up the lower trigram. He has no further worries or apprehension from the threat of advance by 1-9, since he has secured the support of the high and powerful ally (5-9). He will incur no error or blame for his action.

Divination Direction

It is the time for you to make a move. Your plight is about to improve, as your efforts receive due recognition from other people. Keep up with your course of action with sincere and persistent efforts, and you will find that your situation will keep improving.

Line 5-9: This yang line is properly positioned at the center of the upper trigram, powerful in the status of ruler.

The images signify that the ruler practices the Mean. He does not monopolize his power and wealth. He lends his support to his worthy neighbor (4-6) who is trying to restrain the aggressive advance of the yang lines. The ruler gives 4-6 his trust, and the subject gives the ruler his loyalty, doubling the benefits.

Divination Direction

You will be able to find a supporter with resources willing to lend you a helping hand in your efforts. You should be grateful to him. Your cooperative efforts with other people will lead you to good fortune.

Line 6-9: This yang line is improperly positioned at the top of the Minor Restraint hexagram.

The images signify that, in the time sequence of this hexagram, the rain has come and gone, like the carriage that, having been separated from its binding strap (refer to 3-9 above), has been repaired and is moving ahead with a load. In the case of the wife (4-6), she has successfully restrained her husband's (3-9) aggressive behavior and has begun to contemplate whether she should moderate her attitude toward him before it is too late. When the moon (4-6) attains its fullness, it wanes, but it has yet to reach its fullness. To continue one's efforts to attain fullness will bring misfortune. Thus, 6-9 will have misfortune if he insists on using his power with self-righteous attitudes and keeps moving ahead without some restraint, because his behavior will make others suspicious of him.

Divination Direction

It is the time to reflect. Cultivate the virtues of self-restraint and refrain from over-indulging in your self-righteous actions. Be content with your present success and respect the opinions of those close to you.

10. The Treading 履 (Li) Hexagram

Key attributes: Treading carefully, symbol of deliberate action

Judgment

"(*Li* suggests the idea of) one treading on the tail of a tiger, which does not bite him. There will be progress and success." (James Legge, *The I Ching*, 78.)

Essence of Hexagram

This hexagram explains the *Tao* of governance as the paradigm for proper ranking of the governed and a careful exercise of power and authority by those in power in order to provide peace of mind to the governed.

Hexagram Image(s)

Heaven above and Lake below stand for the images of the Treading hexagram. The wise and noble uses the images as his guide for understanding the power (tiger) of the sovereign and the needs of the governed who follow him, in order that they will live with joy and in peace.

Hexagram Analysis

This hexagram consists of the upper trigram Heaven and the lower trigram Lake and indicates two situations: the weak (lower trigram) following the strong (upper trigram), and the strong (5-9) exercising its power to govern the people represented by the lower trigram with the yin line with proper understanding and discrimination. The three yang lines of Heaven represent extraordinary strength and symbolize the tiger. The lower trigram Lake symbolizes being soft, gentle, and joyful. The combined images of the two trigrams portray one of lower ranking treading on the tail of a tiger (high ranking) lightly and joyfully. 3-6 is the only yin line; it is a directive lead line and forms a contiguous relationship with its powerful neighbors, 4-9 and 5-9.

The lead lines of this hexagram are 3-6, directive, and 5-9, structural.

Interpretation of Judgment

The soft or weak (yin) following the strong (yang) stands for the image of the Treading hexagram. The joyful (Lake) resonating with the strong (Heaven) is analogous to the weak who treads on the tail of a tiger, which does not bite him. It means good fortune. In governing the people, the strong (5-9) occupies the center and abides by the correct virtues of the Mean. In exercising his sovereign authority, this virtuous ruler is careful, as if he were treading on a tiger's tail. His virtues will shine gloriously, and he will be respected.

Divination Direction

You feel unsure of success in your endeavor. First, assess the current situation calmly and set up your action plans, and then apply yourself fully to carry them out. You will make good progress.

Individual Lines: Analysis, Interpretation, and Divination Direction

Line 1-9: This yang line is properly positioned at the beginning of the treading process of this hexagram. There is no contiguous or correlating line.

The images signify that he has to begin treading alone in his accustomed path. He does this with the attitude of modesty and sincerity. There will be no blame.

Divination Direction

Stay within your means and try to attain your goals through conscientious efforts. You will not find anyone willing to help you, but continue with your efforts to befriend other people. Be cautious not to engage in a squabble with other people.

Line 2-9: This yang line is the center of the trigram. Though improperly positioned, it possesses the merits of being yang and strong with the virtues of the Mean.

The images signify that this hermit treads along the smooth, level path with peace of mind, although the sovereign (5-9) has not called for his service. He maintains the virtues of *Tao* firmly without being confused or spoiled by any worldly success. It will bring good fortune.

Divination Direction

You will not find anyone willing to help you. You are doing your best to attain your modest and conscientious goal. As long as you keep doing your best with peace of mind, things will work out in your favor.

Line 3-6: This is the only yin line and the directive lead line of this hexagram. It is improperly positioned, as the weak occupies the position of the strong.

The images signify that the one with weak internal strength who acts as if he were strong is like the one-eyed person who pretends to see well or the lame that pretends to tread well. The pretentiousness will bring misfortune, as the tiger will bite him if he treads on the tiger's tail. It can be compared to a warrior who is audacious and passes himself off as a great ruler.

Divination Direction

Do not feel intimidated by your competitor just because he acts powerfully. However, guard yourself against undertaking an action beyond your means and capability simply because you feel everything is proceeding in your favor. An overambitious undertaking will lead you to misfortune.

Line 4-9: This yang line is improperly positioned, symbolizing that its nature is gentle and obedient, but it has a strong desire for advancement.

The images signify that one who is overambitious and close to the ruler (5-9) always takes the risk of offending the ruler, like the one who follows a tiger is running the risk of treading on the tiger's tail. If he is always aware of the danger and is cautious in serving the ruler, it will result in good fortune.

Divination Direction

Though you are competent and talented, you are in a precarious position. Always keep in mind to be respectful to other people in order for you to gain their respect. If you continue to be sincere and harmonious with other people, you will soon gain their recognition, and you will be successful.

Line 5-9: This yang line is properly positioned in the high status line of the ruler who practices the virtues of the Mean. It does not correlate with 2-9, which means that the ruler has no reliable subject to assist him.

The images signify that the ruler possesses the power, prestige, and the virtues of the Mean and carries out state affairs resolutely by himself. There is inherent danger in the use of dictatorial power, and he must use this power resolutely with firmness and humility, always being aware of its danger. If he becomes self-righteous and fails to listen to his subjects, he will face peril.

Divination Direction

Although you are capable and feel confident in yourself, be generous and harmonious with other people. Listen to their opinions with sincerity. Guard especially against your tendency to become stubborn and self-righteous.

Line 6-9: This yang line is at the apogee of the Treading hexagram and at the turning point for the beginning of a new cycle of *Tao*, Peace.

The images signify that, having reached the apex of one's conduct in the process of dealing with a life situation, he looks back on the entire course that he has taken and its consequences. If he has carried out the spirit of *Tao*, there will be great blessing of fundamental good fortune.

Divination Direction

You are at the vantage point of harvesting the benefits of your experience as well as that of other people. For further success, make your plans based on the collective experience that you have gained and carry them out with confidence. You will succeed in a big way!

11. The Peace 泰 (Thai or T'ai) Hexagram

Key attributes: Peace, progress, the symbol of success

Judgment

"In *Thai* (we see) the little gone and the great come. (It indicates that) there will be good fortune, with progress and success." (James Legge, *The I Ching*, 81.)

Essence of Hexagram

This hexagram explains the *Tao* of peace as the paradigm for prosperity and harmonious living.

Hexagram Image(s)

The interactions of the Heaven and Earth energies stand for the images of the Peace hexagram. The ruler applies this principle of interaction between the Heaven and Earth energies in his governance to produce mutual benefits for the ruler and the ruled.

Hexagram Analysis

This hexagram consists of the lower (inner) trigram Heaven and the upper (outer) trigram Earth. Heaven represents greatness, and Earth, obedience. As the great energy of Heaven arrived from above, Earth complied, and there was a harmonious exchange of energies. Heaven under Earth, the reverse of their usual positions, symbolizes the interactions of the Heaven and Earth energies, which produce harmonious existence and growth, resulting in great good fortune.

When the Heaven and Earth trigrams are in their usual positions with Heaven above Earth, the hexagram that is formed is the next hexagram in the sequence, Hexagram #12, Stagnation, where no interaction exists between the two trigrams.

Heaven under Earth also symbolizes the close communication between the ruler (Heaven) and the people (Earth).

This hexagram represents the month of January, which starts a New Year with the blessing of peace.

2-9 and 5-6 act as both directive and structural lead lines of this hexagram.

Interpretation of Judgment

The departure of the petty (yin) and the arrival of the great (yang) stand for peace and prosperity. It represents good fortune. The interactions of the Heaven and Earth energies make it possible for everything in the universe to relate with each other. When people in high and low positions interrelate, they come to understand each other.

The ruler provides virtuous leadership in order that the people maintain harmonious order, and he utilizes resources for the benefit of all. The ruler understands the spiritual needs of the governed, and he points the governed in the direction of correct *Tao* to follow for their own benefit.

This hexagram depicts a person who is gentle in manner and has strong inner integrity. Another depiction is that of a noble man who follows *Tao* and thrives, while the fortune of the petty man deteriorates.

Divination Direction

It augurs great good fortune. Everything is in your favor, and you must maintain your integrity and harmonious relationships with others without becoming selfish and greedy. Continue with your well-intentioned efforts. Everything will work out in your favor, leading to great success. Your health problem will improve soon. It is a favorable time for marriage, a move, and travel. An expectant mother will give birth to a baby with auspicious fortune.

Individual Lines: Analysis, Interpretation, and Divination Direction

Line 1-9: This yang line is the first line of the Peace hexagram that forms the lower trigram of Heaven with the other two yang lines.

The images signify that in this time of peace, the noble and competent (1-9), though unrecognized and low in status, proceeds to serve the state. The other two competent noble men (2-9 and 3-9) who share his aspirations will go along with him to serve the state. This is likened to the rush plant,[22] which has interconnected roots; when one stalk is pulled out, other roots connected to it come up with it. The people of the state (outer trigram) cooperate because the noble men have the high-minded intent to help them. The actions of the noble man (1-9) will bring good fortune.

Divination Direction

The time has come for you to act with a plan. Proceed with your well-motivated endeavor, and you will succeed.

Line 2-9: This yang line is at the center of the lower trigram and correlates with 5-6. He is competent and practices the virtues of the Mean, enjoying the full confidence of the ruler (5-6), who delegates important responsibilities to him.

The images signify that he is magnanimously virtuous. He is so resolute that, if necessary, he will cross a river by wading not by using a boat. He reaches out to those who are wise but neglected and who live scattered in distant places. He will not become involved with factional groups. He is disciplined enough to forego his personal needs, even the loss of his friends, in order to serve justice. Even the uncouth are accommodated. In these ways he practices the great virtues of the Mean.

Divination Direction

It augurs well. Move ahead with what you have been planning and preparing for. Be generous and impartial. It is especially auspicious to engage in the activities that will be of service to other people, such as public service. You will be successful.

Line 3-9: This yang line is at the apex of the Heaven trigram, bordering the Earth and Heaven trigrams. These energies of Heaven and Earth interact to bring about the blessings of peace.

This line borders on the upper trigram and is at the junction of a turnaround. The images signify that there is nothing level that does not eventually tilt. There is nothing that goes away that does not return. There is no state of peace that will not be disrupted. A virtuous man who understands this principle of recurring changes will maintain his *Tao* firmly and will be able to overcome the difficulties that are brought about by the changes. He will commit no error and will enjoy the blessings of bountiful sustenance.

Divination Direction

Your present situation may not be as smooth as it has been, and you may run into difficulties in your endeavor. Proceed at a deliberate pace with good motive and a sincere attitude. You will be successful in the end. You will also get back what you have lost.

Line 4-6: This yin line is the first line of the Earth trigram, properly correlating with 1-9.

The images signify that this man is virtuous and humble in his high-status position as prime minister. He seeks the advice of the three wise men in lower status (the three yang lines of the lower trigram) without imposing his status or wealth. Like a flock of fluttering birds, his neighbors (5-6, 6-6) come and join him to listen and learn from the three wise men with mutual trust.

Divination Direction

It is wise to seek the advice of other people with an open mind so that your tendency toward obstinacy will not bring harm to your endeavor. Other people will be willing to cooperate with you if you treat them with respect.

Line 5-6: This yin line is at the center of the upper trigram Earth, correlating with 2-9.

The images signify that the ruler (5-6) trusted his strong and wise subject of lower status (2-9) so much that he gave his daughter to him in marriage.[23] It resulted in blessings and great good fortune. Such an act of trust was possible because the ruler possessed the virtues of the Mean. He further decreed that, as with all wives, daughters of the royal families must obey their husbands who are of lower status.

Divination Direction

Before long, the time of peace will face the time of its decline. You must keep in mind that today's prosperity will not last forever. Find someone experienced and trustworthy to delegate your business, and you will be successful and happy.

Line 6-6: This yin line is at the top of the Peace hexagram. Peace is about to give way to the new cycle of retrogression and stagnation.

The images signify that the state is in disorder and is on the verge of collapse, like the city wall that crumbles down to the moat[24] below. Signs of disorder begin to appear in the state; people begin to disobey the orders from above. It is not the proper time to mobilize the mass in order to use military force to rule the state because it will not work; the changing tide is inevitable. It is better for the ruler to control the disorder within his own city or his own close circle by issuing necessary orders. If the ruler insists on his righteousness and persists in resisting the change, he will have cause for regret.

Divination Direction

At this juncture, nothing you do will work successfully. Concentrate your efforts to maintain what you already have. It is not the proper time to expand your endeavor or start a new enterprise. Take this time to reflect upon yourself and prepare for the future.

12. The Stagnation 否 (Phi) Hexagram

Key attributes: Stagnation, retrogression, the symbol of failure

Judgment

"In *Phi* there is the want of good understanding between the (different classes of) men, and its indication is unfavorable to the firm and correct course of the superior man. We see in it the great gone and the little come." (James Legge, *The I Ching*, 83.)

Essence of Hexagram

This hexagram explains the *Tao* of proper conduct as the paradigm for dealing with the time of chaos.

Hexagram Image(s)

The lack of interaction between Heaven and Earth stands for the images of the Stagnation hexagram. The wise and noble uses the images as his guide in applying the virtue of withdrawal at this time of stagnation to guard himself against harm coming from the petty. He should not expect to be effective and satisfied in serving in the government at this time when the petty is ascending and overriding the virtuous.

Hexagram Analysis

This hexagram is made up of the upper trigram Heaven and the lower trigram Earth, indicating that the energies of both trigrams are maintaining their established positions without interacting. Therefore, there is no growth or transformation. It is this stagnation or retrogression that creates the dark ages in human society.

The opposite of the Stagnation hexagram is Hexagram #53 Progressive Advance. The yin or the petty of the Progressive Advance hexagram (line 4) comes down to the inner trigram of Hexagram #12 to form the Earth trigram, and yang or the great (line 3) moves up to the outer trigram to form the Heaven trigram.

"The great gone and the little come" in the judgment is derived from the hexagram. The three yang lines, symbolizing the great men, are driven away to the outer trigram, and the three yin lines, symbolizing the petty men, occupy the inner trigram. Thus, harmonious interactions between the ruler and the subjects are blocked.

2-6, the directive, and 5-9, the structural, are the lead lines of this hexagram.

Interpretation of Judgment

The Stagnation hexagram symbolizes adverse human condition. When the Heaven and Earth energies fail to interact with each other, all things in heaven and earth stagnate. When the ruler fails to interact with the governed, remaining in the dark about the hard times the governed are facing, the government and society become chaotic. Then, the petty and incompetent (yin lines of the inner trigram) push the noble and competent (yang lines of the outer trigram) out of government services. It is the time when yin occupies the inside and yang the outside, the weak the inside and the strong the outside, the petty man the inside and the great man the outside.

The month of July is represented by this Stagnation hexagram. The opposing energies of the all-yin Earth trigram and the all-yang Heaven trigram are at a stalemate, each in its established position. However, the yin energy is in ascendancy, with the petty (yin) gaining its momentum progressively over the great (yang). The petty is beginning to thrive, and the noble and competent are being pushed away in progressive stages.

This is not a propitious time for the noble man who pursues the correct *Tao*. This is the time for the noble to withdraw and keep his energies on reserve.

Divination Direction

It augurs ill. It is not the proper time for you to begin a new enterprise or expand the present one. Refrain from rushing into an action; take your time and wait patiently for a new opportunity.

Individual Lines: Analysis, Interpretation, and Divination Direction

Line 1-6: This first line is yin and improperly positioned at the lowest position of the Stagnation hexagram and correlates with 4-9. Though weak and low in status, he will receive the recognition and support of 4-

9 if he follows the constancy of *Tao* and the leadership of 4-9 to serve the ruler (5-9).

The images signify that if he makes a move to advance, the other incompetents (2-6, 3-6) will come along with him, like the interconnected roots of the rush plants where, when one plant is pulled, the others come up with it. In this chaotic time, he needs to be disciplined enough to distinguish himself from the other incompetents by remaining inactive or retired (stagnant), practicing *Tao* and being loyal to the ruler. Only then will there be good fortune and progress in the future.

Divination Direction

Be mindful that it is the time of stagnation and chaos. Be especially careful not to team up with the incompetent or people of bad influence. It is the time for you to take a step backward and preserve your resources and prepare for the opportunity that is to come.

Line 2-6: This yin line is properly positioned at the center of the lower trigram and properly correlates with 5-9, the ruler, in this time of stagnation and chaos.

The images signify that although he is small and incompetent, he possesses the virtues of the Mean and shows his obedience toward the great (follows the virtuous conduct of the great). It will bring good fortune. In this time of obstruction of the great, if the great comports himself according to the *Tao* of the time of stagnation without being misled by the petty who surround him, the great will prevail.

Divination Direction

Cultivate your self-discipline and only pursue the justifiable cause that is within your means. Listen carefully to the advice of those with experience and knowledge and follow their advice with diligence.

Line 3-6: This top line of the inner trigram is improperly positioned in the era of stagnation.

The images signify that the petty and incompetent (3-6) is serving at a high level in the government. Although he feels a sense of shame because of his inadequacy, he remains in his position, compounding his shame and continuing the advance of the petty man.

Divination Direction

You have many worries because your undertaking has some fundamental weaknesses. The situation will keep deteriorating. It is not a proper time for you to start a new undertaking. Settle whatever you are doing as quickly as possible and wait for a better opportunity.

Line 4-9: This yang line is the first line of the upper trigram and improperly positioned; it correlates with 1-6.

The images signify that the period of stagnation is on the verge of ending, which will open up an opportunity for the great to advance. However, the strong and competent is holding back his efforts to bring a turnaround in the chaotic affairs of the state. He is gauging the timing of his mission to conform to the ordination of Heaven or the ruler. By following this ordination, he will not commit an error. When the stagnation is checked and order is restored, all his friends and supporters (1-6, 5-9, 6-9) will share the blessings.

Divination Direction

You are at the turning point when your suffering will end. It is the time of strategic thinking to get ready for the opportunity that is on its way. When you act properly, many will be willing to cooperate with you, and you will succeed.

Line 5-9: This yang line is properly positioned at the center of the upper trigram.

The images signify that the great man (the competent ruler) who possesses the virtues of the Mean is bringing about a change from chaos to order. However, in this period of change, he must take heed of the perils of regressing and losing whatever gains he makes that are inherent in any change. In the process of restoring order, one must be as cautious as hanging heavy objects (the heavy responsibilities of state affairs) on the new sprouts and the slim branches of a mulberry tree.

Divination Direction

Your time of hardship is about to end. Renew your resolve and double your efforts to attain your goal without becoming careless and lax over small successes.

Line 6-9: This yang line is the last line of the Stagnation hexagram. It has strong and competent qualities but is improperly positioned.

The images signify that this competent man works hard to accomplish the task of reversing stagnant and obstructive state affairs. The days of stagnation and obstruction will not last too much longer. Order and harmony will follow chaos and obstruction, and there will be joy and happiness among the people.

Divination Direction

In the beginning, you will experience some difficulties in your endeavor, but take heart; your resolve and steady efforts will bring successful results, which will bring benefits not only to you but also to others who have cooperated with you.

13. The Companionship 同人 (Thung Zan or T'ung J'en) Hexagram

Key attributes: Companionship, the symbol of community or cooperation

Judgment

"*Thung Zan* (or 'union of men') appears here (as we find it) in the (remote districts of the) country, indicating progress and success. It will be advantageous to cross the great stream. It will be advantageous to maintain the firm correctness of the superior man." (James Legge, *The I Ching,* 86.)

Essence of Hexagram

This hexagram explains the *Tao* of cooperation as the paradigm for achieving great harmony through common objectives among different groups of people.

Hexagram Image(s)

Heaven above Fire stands for the images of companionship. The lower trigram Light (Fire) symbolizes civility and enlightenment. In accomplishing the great mission, only the noble man who practices the virtues of the Mean can bring about harmony and fellowship in the world because he does it with civility and enlightenment. The noble man possesses the ability to understand the individual attributes and different capabilities of people and all other things on earth, and he brings them together to work in harmony.

Hexagram Analysis

This hexagram consists of the lower trigram Fire and the upper trigram Heaven, with 2-6, the noble man, as the only yin line of the hexagram. The spirit of companionship pervades in this hexagram. The five yang lines cooperate with the lead line of 2-6, which correlates properly with 5-9, thus forming a strong and harmonious alliance. The upper trigram Heaven and the lower trigram Sun (Fire) are in harmony, as Fire burns upward to Heaven; they entertain the same objective of bringing benefits to the whole world. 2-6, the directive, and 5-9, the structural, are the lead lines of this hexagram.

Interpretation of Judgment

The soft (yin) occupies the center position. Heaven resonates with it to present the images of the Companionship hexagram. The noble man (2-6) practices the virtues of the Mean and attracts the fellowship of others. His conduct is fair, and his mind and heart have as open and unrestricted a view in dealing with people as the unrestricted view of the wide open field.[25] He will prevail. The upper trigram Heaven symbolizes the great strength, suspiciousness, and progression with which one undertakes such a great enterprise as running state affairs. There are always many perils to overcome in the course of accomplishing the mission, as with crossing a great river. It is the time of cooperation and harmony. The time has come to venture crossing the river, as it is the time for the noble man to carry out the great enterprise of state affairs.

Divination Direction

If your motivation is good without greed or harm to others, you will be successful. Be fair and cooperative with other people. In turn, they will cooperate with you to overcome your difficulties.

Individual Lines: Analysis, Interpretation, and Divination Direction

Line 1-9: This yang line is properly positioned as the beginning line of the Companionship hexagram, not correlating with any line.

The images signify that he is free of any encumbered relationship, and he goes out the gate of his house and forms a wide fellowship in the community with a fair and unprejudiced approach. There will be no error in his conduct or any blame on him.

Divination Direction

Do not dwell on petty emotional attachments. Watch your speech or conduct that might arouse jealousies in other people. Listen to the opinions and advice of other people with sincerity. Carry out your undertaking in a cooperative spirit with other people to attain favorable results.

Line 2-6: This is the only yin line of the Companionship hexagram, and it correlates with 5-9.

The images signify that a collaborative relationship exists between the two correlating lines (the noble, 2-6, and the ruler, 5-9), both of whom practice the virtues of the Mean. 2-6 makes special efforts not to restrict his relationships to his family and his clan. Confined companionship can lead to prejudice against others and to factionalism, which will be a barrier to unity in the state and a source of regret.

Divination Direction

The collaborative relationship you have established with the ones you trust is an important base from which to launch your plan. Be generous and fair in dealing with other people, and you will be successful.

Line 3-9: This yang line is properly positioned at the top of the lower trigram, contiguous to 2-6 and not correlating with 6-9.

The images signify that distrust among people destroys fellowship, and this strong and ambitious person who lacks in the virtues of the Mean wants to advance aggressively against 6-9, with whom he has an antagonistic relationship. However, he finds no one who is willing to support him. He desires to form a fellowship with the contiguous 2-6, but he finds this impossible because 2-6 is already in alliance with the powerful 5-9. Under the circumstances, he decides to hide his armed troops in the thicket, and he surveys 6-9's situation from high ground. He continued his vigilance for three years, but he was not able to obtain a vantage point for his uprising. His ambition will remain unfulfilled.

Divination Direction

Reflect upon yourself as to whether you will go to the extent of using dishonesty or chicanery to fulfill your ambitions. If you consider doing this, you must cast that aside, as you will be setting your own trap for failure.

Line 4-9: This is a yang line and the first line of the upper trigram, improperly positioned with no correlating line.

The images signify that the efforts of reconciliation promote fellowship, and he has a gentle and reflective mind with an ambition to advance. He wants to form an alliance with 2-6, but from his position on a high wall, he discovers that 3-9, who is contiguous to 2-6, has already deployed his armed troops. He realizes that it is not propitious for him to interfere in the present situation, as it will create dissension among the people. With the wall of distrust in 3-9, he was sensible and resolute enough to give up this ambition. He turned the difficult situation into a sensible resolution, and he will enjoy good fortune.

Divination Direction

You have a correct plan but it is not timely, and an attempt to carry out the plan will be in vain at this point in time. Retreat a step at once and set up a new plan that is within your means and which relies solely on yourself to achieve it, and you will be successful.

Line 5-9: This yang line is properly positioned at the center of the upper trigram, correlating with 2-6. There are two yang lines between the two correlating lines, which covet an alliance with 2-6.

The images signify that nothing is powerful enough to destroy the genuine human desire for fellowship. Circumstances separate 5-9, the ruler, who wants to establish a strong relationship with 2-6; both are virtuous men who practice the virtues of the Mean. The ruler meets strong opposition from the opposing forces of 3-9 and 4-9 in establishing the relationship. Realizing that he first needed to bring the opposing forces within his circle, he used his military force to quell them and bring them into his circle. After his victory, he was able to establish a strong relationship with 2-6.

The judgment text says, "For the fellowship, there is first howling and wailing, but afterward, laughter." The "howling and wailing" are those of 5-9 and 2-9 when they were thwarted from their fellowship; the "laughter" refers to a later time when they were able to enjoy the fellowship.

Divination Direction

It augurs well. You will find favorable solutions to your problems, and the time is here to expand your plan and activities. Be friendly and generous to other people, and they will cooperate with you.

Line 6-9: This yang line is improperly positioned at the top of the outer trigram, correlating with no line.

The images signify that he locates himself in the countryside where he finds a few people living nearby with whom he can form a fellowship. This is not the kind of fellowship that can influence a large of number of people. He is far removed from the strife in the city and has only a few regrets about this move. However, being away from the city is not conducive to achieving his ambition to bring all the people together.

Divination Direction

It will be to your advantage not to seek to achieve your ambition aggressively at the present time. Be content with what you have and conserve your energy and resources until an opportunity presents itself for you to make a move with confidence.

14. The Great Possession (Abundance) 大有 (Ta Yu) Hexagram

Key attributes: Great possession, the symbol of abundance

Judgment

"*Ta Yu* indicates that (under the circumstances which it implies), there will be great progress and success." (James Legge, *The I Ching,* 88.)

Essence of Hexagram

This hexagram explains the *Tao* of abundance as the paradigm for bringing about prosperity through self-development and great statesmanship that encourages the good and suppresses the evil.

Hexagram Image(s)

Fire above Heaven stands for the images of the Great Possession hexagram. The upper trigram Sun and the lower trigram Heaven symbolize the sun in heaven lighting the whole world, like the virtues of the noble sovereign that shine throughout the state. He distinguishes the good from the evil and suppresses evil and promotes good, in compliance with the will of Heaven.

Hexagram Analysis

This hexagram consists of the lower trigram Heaven that symbolizes strength and greatness, and the upper trigram Light, enlightenment. 5-6 of the upper trigram with the status of a sovereign is the only yin line of the hexagram and correlates with 2-9. The soft 5-6 that occupies the center position of the upper trigram is virtuous, and the strong and great 2-9 with which it correlates is also virtuous, as indicated by its position in the center. 2-9 and the other four yang lines in this hexagram represent the strong and competent subjects who respond to the call of the ruler, producing the era of Great Abundance.

5-6 is the sole lead line of this hexagram.

Interpretation of Judgment

The ruler, who is humble and yielding, achieves his greatness by practicing the virtues of the Mean. As a virtuous and enlightened ruler, he follows Heaven's will by taking timely action to benefit the ruled. The special collaborative relationship between the ruler above (5-6) and the virtuous and great below (2-9) encourages the other strong and competent subjects to support the ruler. This resonance and support will result in great prosperity for all in the era of the Great Possession.

Thus, the Great Possession hexagram means prevailing good fortune with great progress and success.

Divination Direction

It augurs very well. Everything is going well with you. It is the time of prosperity and contentment and is especially favorable for financial dealings and business. However, you must live up to the spirit that this hexagram teaches, which is to maintain the attitude of humility and modesty in the midst of prosperity and abundance. It is also the time to prepare for the hard time that will come in the future.

Individual Lines: Analysis, Interpretation, and Divination Direction

<u>Line 1-9</u>: This is the yang and first line of this hexagram, properly positioned with no correlating line. It indicates that this man in the lowest status has no one from whom he can receive support. It is neither

contiguous to 2-9 nor correlative with 4-9, as both are yang lines. The only saving grace for this line is the fact that it is properly positioned (a yang line in yang position), thereby escaping blame.

The images signify that he has no one from whom to draw support. It is hard and hurtful for this competent person to remain in the lowest status at the time of great prosperity. He must have a great deal of self-awareness and patience in order to overcome his hardship. If he endures and works steadfastly to make small but steady progress step-by-step, he will commit no error.

Divination Direction

It is not the time to entertain high aspirations and work actively to achieve your goal. You will experience many hurdles without support or cooperation from other people. This lack of support challenges your patience, but you must endure it while it lasts. In the meantime, be content with your daily routines and small accomplishments.

Line 2-9: This yang line is improperly positioned at the center of the lower trigram and correlates with 5-6, the ruler.

The images signify that the noble with the virtues of the Mean is competent and humble in his attitude. He enjoys the full confidence of the ruler, who delegates many important state affairs to him. He is like the person who is charged with transporting a heavy load on a big wagon. There is hardly any danger of the wagon breaking down, as this competent official maintains the constancy of the Mean, irrespective of the weight of the responsibilities. He will carry the load as far as necessary without making any blamable error.

Divination Direction

It augurs well. The opportunity to achieve your aspiration is around the corner. Keep on making steady efforts, and you will find many friends to help you succeed.

Line 3-9: This yang line is properly positioned at the top of the lower trigram, the high-status position of nobility.

The images signify that the noble is competent and loyal to the ruler. He shares his possessions with the ruler and the people of the state. The ruler entertains him and gives him due recognition for this. On the other hand, the petty man (incompetent and disloyal) keeps all his possessions for his personal use, and his selfish actions are harmful to the state. He will not be worthy of the ruler's hospitality.

Divination Direction

Presently, you may be enjoying a desirable position, privilege, or possession. You must make extra efforts to learn and cultivate your virtues in order to carry out your responsibility competently and forestall losing what you already have.

Line 4-9: This yang line is improperly positioned at the position close to the ruler.

The images signify that this person is wealthy and talented. He is wise and intelligent and is able to properly distinguish the status and responsibilities of the ruler and himself. He is able to restrain himself from becoming arrogant and abusing his wealth and talents. He will commit no error.

Divination Direction

You are enjoying the confidence of your superior. Increasingly, your superior has been delegating more responsibilities to you. Be mindful not to become arrogant or lax in your self-discipline to avoid your favorable situation from becoming unfavorable.

Line 5-6: This is the only yin line of this hexagram at the center of the upper trigram Fire, correlating with 2-9. The ruler practices the virtues of the Mean and is humble in his attitude. His mind is bright and devoid of selfishness, like fire that is void in the center while burning brightly outside. Such a ruler, though gentle and humble, manifests the true authority of a sovereign.

The images signify that the ruler is sincere and trustworthy. He assigns important state affairs to his wise subject (2-9), based on mutual respect and understanding. When called upon to serve, every competent subject in the upper state as well as the lower state responds to the call willingly. He is well suited to be the ruler in the time of the Great Possession. His authority is meritorious, and he is gracious to his subjects. He is unassuming and approachable, and there is no need for his subjects to be cautious or afraid of him. There will be good fortune.

Divination Direction

It augurs well. The time has come for you to put your ideas and plans into action. Constantly discipline yourself to follow the virtues of sincerity and trustfulness in your everyday life, and you will have many blessings.

Line 6-9: This yang line is at the top of the Great Possession hexagram, contiguous to 5-6, the ruler, indicating that he is an official of high status in the time of great riches and abundance.

The images signify that Heaven helps the ruler (5-6) who is obeisant to the will of Heaven. Likewise, this official, although in a high and powerful position, respects the ruler and his wisdom. The one who follows the way of *Tao* will enjoy good fortune in every respect.

Divination Direction

Your good fortune will be multiplied if you help the people, especially those who are lower in status and less fortunate than you, and you treat them with respect and sincerity. You will be amply rewarded for these actions.

15. The Modesty 謙 (Khien) Hexagram

Key attributes: Modesty, the symbol of humility

Judgment

"*Khien* indicates progress and success. The superior man (being humble as it implies), will have a (good) issue (to his undertakings)." (James Legge, *The I Ching,* 89.)

Essence of Hexagram

This hexagram explains the *Tao* of modesty as the paradigm for attaining equitable distribution and balance, avoiding either extreme.

Hexagram Image(s)

The Mountain that positions itself lower than the Earth stands for the images of the Modesty hexagram. The wise and noble uses the images as his guide to equalize benefits among all by adding to those who are less fortunate with what is reduced from those who have more.

Hexagram Analysis

This hexagram consists of the lower trigram Mountain and the upper trigram Earth. It has only one yang line at the top of the lower trigram directly under the upper trigram Earth. This indicates that the heavenly energy (3-9) positioned itself lower than the obedient and humble earth energy of the upper trigram, giving this hexagram its theme of modesty. The one yang line takes the commanding role over all the yin lines of the hexagram, but it is modest and does not assume a superior attitude over them.

3-9 is the sole lead line of this hexagram.

Interpretation of Judgment

Modesty is making lower what is high and making higher what is low. It brings both ends of the extreme to meet at the center to bring about transformation.

This hexagram presents images of modesty. In this hexagram, the energy of heaven (3-9) comes down from its exalted position to the earth, enabling everything on earth to grow. The energy of earth thrusts itself upward from its depth to bring forth growth. Thus, both heaven and earth radiate their modesty by moving from their extreme positions to interact to create and maintain life.

As represented in the hexagram, the virtue of modesty is considered the highest virtue for all men, regardless of their status. The *I Ching* texts describe modesty in the following ways: "The *Tao* of Heaven reduces from the full for the benefit of the modest. The *Tao* of Earth changes the full to make it flow to the modest. Deities harm the full but enrich the modest. Man hates the full but likes the modest. Modesty makes a man noble and ennobles him to radiate with virtues, maintain his humility, and stay on the virtuous course to the end."

Divination Direction

The time is not ripe for you to proceed with any active undertaking. Conserve your resources to prepare for the opportunity that is approaching. It is not a time for a business expansion. At present, you are having a difficult time, but the situation will gradually improve in your favor. Endure your hardship with modesty and patience. A slow-paced but deliberate trading practice will result in your favor with good-sized profits. The financial market is in decline. It is favorable to conclude a marital arrangement but guard against a frivolous romantic involvement.

Individual Lines: Analysis, Interpretation, and Divination Direction

<u>**Line 1-6:**</u> This yin line is the lowest line of the Modesty hexagram with no line correlating. The lower trigram of its primary nuclear hexagram is Water, and the upper trigram, Thunder, the symbol of wood or boat.

The images signify that the noble man is the model of modest virtues. He is virtuous and disciplined, and he is morally equipped to cross the great stream. This means that he can undertake a great enterprise that entails great many risks. There will be good fortune.

Divination Direction

Proceed with confidence in dealing with problems and difficulties that you face in pursuing your goal. Continue with your steady efforts to attain your goals with the attitude of modesty and sincerity, and you will succeed.

<u>**Line 2-6:**</u> This yin line is properly positioned at the center of the lower trigram, contiguous to the lead line 3-9. The upper trigram of its primary nuclear hexagram is Thunder, the symbol for sound.

The images signify that a modest and sincere heart expresses itself in one's conduct. 2-6 practices the virtues of the Mean and is modest, and he is in a contiguous relationship with 3-9. He recognizes that 3-9 is capable, wise, and modest. This virtuous man (2-6) praises the virtues and wisdom of 3-9 and expresses his wish that the ruler will utilize 3-9 to help run the state. 2-6's sincerity and modesty will result in good fortune.

Divination Direction

A wise man understands when and how to seek help from a right person. Get help or advice from the one that you trust. Always be sincere in your attitude and respect your superiors and virtuous people, and you will be successful.

Line 3-9: This is the only yang line and the sole lead line of this hexagram. The lower trigram Water of its primary nuclear hexagram symbolizes diligence, and its upper trigram Thunder, movement.

The images signify that the noble man works diligently and achieves much with modesty. He stays on the course of humility to the end, and everyone (all the yin lines) respects and supports him. There will be good fortune.

Divination Direction

You must concentrate your efforts to solve your own difficulties. You cannot achieve your goal easily but will succeed in the end through diligent efforts. Do not be discouraged and give up your efforts because of minor difficulties but work for your goal with renewed determination to succeed.

Line 4-6: This yin line is properly positioned just above the lower trigram Mountain (halt) as the lowest line of the upper trigram Earth (obedience). The combination of the two attributes, halt and obedience, represents utmost modesty. The upper trigram of the primary nuclear hexagram is Thunder (movement), and its lower trigram, Water (peril). The combined images require one to have utmost modesty in order that he can make careful and deliberate moves (instead of reckless, arrogant moves) to overcome the perils that accompany any situation.

The images signify that the virtue of modesty in serving the ruler (5-6) above him and in respecting the competence of 3-9 below him must be demonstrated through sincere efforts in the course of performing his duties.

Divination Direction

It is to your advantage to maintain disciplined behavior of modesty and patience, rather than aggressive and competitive behavior. Make efforts to be helpful to other people, as your cooperation with them will bring successful results to your endeavor.

Line 5-6: This yin line is at the center of the upper trigram and symbolizes that the ruler is modest in nature with the virtues of the Mean.

The images signify that the modest ruler does not show off his power or wealth to his neighbors (4-6, 6-6). He entrusts his competent subject (3-9) with many important state responsibilities. His senior officials (4-6, 6-6) also respect 3-9 with genuine modesty and work together with him. Under certain circumstances like a rebellion, the ruler utilizes military force; this action is favorable because it is done with modesty and objectivity.

Divination Direction

Remember there is more than one way to deal with a problem. In dealing with your opponent, choose an alternative that maintains your attitude of modesty and fairness.

Line 6-6: This yin line is properly positioned at the top of the Modesty hexagram. As the top line of the upper trigram Earth, it symbolizes territory, such as the city, state, or country.

The images signify that one's modesty expresses itself in his proper conduct that promotes peace and order. This feudal lord praises and expresses support for the competent 3-9 to serve the ruler (5-6) to help the ruler achieve his goal. If the feudal lord has anyone who rebels against his authority in his feudal state, it will be appropriate for him to use his military force to suppress the rebellion because his action is based on modesty, since force will be used only to maintain peace.

Divination Direction

Your progress is not smooth, with many obstacles to overcome, requiring your strong determination and courage. Refrain from any activity that might arouse suspicions or jealousies in other people. Maintain your reasonable expectations and proceed at a modest pace. However, you have to take action to defend yourself when necessary.

16. The Harmonious Joy 豫 (Yu) Hexagram

Key attributes: Harmonious joy, the symbol of enthusiasm

Judgment

"*Yu* indicates that (in the state which it implies), feudal princes may be set up, and the host put in motion, with advantage." (James Legge, *The I Ching,* 91.)

Essence of Hexagram

This hexagram explains the *Tao* of harmonious joy as the paradigm for movements that inspire enthusiasm in people's minds.

Hexagram Image(s)

Thunder rolling above and the earth responding with resonant activities stand for the images of the Harmonious Joy hexagram. Using the images as his guide, the former king made music (Thunder) to ennoble the ancestors (Water) and glorify the Supreme Deity (Thunder) in the course of worshipping the ancestors.

Hexagram Analysis

The hexagram consists of the lower trigram Earth (compliance) and the upper trigram Thunder (movement). The only yang line (4-9) in the hexagram roars with a thunderous rolling sound above Earth, and all the yin lines of the hexagram are compliant to its command. The images represent summer, when thunder activities occur. This release of yang energy brings joy, contentment, and relaxation.

Thunder is also the symbol of feudal princes. The lower trigram Mountain of the primary nuclear hexagram symbolizes virtues, and its upper trigram Water, the spirit of the deceased. The image of music for the primary nuclear hexagram and the upper trigram Thunder portrays the ceremonial dedication to honor the ancestral spirit.

The lower trigram Earth also symbolizes the multitude or the army. When combined with the image of the upper trigram Thunder for movement, the hexagram portrays the image of military mobilization.

4-9 is the sole lead line of this hexagram.

Interpretation of Judgment

The mighty (yang line) resonates with everyone (all the yin lines) to attain good governance by following the laws of nature, bringing forth enthusiasm and harmonious joy. Heaven and Earth move in harmony following the natural principle of compliance and devotion. The cycle of the sun and the moon moves with regularity, and the four seasons arrive and depart with unerring timing. So must the feudal princes govern in accordance with the laws of nature, resulting in the people in their feudal states following their leadership with enthusiasm and joy. The same law applies in mobilizing the mass to pacify when rebellion arises. The sage ruler acts in compliance of *Tao* and carries out justice with clearly defined and just rules so that the people will respect and obey them.

This hexagram represents four different images relating to a major principle of governance that must be implemented in the spirit of the hexagram theme of Harmonious Joy (of the governed) and the dependability of nature. The first priority in governance is to establish leadership; the second, the national defense; the third, law and order; and the fourth, which is the main overriding image, religious observance that connects human spirit with that of deity.

Divination Direction

It augurs well. Good times are on the way. If you stay on your course of action with a careful business plan, you will be amply rewarded. Financial investments are on an uptrend for the time being. It is a favorable time for you to start a business, move, or seek a promotion.

Individual Lines: Analysis, Interpretation, and Divination Direction

Line 1-6: This yin line is properly positioned at the lowest line of the hexagram, correlating with 4-9.

The images signify that the incompetent in the lowest status proclaims his joy and contentment by indulging in personal licentious pleasures, taking advantage of his alliance with the high official in power (4-9). His disregard for the harmonious joy will bring him misfortune. He will be frustrated in his effort to achieve his ambition.

Divination Direction

It augurs ill. To your disappointment, you are in a period of falling fortune. It is not the time for you to depend on other people to help you out. You must cultivate self-discipline and prepare for an opportunity to succeed.

Line 2-6: This yin line is properly positioned at the center of the lower trigram Earth and the first line in the lower trigram Mountain of the primary nuclear hexagram that symbolizes rock.

The images signify that this man is firm as a rock in his practice of the Mean and does not indulge himself in unwholesome pleasures like the others (1-6, 3-6). Like a sage, he is aware of any change that is in its incipient state and of its possible consequence. He acts on it immediately, not even putting off his action for later in the day. He will enjoy good fortune.

Divination Direction

You need to implement your plans. Stay firmly on the course of self-discipline and not become greedy. Be alert and do not hesitate to make necessary decisions and act upon them.

Line 3-6: This yin line is improperly positioned at the top of the lower trigram, with a contiguous relationship with 4-9.

The images signify that this person, proud and haughty in his attitude, is looking for favor from the high official in power (4-9) and feels self-important, and he misses the timing for seizing his good opportunity. Unless he becomes remorseful and repents his conduct soon, he will suffer regret, as he occupies an inappropriate position, especially with arrogance in his mind-set.

Divination Direction

First, make sure you do not harbor negative ideas and emotions toward other people. Make concerted efforts to get along harmoniously with other people. Stay within your means without becoming greedy or overambitious.

Line 4-9: This is the lead line and the only yang line of this hexagram. He commands the friendship and respect of everyone (all the yin lines). If the three yin lines below him are compared to strands of hair, he is the hair clasp that holds them together. In the social strata, this is the position of the prime minister.

The images signify that this virtuous person of high status is the source of pleasure and joy. He can bring about great achievements, as everyone is willing to follow his leadership. He is virtuous and competent in the high position and loyal to the ruler (5-6), even though the ruler has a weak personality. He does not harbor any suspicion toward other people, for they come together to follow his leadership, as a hair clasp holds strands of hair together.

Divination Direction

It augurs well. Finally, your aspirations will be realized. Many people will be willing to cooperate with you to help achieve your goal. It is to your advantage to be fair and friendly with them and proceed in a comfortable, natural pace.

Line 5-6: This yin line is improperly positioned at the center of the upper trigram. The upper trigram Water of the primary nuclear hexagram symbolizes peril or worry.

The images signify that the ruler is weak and suffers from the unsound enthusiasm for the chronic malady of pleasure seeking. However, a competent and loyal subject (4-9) helps run the affairs of the state. The ruler is unable to change his ways, but he will not lose his position as ruler.

Divination Direction

Good preparation can reduce many worries later. You have many worries, since your plans did not work out as you had planned. Prepare yourself with manageable plans and more resources. Learn to be more flexible, and move at a steady pace with one small success at a time.

Line 6-6: This yin line is at the apogee of the Harmonious Joy hexagram, as well as the top line of the upper trigram Thunder, which symbolizes movement or change.

The images signify that the unsound enthusiasm for pleasure-seeking activities of 6-6 continued for a long time, and his mind has become benighted. He can still change his way of living and have no regret. However, at the apex, how much longer can he continue with his indulgence in pleasurable activities?

Divination Direction

Refrain from putting a big plan into action fast. Go slowly but at a steady pace to achieve your modest goal. Watch yourself for enjoyment from any addictive behavior. Unless you can rein in your intemperate behavior soon, it will lead you to ruin.

17. The Following 隨 (Sui) Hexagram

Key attributes: Following, the symbol of succession

Judgment

"*Sui* indicates that (under its conditions) there will be great progress and success. But it will be advantageous to be firm and correct. There will (then) be no error." (James Legge, *The I Ching*, 93.)

Essence of Hexagram

This hexagram explains the *Tao* of adaptation as the paradigm for meeting the demands of time through disciplined leadership to maintain integrity and achieve harmony. A leader should learn how to follow before he can lead.

Hexagram Image(s)

Thunder (summer) hiding in the Lake (autumn) stands for the images of the Following hexagram and portrays the end of summer thunder activity and the advent of autumn (Lake). The sun has traveled from the east (Thunder) to the west (Lake), and it is getting dark. With the images of the lower trigram Mountain (halt) of the primary nuclear hexagram and its upper trigram Wind (entering), the combined images depict how one activity of nature follows it; e.g., from hot to coolness, and from light to darkness.

Following the course of nature, the noble man continually adapts himself to meet the demands of the time for his service by engaging in tireless activities during the day, and returning home at nightfall for rest and recuperation.

Hexagram Analysis

This hexagram consists of the lower trigram Thunder, which symbolizes the eldest son, and the upper trigram Lake, the youngest daughter or a young girl. The hexagram title "Following" is derived from the unconventional characterization of this hexagram in which the yang follows the yin, the older follows the younger, instead of the usual order. This reversal of order requires extraordinary discipline and integrity on the part of the strong (yang) and the old (more experienced), which symbolizes the principle of effective leadership in adapting to the reality. When a leader demonstrates this quality in leadership, the gentle follows with joy (Lake) and enables the strong (Thunder) to carry out the demands of the time. This is the way the strong demonstrates the inner leadership quality of following the correct advice of the gentle.

The same principle applies in the management of family affairs. The spirit of gentleness has to prevail over coercion in order to maintain family harmony. The sincerity of the family leader who listens to the voice of family members elicits their joy as they follow his leadership. The principle is represented in this hexagram by the lower yang trigram Thunder following the upper yin trigram Lake with the single yang line (1-9) leading the lower trigram, or the eldest brother following the youngest sister. The yang line of 1-9 follows the yin line of 2-6; the yang line of 5-9 follows the yin line of 6-6. Nowhere else in *I Ching* is such a reverse order found.

1-9, directive, and 5-9, structural, are the lead lines of this hexagram.

Interpretation of Judgment

The strong (yang) joyfully taking its position below the weak (yin) stands for the images of the Following hexagram. The concept of "Following" to meet the demands of time is of great significance. The strong exercises the virtues of modesty and follows the advice of the gentle; the one in higher status follows the advice of the one in lower status. However, a "Following" should not be carried out blindly but through the correct practice of *Tao* to meet the demands of time without committing an error. The lower trigram Thunder (movement) and the upper trigram Lake (joy) portray that the act of "Following" is the source of great joy and good fortune when it follows consistent virtuous conduct. The exemplary conduct of the leader must be consistent to motivate a large number of people in the world to follow.

Divination Direction

It augurs well. Maintain a course of action that you consider beneficial to both yourself and the other party. Be flexible so that you can take advantage of the available opportunities. Be cooperative with other people for mutual benefits. It is a favorable time for finding a job, starting a business, or traveling.

Individual Lines: Analysis, Interpretation, and Divination Direction

Line 1-9: This yang line is properly positioned as the lowest in this hexagram, not correlating with any line. The lower trigram Thunder (movement) represents the government official (one yang line governs the two yin lines) and change. The lower trigram Mountain of the primary nuclear hexagram symbolizes gate. The combined images of the lower trigram portray the act of leaving home to associate with other people to listen to their opinions and advice.

The images signify that one must be able to adapt to changing reality by following a wide range of opinions with wisdom and sincerity. For the government official in a low status who will have a change in his status, he will have good fortune if he follows the correct path of *Tao*, since he is competent and virtuous. He will have meritorious achievements if he goes beyond his gate to associate with other people (2-6) for their opinions and advice, since he has followed the correct path of *Tao*.

Divination Direction

The time has come for you to implement what you have been planning and preparing for. You are competent and conscientious and will have a promotion. Actively associate with other people for mutual cooperation, and you will have good fortune.

Line 2-6: This yin line is properly positioned at the center of the lower trigram and correlates with 5-9.

The images signify that this person who practices the virtues of the Mean has the choice of following one of the two yangs, 1-9 or 5-9, in this era of "Following." It is not possible to follow both. If he cannot cut his attachment to the little boy (1-9) (immature, unworthy man), he will end up losing the mature man (5-9). Likewise, a man cannot pursue both right and wrong at the same time, nor can he achieve something great while dwelling on a trifling matter.

Divination Direction

It is to your advantage to have a choice and make the choice with a positive outlook. Assess your situation accurately. Be decisive in your move and follow the course of the greater cause.

Line 3-6: This yin line is improperly positioned, contiguous to the line above and with no correlating line. The primary nuclear hexagram of this hexagram consists of the lower trigram Mountain (halt or staying) and the upper trigram Wind (benefits or gain).

The images signify that this man chose to follow the mature person with the higher status (4-9) instead of the little boy (1-9) (inferior or immature man), thereby gaining what he was seeking. It is to his advantage to stay in the constancy of *Tao*.

Divination Direction

Wisdom is knowing what to choose when. Assess your situation accurately and choose the option that will bring the greater gains to you. Refrain from acting on many plans simultaneously.

Line 4-9: This yang line is improperly positioned at the high status of prime minister, contiguous to 3-6 who chooses to follow him.

The images signify that only sincere and unselfish following will result in success. This strong and competent prime minister serves the ruler, 5-9, who is also strong in character. At the same time, the minister fosters his own followers. If the prime minister continues to strengthen his own power, he will arouse suspicion in the ruler's mind, which would lead to his ruinous misfortune. Success often makes a person arrogant, leading him to ruin. Therefore, it is essential that he demonstrate his loyalty to the ruler clearly by being sincere and following the correct path of *Tao* so that he will not commit any error.

Divination Direction

Examine your mind-set to see if you harbor any desire to promote factions among people to take advantage of them. If so, change your mind-set, for it will bring misfortune to you.

Line 5-9: This yang line is properly positioned at the center of the upper trigram, correlating with 2-6, the centerline of the lower trigram.

The images signify that the sincere following is powerful enough to bring people intimately close. This able and virtuous ruler who practices the Mean trusts his virtuous subject, 2-6, deeply with all his sincerity, and the close, intimate relationship between the two is likened to that of husband and wife. There will be good fortune.

Divination Direction

First try to establish a trusting relationship with others. Work toward your goal with sincerity, and you will succeed. When necessary, you will find help if you seek it.

Line 6-6: This yin line is properly positioned at the top of the Following hexagram. The upper trigram Lake represents west in direction. The lower trigram Mountain of the primary nuclear hexagram symbolizes hand, and its upper trigram Wind, string.

The images signify that the wise and gentle senior advisor to the ruler is about to retire after a successful career helping the ruler with wise advice. The ruler is trying very hard to persuade him to change his mind and stay on to help him; it is as if the ruler is tying him up with strings and not letting up. Finally, the loyal senior official accepts the honor the ruler offers him to be the master priest for the royal family's temple of ancestors on the west Mountain, the sacred ground of the *Chou* dynasty. He was obliged to accept this position, which is the highest that a subject can have in the state.

Divination Direction

Do not dwell on your petty emotional attachments but have a wider perspective in making your choice. At present, everything is going well with you. You will be able to find a good supporter when you need one.

18. The Decaying 蠱 (Ku) Hexagram

Key attributes: Decaying, destroying, the symbol of major power

Judgment

"*Ku* indicates great progress and success (to him who deals properly with the condition represented by it). There will be advantage in (efforts like that of) crossing the great stream. (He should weigh well, however, the events of) three days before the turning point, and those (to be done) three days after it." (James Legge, *The I Ching*, 95.)

Essence of Hexagram

This hexagram explains the *Tao* of revitalization as the paradigm for correcting what has been corrupted.

Hexagram Image(s)

Wind below Mountain stands for the images of the Decaying hexagram. The wise and noble uses the images as his guide to motivate the governed to revitalize the society by listening and responding to them and cultivating their spirit and virtues.

Hexagram Analysis

The Chinese character for the Decaying hexagram is hieroglyphic, consisting of three worms (🐛)in a vessel (▬), and it has various meanings: decay, toxic, and intestinal worms.

The Decaying hexagram results when the Following hexagram is overturned.

The successful and joyous era of "Following" makes people complacent and eventually results in the habit of indulgence, with decadence as the consequence. This hexagram consists of the lower trigram Wind with the meaning of compliance, and the upper trigram Mountain, halt or immovability. This image indicates that wind is not penetrating the foliages of the mountain, for there is no interchange between the two trigrams. The upper trigram of halt means it does not intend to change its habit of indulgence (the success in the era of "Following"), and the lower trigram is complacent with what the mountain is doing and does not motivate it to change its ways. The Wind is obstructed from blowing through the Mountain freely, causing the trees and the vegetation on it to decay and die. Furthermore, 6-9 of the upper trigram has no line to correlate with in the lower trigram, and 1-6 of the lower trigram has no line to correlate with in the upper trigram. These factors further reinforce the sign of the time that things are stale and corrupt with wealth, power and pleasure-seeking activities. This is a natural consequence after the Following hexagram has reached its apex.

1-6, directive, and 5-6, structural, are the lead lines of this hexagram.

Interpretation of Judgment

The time of crisis demands great leadership to bring about the necessary changes to reestablish law and order in the society. The time of crisis will produce such a leader, for complete corruption is the sign of a new beginning that will follow. For this reason, the judgment text says:

"*Ku* indicates great progress and success." It is the time when such a leader must risk much and govern as if he were crossing a great river. In order to take advantage of the sign of a new beginning to bring about change, not only must he have the courage but the wisdom to select the right timing and make feasible plans for his undertaking.

The reference to the three days in the judgment text (the "three" is symbolic) emphasizes the importance of timing and careful planning. The Chinese zodiac calendar is based on a sixty-year cycle and has ten characters representing heavenly attributes and twelve characters representing earth animals supporting the heavenly attributes. The "three days before the turning point" in the judgment text refers to three days before the beginning of the cycle and is the eighth character representing one of the heavenly attributes, which is a yin character for planning with proper deliberation rather than acting without planning. The "three days after it" is three days after the cycle begins and is the fourth character representing one of the heavenly attributes, also a yin character. It connotes looking back at the past to counter the stagnation. In order to achieve the goal, one must first correctly assess the starting phase for stirring the desire of people for reform, like the blowing wind (lower trigram Wind), and to establish a just and principled state with a strong and firm foundation like a mountain (upper trigram Mountain).

Divination Direction

It augurs ill. It is the time of worries and losses due to personal, family, health, and financial problems. These problems are rooted mainly in your own conduct. Examine yourself closely to see if you are unfriendly, disorganized, and corrupt in your dealings. If so, you need to take speedy and decisive actions to change your conduct and wait for a better time to come. The financial market will decline dramatically as the prelude to a sharp upturn.

Individual Lines: Analysis, Interpretation, and Divination Direction

Line 1-6: This yin line is the beginning line of the Decaying hexagram and does not correlate with any line. It is the directive lead line of the hexagram. The primary nuclear hexagram is made up of the lower trigram Wind and the upper trigram Thunder, both with the meaning of wood, symbolizing here the sturdy pillar (of wood) that does not bend, or the one who rights the wrong.

The images signify that the rigid practice of tradition results in decay. In this case, the son straightens out the family troubles (past wrongs on social matters) that his father had caused. His motive is to fulfill his duty of filial piety toward his father by correcting the ills in such a way that the correction will not bring the disgrace of blame upon the father. Despite the difficulties and risks inherent in such a task, the well-motivated son will have good fortune in the end.

Divination Direction

It augurs ill. You are put in a difficult position to work on the vexing problem that you did not create. Do your best to understand the problem to solve it. The sooner you take decisive action to solve the problem, the better it will be for all concerned.

Line 2-9: This yang line is improperly positioned at the center of the lower trigram and correlates with 5-6. In terms of the family hierarchy, 2-9 is the son and 5-6 the mother.

The images signify that the lack of proper leadership results in decay. In this case, the son straightens out the family trouble (family matters) that was caused by his mother. He does this by practicing the virtues of the Mean without being righteous, and being gentle in his attitude.

Divination Direction

You are hard at work to resolve the problem that you did not create. You need to study the situation closely and clarify the problem before you try to solve it. Since you are capable, you will succeed in your efforts.

Line 3-9: This yang line is properly positioned, correlating with no line.

The images signify that a corrective action accompanies difficulties and needs wisdom and tact. In this case, the son in this family is competent but too aggressive in his approach. The son straightens out the family trouble that was caused by his father, but in a very aggressive manner. His overaggressiveness will cause a little regret, but it will not lead to any grave error.

Divination Direction

You need to use your fine sensitivity so that you do not unnecessarily hurt other people in your efforts to correct the situation. You need to take a decisive action with a temperate attitude to correct the problem without wasting time in order to forestall the problem before it spreads.

Line 4-6: This yin line is properly positioned, correlating with no line. It is the first line of the upper trigram Mountain that symbolizes halt, inaction, or leniency.

The images signify that the son has the correct motive to remedy the family problem that his father caused, but he is too weak and lacks the ability to carry out his intentions. If he continues to proceed in this manner, he will not be able to succeed.

Divination Direction

It will be difficult for you to prevent the problem from getting worse. Let each problem run its course. Meanwhile, prepare yourself for a new opportunity that is sure to come.

Line 5-6: This yin line is improperly positioned at the center of the upper trigram and correlates with 2-9.

The images signify that collaborative efforts are necessary to correct the past wrongs of the government. In this case, the ruler practices the virtues of the Mean and has the ability to exercise his power with a proper balance. By his virtuous governance with the help of his trusted competent subject (2-9), he successfully brings about reform and restores the authority of the government, which had been damaged by his father.

Divination Direction

It augurs well. Make a move to handle the most difficult problem thwarting your progress. You are about to resolve the knotty problems that have been troubling your mind. The one in whom you have trust will be able to help you out.

Line 6-9: This yang line is at the top of this hexagram, correlating with no line. Here, the upper trigram Mountain symbolizes loftiness.

The images signify that one can make important contributions toward correcting the past wrongs in the society through his lofty pursuit of *Tao* for self-realization. This person entertains a higher aim of contributing to mankind through self-realization, rather than through serving the ruler (5-6) or the feudal lord (3-9). He engages in the lofty pursuit of *Tao*, which will set a good example for people to follow.

Divination Direction

The time has come for you to bring your endeavor to a conclusion. You deserve to relax and enjoy your life before you start with a new and greater plan.

19. The Advance 臨 (Lin) Hexagram

Key attributes: Approach, the symbol of advance

Judgment

"*Lin* (indicates that under the conditions supposed in it) there will be great progress and success, while it will be advantageous to be firmly correct. In the eighth month there will be evil." (James Legge, *The I Ching*, 97.)

Essence of Hexagram

This hexagram explains the *Tao* of advance as the paradigm for success and progress through constant proper restraint in one's conduct.

Hexagram Image(s)

The lower trigram Lake and the upper trigram Earth stand for the images of the one who is standing on the shore (Earth) overlooking the Lake joyfully. The wise and noble uses the images as his guide to make utmost efforts to enlighten the people, for his magnanimity toward the governed is limitless.

Hexagram Analysis

This hexagram consists of the lower trigram Lake that symbolizes joy and the upper trigram Earth, obedience. The two yang lines are the lead lines (1-9 and 2-9) of the hexagram, and each correlates respectively with 4-6 and 5-6 of the upper trigram. In November, yang returns to the bottom of the hexagram. It advances to the second yang line in December and keeps advancing until it reaches its apex in April. It is from this advance of the yang that the hexagram derives its name "Advance."

1-9, directive, and 2-9, structural, are the lead lines of this hexagram.

Interpretation of Judgment

The Advance hexagram depicts the era when the great man (yang) advances, while the petty man (yin) obeys (Earth) joyfully (Lake). The strong (2-9) occupies the center, while the gentle (5-6) in the higher status resonates with the strong. Therefore, the hexagram Advance stands for the fundamental good of being in the constancy of *Tao*, the principles of Heaven and Earth. The joyous season of spring is near, and the great continues to advance with success. However, one must work diligently to make good use of this opportune time. The yin and yang cycle will reverse the yang advance in the eighth month when yin (the petty man) takes over yang (the great man), and this will result in misfortune. Following the six months in which yang steadily advances, yin returns to the bottom of the hexagram in the seventh month (refer to Hexagram #44 Encounter) and begins its advance, reversing the yang position of this hexagram in the eighth month.

Divination Direction

It augurs well. Your efforts will result in success after success. You can attain a leadership position. It is favorable for your business, trading, move, and marriage. A depressed financial market will stage a dramatic rise. Guard against a romantic involvement. An expectant mother will have an easy delivery of a daughter. You must remember that this is the time to prepare for the rainy days, as the sunny days will not last forever.

Individual Lines: Analysis, Interpretation, and Divination Direction

Line 1-9: This yang line is properly positioned as the directive lead line of the hexagram and correlates with 4-6.

The images signify that this man, though low in status, is virtuous and competent and gets the support of a higher official (4-6) for his advance. Since he pursues his goal in the rectitude of the constancy, showing impartiality to everyone, there will be good fortune.

Divination Direction

The better prepared you are, the greater success you will enjoy. You are on the threshold of success in your efforts. You will be able to get the help of others when necessary.

Line 2-9: This yang line is the lead line of this hexagram at the center of the lower trigram and correlates with 5-6.

The images signify that this virtuous man who practices the Mean is competent and strong, and he receives the ruler's support. He will have good fortune in every way because he follows the principle of *Tao*, even though everything is in constant change, and every rise has a fall.

Divination Direction

It augurs well. Do not dwell on your past failures or unpopularity. Your abilities are well recognized by others, and you will be given the opportunity to promote. You will be successful.

Line 3-6: This yin line is improperly positioned at the top of the lower trigram Lake that symbolizes mouth and tongue.

The images signify that this incompetent high official has made an easy advance to a position to which he is not qualified. He tries to impress the two advancing competent men (1-9 and 2-9) with flattery, but no advantage results. He should realize that he is holding the wrong position (yin line in the yang position) and should be concerned enough to change his wrong attitude and be remorseful; if he does that, his worrisome situation will not last long.

Divination Direction

Sweet words or flattery will not do you any good. Make efforts to cultivate the virtues of honesty and sincerity. With a correct mind-set, assess your situation thoroughly and do your best with sincerity in order to succeed in your undertaking.

Line 4-6: This yin line is properly positioned, high in status, correlating with 1-9.

The images signify that this person who holds a high status position is virtuous. He gives appropriate recognition to his able subordinate (1-9), leading both to have the full measure of progress and advance. Because of his proper conduct, there will be no error.

Divination Direction

Good, talented people will not remain with you all the time. It is the best policy to be fair with everyone. Have the wisdom to utilize the talents of other people to carry out your plans successfully.

Line 5-6: This yin line is at the center of the upper trigram and correlates with the virtuous 2-9, who is both competent and wise.

The images signify that this ruler, who practices the virtues of the Mean, has a deep trust in the loyalty and abilities of his subject, 2-9. The ruler delegates important state affairs to him, in order to govern the state with wisdom and intelligence. The ability of the ruler to utilize this subject's talents to achieve his objectives is his most important imperative.

Divination Direction

It augurs well. Establish clear plans and action directions. Provide the leadership to foster cooperation among the competent people in order to get the help that you need, and you will be successful.

Line 6-6: This yin line is at the top of both the upper trigram Earth that symbolizes sincerity, honesty, and obedience and the Advance hexagram. It correlates with no line.

The images signify that this person has advanced to the highest degree of self-realization with integrity and peace of mind. This man teaches the capable young officials (1-9, 2-9) with sincerity and grace. There will be good fortune, and he will commit no error. As his competent subordinates (1-9, 2-9) advance with the full trust of the ruler (5-6) and the prime minister (4-6), in the beginning he will not receive full appreciation from the competent subordinates, but he eventually will.

Divination Direction

You may experience difficulties by being misunderstood by other people. If this is so, do not feel upset and frustrated; instead, deal with them with sincerity and honesty. This will help you win their trust and build confidence in you.

20. The Observation 觀 (Kwan) Hexagram

Key attributes: Observation, the symbol of contemplation

Judgment

"*Kwan* shows (how he whom it represents should be like) the worshipper who has washed his hands, but not (yet) presented his offerings: with sincerity and an appearance of dignity (commanding reverent regard)." (James Legge, *The I Ching*, 99.)

Essence of Judgment

This hexagram explains *Tao* of observation as the paradigm for understanding nature's way and the people. One is to view the world as it appears, and the other is to view oneself (self-contemplation), in order to cultivate one's mind to follow the correct path in life.

Hexagram Image(s)

Wind blowing above Earth stands for the images of the Observation hexagram. With these images in mind, the former kings went on observation tours throughout the state to learn about the actual conditions of the governed to implement government policies accordingly.

Hexagram Analysis

"Kwan," the Chinese name for this hexagram, is a spiritual temple, and it symbolizes the spiritual shrine of one's mind. This hexagram deals with contemplation (mind-set) and conduct. If one has a proper mind-set based on *Tao,* good conduct will follow.

This hexagram consists of the lower trigram Earth, which here symbolizes such attributes as obedience, cow, or a sacrificial offering, and the upper trigram Wind, which represents compliance, cleanliness, or ablution. It has the images of the upper two yang lines observing (looking down) the four yin lines below, which, in turn, are looking up, observing the top two yang lines. The upper trigram Mountain of the primary nuclear hexagram has various symbolisms, such as halt, gate, hands, and observation.

5-9, structural, and 6-9, directive, are the lead lines of this hexagram.

Interpretation of Judgment

The great observer (5-9) occupies the high position of sovereignty. He complies with the principles of *Tao* and observes the governed through his virtuous practice of the Mean.

The Observation hexagram also presents the image of the sovereign who has just completed the ritual of ablution[26] prior to his sacrificial offering in the ancestral temple ceremony. The first part of the ceremony, the ritual of ablution, is the occasion for the sovereign as the chief priest to conduct himself most sincerely and solemnly with the proper mind-set.

THE SIXTY-FOUR HEXAGRAMS ❀ 147

After he completes the careful and deliberate preparation, he makes the sacrificial offering in a short ceremony.

This two-part ceremony emphasizes that the preparation for the offering with a proper mind-set is as important or more important than the offering itself.

When the subjects observe the sovereign dedicating his heart and mind to his ancestors, they are morally and spiritually inspired to follow his example. In this way, the people learn about the deity who created and governs nature, as represented in the four seasons, which never deviate from the deity's law of nature. Just as nature submits itself to the deity, so does everyone on earth submit himself to the authority of a sage ruler who follows *Tao* and whose influence spreads like the wind blowing over the earth.

Divination Direction

It augurs some drastic changes in your life. There will be fluctuations in the financial market. An observant business transaction will result in a windfall. In general, you may not be blessed with material things, but you have a sound spiritual mind, which is your important asset. You can overcome your worries by lowering your expectations and engaging in nonmaterialistic occupations. Be faithful to other people in carrying out your plans, and maintain your humble attitude. It is favorable to travel, but unfavorable for marital or childbirth events.

Individual Lines: Analysis, Interpretation, and Divination Direction

Note: Each line of this hexagram moves progressively toward a more mature level of self-cultivation.

Line 1-6: This yin line is improperly positioned at the beginning of this hexagram and represents a child or a petty man.

The images signify the different depths in observation, such as observing the actions of a child who does not yet have a depth of understanding. If the thoughtless masses or a petty man conducts himself like a child, he cannot be blamed; however, it would be regrettable if a noble man acts in a childish manner, instead of contemplating and conducting himself more thoughtfully.

Divination Direction

At this time, it is not easy for you to maintain even the status quo, and it is better for you to be content with your everyday routine and small undertakings to support your family. It is not the proper time for you to launch a risky or ambitious venture.

Line 2-6: This yin line is properly positioned at the center of the lower trigram and correlates with 5-9. The lower trigram Earth has the meaning of closing the door, and the upper trigram Mountain of the primary nuclear hexagram, the gate.

The images signify that the observation is limited because the observer is peering through the crack in the door. This yin line symbolizes softness, weakness, or female. Despite the fact that this man practices the Mean and has the correlative relationship with the ruler, his limited observation and lack of introspection give him only a narrow, self-centered point of view. Like the woman in the family, it will be to his advantage if he is gentle and compliant with the rectitude of *Tao* and not undertake a great enterprise. However, such limited self-centered observation (perspective) is unfitting and regrettable for a noble man.

Divination Direction

Understand the fact that you are self-centered and shortsighted. First make efforts to cultivate more open-mindedness. Concentrate your efforts to carry out your family routines successfully. It is not a proper time for you to engage in a risky or ambitious venture.

Line 3-6: This yin line is at the top of the lower trigram bordering with the upper trigram Wind. It symbolizes a juncture of advancing or retreating. (Which way does the wind blow?) It has no correlating line and is at equal distance from 1-6 and 5-9.

The images signify that observation needs to be directed to oneself. He should first undertake an intense self-examination of his own life and activities before making the decision to advance or retreat. He will avoid committing an error by choosing the correct course of action that is in compliance with *Tao*.

Divination Direction

Examine your motive and assess your resources so that you stay within your means and have the right motivation in launching your undertaking.

Line 4-6: This yin line is properly positioned for the high status of the prime minister, contiguous to the sovereign. The lower trigram Earth represents the state.

The images signify that this person observes the state from a high level. Having a wide perspective, he is able to exert influence and extend the glory of the state under the competent rule of the virtuous sovereign who practices the Mean. It is fitting that this man be honored with an important government position, or as a guest of the ruler, in the tradition of a sovereign honoring the wise and virtuous by having him as his personal guest.

Divination Direction

You have a chance to be promoted if you stay with your present job. Your good efforts will gain the recognition of your superiors. The matters of your concern will develop in your favor at a gradual pace, so carry out your assignments with sincerity.

Line 5-9: This yang line is at the center of the upper trigram. The upper trigram Mountain of the primary nuclear hexagram symbolizes the mind that stays inside (to stay where it belongs and to be introspective) for self-observation.

The images signify that the one in the position of influence needs to have constant self-examination. This virtuous ruler observes and reflects on his own virtues and conduct. If he finds that he is practicing the rectitude of *Tao* worthy of a noble man, he will not fall into error. His attitude and conduct as the ruler affect everyone within the four corners of his state. His observations and actions touch all of the governed (four yin lines below), and they look up to him and submit themselves to his rule.

Divination Direction

Be exemplary toward other people by being sincere and reliable to them and open-minded in accepting their new ideas. Refrain from engaging in selfish activity.

Line 6-9: This yang line is at the top of the Observation hexagram, indicating that this high official is at the retirement stage and free from worldly affairs. He devotes himself to perfect his self-realization, although he is still competent enough to carry out important assignments advising the ruler. There are four yin lines below this yang line.

The images signify that the enlightened one has the role to play above and beyond one's personal gains. This noble and competent high official performs the important task of assuring (observing) that the sovereign stays on the virtuous and correct course of governance. In return, the ruler and all the common people of the state are observing his virtuous and spiritual conduct as an example to follow. He provides a model for others as he pursues *Tao* in depth.

Divination Direction

Your mind is not at ease, as you have many things that cause you concern. Maintain a positive attitude and carry out each task step-by-step with conviction and sincerity, and you will be successful.

21. The Biting through 噬 嗑 (Shih Ho) Hexagram

Key attributes: Biting through, the symbol of criminal proceedings

Judgment

"*Shih Ho* indicates successful progress (in the condition of things which it supposes). It will be advantageous to use legal constraints." (James Legge, *The I Ching*, 101.)

Essence of Hexagram

This hexagram explains the *Tao* of justice as the paradigm for managing criminal litigation to overcome barriers and obstacles created by criminals in the society.

Hexagram Image(s)

Thunder and Lightning (the upper trigram Light) stand for the images of the Biting-through hexagram. Former sage kings used the images of this hexagram as their guide to govern their states with the clarity of Lightning in establishing laws, and with the authority of Thunder in meting out the clearly defined punishment to the criminals.

Hexagram Analysis

This hexagram consists of the lower trigram Thunder, the symbol of movement or action, and the upper trigram Light, the symbol of intelligence. The two yang lines, one at the bottom and the other at the top, present the images of the lower and upper jaws. The third yang line between the two represents a barrier or an obstacle in the mouth to "bite through" and eliminate. In this hexagram the upper trigram Water of the primary nuclear hexagram symbolizes peril, law, or prison.

5-6 is the sole lead line of the hexagram.

Interpretation of Judgment

The upper and lower jaws and the object in the mouth between the jaws stand for the images of the Biting-through hexagram. The "biting" symbolizes successful progress in an action taken to eliminate an obstacle. The combined images of the lower trigram Thunder (movement) and the upper trigram Light represent the action being carried out with intelligence. The combination of the action (the lower trigram) and the intelligence (the upper trigram) brings about sound justice by eliminating the obstacles (4-9) in the society that criminals create. The soft (5-6) attains the center of the upper trigram, symbolizing the ruler who practices the virtues of the Mean and administers a fair and virtuous criminal justice system by correctly distinguishing right from wrong.

Divination Direction

You have some obstacles and difficulties to overcome in your life. You will experience some marital and other human relationship problems, but this will not last long. Your financial situation will improve gradually. You do not need to get discouraged over your current hardships. Calmly analyze the situation and, based on your assessment, attack each problem with persistence. You will succeed.

Individual Lines: Analysis, Interpretation, and Divination Direction

Line 1-9: This yang line is properly positioned at the beginning of the hexagram. It symbolizes the start of criminal proceedings. The lower trigram Thunder has the meaning of wood; here it represents the wooden stock or fetter. 1-9, the lowest line, represents the ankle in the human body.

The images signify that this man is at the beginning stage of a criminal proceeding. For a small first offense that he committed, he is made to wear the wooden stocks on his feet, restraining the movement of his toes. Consequently, his toes are injured, and he is unable to walk. This punishment and consequence will deter him from committing more offenses. For this reason, he becomes a person of no blame. If a small disability prevents him from committing more serious offense, it is a good fortune.

Divination Direction

Your current direction in your efforts is misleading you, and you will be better served if you change your direction.

Line 2-6: This yin line is properly positioned at the center of the lower trigram. The three yin lines of the hexagram represent teeth between the two jaws or the magistrates, and the two yang lines, one at the bottom and the other at the top, the criminals.

The images signify that this is one of the low-level magistrates who deal with criminals who are being tried for relatively light offenses. This magistrate is virtuous and well qualified for the task. He metes out soft punishment to petty criminals (1-9), avoiding the folly of "destroying one's nose for biting through a piece of tender meat" with such great force that the tender meat touches the nose (too harsh a punishment for a light offense). By his fair administration of justice, he will be able to motivate the criminals (1-9) to reform. He will commit no error.

Divination Direction

Always examine a better alternative in dealing with a difficult problem. You may get involved in disputes. Pursue your goals with a friendly and cooperative attitude with other people, and you will be successful.

Line 3-6: This yin line is improperly positioned at the top of the lower trigram.

The images signify that this magistrate is neither virtuous nor well qualified for the high position. The difficulty he faces in meting out punishment to the hardened and rebellious criminals is analogous to gnawing dried meat, which has some spoiled parts. The misplacement of this magistrate to deal with hard criminals will present him with some regrettable difficulties (dealing with poisonous hatred directed toward him because of his inexperienced administration of justice), but he will not commit any serious error nor incur blame in meting out the required punishment.

Divination Direction

It is not the proper time for you to get involved in a public affair or an ambitious enterprise. Stay within your means in carrying out your plan and be satisfied with small successes.

Line 4-9: This yang line is improperly positioned, correlating with no line.

The images signify that this minister of justice is competent, but he lacks the virtues of the Mean. It is as hard as gnawing dried meat on the bone for him to deal with the most hardened criminals. However, due to his competence, he is successful in getting the criminal's deposit of gold or other metals and arrows as required pledge before the beginning of the criminal proceedings, in accordance with traditional practice. (This practice symbolizes the character of the magistrate to be as hard and unbending as metal and straight as an arrow to handle such criminals adequately.) Though difficult, it is to his advantage to practice the constancy of *Tao*. However, because he lacks in the virtues of the Mean and is improperly positioned, he falls short of achieving glowing merits. If he perseveres to practice the constancy of *Tao*, it will bring good fortune.

Divination Direction

Your situation will get worse before it improves. Presently, the going is difficult for you, but if you work toward your goal with persistence, you will succeed.

Line 5-6: This yin line is improperly positioned, correlating with no line.

The images signify that this ruler practices the virtues of the Mean but lacks the toughness required in dealing with some hardened criminals who come before him. To deal with such criminals is like gnawing dried meat, but these criminals are not as difficult to deal with as the criminals that the minister of justice handles, which is likened to gnawing dried meat that is attached to the bone. However, the ruler's virtuous handling of the criminals with the help of the competent minister results in getting the criminal's deposit of yellow gold and arrows to begin the criminal proceedings in accordance with traditional practice. (The yellow gold symbolizes the administration of justice as fairly as the color yellow, the color of the Mean.) His virtuous and cautious approach is proper for his position, and he will commit no error.

Divination Direction

Your ability to understand your problem objectively will be the key to solving your problem. You are faced with some difficult problems to resolve. You can overcome the difficulties with your sincere and persistent efforts, and you will be successful.

<u>**Line 6-9:**</u> This yang line is improperly positioned at the top of the Biting-through hexagram.

The images signify that he is the most hardened criminal who cannot be reformed. He serves his sentence bearing such a heavy cangue (Chinese neck fetters) that his ears disappear under the cangue. There will be misfortune because he is incorrigible and does not listen to the warnings and the right advice.

Divination Direction

It augurs ill. Behave yourself with modesty and patience or you will suffer.

22. The Ornamental 賁 (Pi) Hexagram

Key attributes: Ornamental, the symbol of model

Judgment

"*Pi* indicates that here should be free course (in what it denotes). There will be little advantage (however) if it be allowed to advance (and take the lead)." (James Legge, *The I Ching*, 103.)

Essence of Hexagram

This hexagram explains the *Tao* of art as the paradigm for attaining beauty (grace, art, ornamental, culture) and substance (virtuous integrity) through the interplays of yin and yang.

Hexagram Image(s)

Light below Mountain that decorates the mountain with bright light stands for the images of the Ornamental hexagram. The wise and noble uses the images as his guide to govern (mountain) the people with a clear understanding of the art of governing (light) and not resorting to the abuse of power. However, in the administration of criminal justice, he strictly adheres to the clearly defined penalties and does not use arbitrary rules of punishment.

Hexagram Analysis

This hexagram consists of the lower trigram Light that symbolizes brightness, civilization and enlightenment, and the upper trigram Mountain that symbolizes halt or standstill. When the middle line of the trigram Heaven is replaced with the soft line (yin line), it becomes the trigram Light. The commentary in *Ten Wings* refers to the yin line as "the soft comes to adorn the hard." What Heaven gives is substance, represented by the hard line (yang line). The substance becomes beautiful when one of the yang lines is exchanged with a soft line (yin line) of adornment. The upper trigram Mountain comes from the trigram Earth, when its top soft yin line is exchanged with the hard yang line. With the addition of the substance (yang), Earth's decorative softness (yin) attains a balance. The panoramic picture of the hexagram, the sun below the mountain, presents the decorative image of sunset.

2-6, structural, and 6-9, directive, are the lead lines of this hexagram.

Interpretation of Judgment

The Ornamental hexagram with its balancing aspect represents progress and success. The images signify that when the soft or decorative (yin) comes to replace the hard or practical (yang) and changes the trigram Heaven into the trigram Light, nature becomes beautiful. When the top soft line of the trigram Earth is exchanged with the middle (hard) line of the trigram Heaven, the trigram Earth obtains the substance to decorate. When the soft decorates the hard (substance), it is a superficial adornment and is fitting for small achievements. The ornament enhances the beauty of the substance when it is utilized only to the degree that it balances the hardness of the substance. Therefore, one should set out to do well on small matters, but not for clearly defined matters such as the administration of criminal justice.

The upper trigram Mountain denotes that the decorative or the nonsubstantive activity in society should have limits. The hard represents the heavenly way or *Tao*, and the soft, the culture or what humanity creates, such as the roles assigned to the ruler, parents, siblings, husband and wife, and other norms of social mores. One comes to understand how nature works by observing the orderliness of nature. In the same way, one comes to understand how a society or a person is transformed through culture and civilization.

Divination Direction

Beware of chicaneries in business dealings and marital arrangements. You must take the time to cultivate self-discipline and develop the ability to distinguish right from wrong in deciding the correct course of action. It is to your advantage to try harder to cultivate your moral and intellectual abilities rather than seek material gains. It is auspicious to engage in an occupation related to art, fashion, body grooming, and advertising. Your sincere, persistent efforts will bring small successes.

Individual Lines: Analysis, Interpretation, and Divination Direction

Line 1-9: This yang line is properly positioned at the beginning of the hexagram and correlates with 4-6. The trigram Water of the primary nuclear hexagram symbolizes carriage.

The images signify that this competent and promising man of low status adorns his feet or "cultivates himself" to prepare himself to respond to a good opportunity. Possessing self-restraint and being humble in his low status, he decides to walk instead of riding in the carriage as the high-ranking officials do. It is morally correct to walk, demonstrating his humble attitude and restraint from luxurious indulgence.

Divination Direction

As yet, no opportunity has come for you to act upon. Continue with your present efforts with sincerity and persistence, and you will have good fortune.

Line 2-6: This yin line is properly positioned at the center of the lower trigram, correlating with no line. It is in a contiguous relationship with 3-9 above, which symbolizes the chin, and 6-9, the upper jaw. 2-6 is directly under the chin, representing the beard, which moves about with the chin.

The images signify that this man, who practices the virtues of the Mean, has no special talent and mainly spends his time tending to his beard or cultivating his dignity and appearance in order to rise to a higher position. He is riding the coattails of the higher official, like the beard that follows the movement of the chin.

Divination Direction

A good opportunity will present itself for you to act upon. Follow your mentor with sincerity, and good fortune will come to you.

Line 3-9: This yang line is at the top of the trigram Light as the symbol of the enlightenment or the civilization attaining its elegance. This yang line is provided adornment by the two yin lines above and the one below it, making the substance balanced with elegance and grace.

The images signify that this man has attained the perfect luster of enlightenment. But he must not let his comfortable life lead him into becoming indolent. The perpetual practice of *Tao* will result in good fortune, since it does not allow any encroachment of danger that might hinder his efforts.

Divination Direction

Keep your mind open for good ideas or advice of your friends. Continue with your efforts to pursue the righteous cause with sincerity and persistence, and you will have good fortune.

Line 4-6: This yin line is properly positioned above the apex of the trigram Light (ornamental); it correlates with 1-9, who is so humble that he sets aside the carriage and walks. This is the beauty of conduct. The upper trigram Thunder of the primary nuclear hexagram symbolizes the horse that neighs and has white spots on its left leg and forehead, while the lower trigram Water symbolizes the robber. 4-6 (woman) feels uneasy because 3-9 (man) wants to steal her relationship with 1-9 for himself, like a robber. The correlative relationship between 4-6 and 1-9 represents the marital relationship.

The images signify the highest forms of beauty in a person are the virtues of sincerity and honesty, like the horse with white spots or the beauty of simplicity. In making an important choice such as the marital partner, one has to listen to one's simple but genuine heart. Although the woman (4-6) has a correlative relationship with this man (1-9), she feels uneasy, as the strong and handsome 3-9 also has a close relationship with her. This puts her in an anxious frame of mind to make the correct choice. Her genuine heart goes to 1-9, who is simple and honest, though low in status. This honest man comes on the back of a white spotted horse, like a robber, seeking a matrimonial alliance. In the beginning he is suspect, but in the end she accepts him and will commit no error.

Divination Direction

Maintain your trusting mind by ridding your distrust of other people. It will be to your advantage to concentrate your efforts on your pursuit, especially artistic and intellectual cultivation, and you will get satisfactory results.

Line 5-6: This yin line is at the center of the upper trigram Mountain, contiguous to the top yang line. The trigram Mountain that stands for halt or restraint refers to the ruler (5-6) with the virtues of the Mean and leniency. He is honest and sincere in the treatment of his subjects. A wise man is referred to as "the sage of the hillside garden" and is represented here by 6-9, who is retired from worldly affairs and lives with the lofty ideal of perfecting self-realization.

The images signify that the virtuous and lenient ruler solicits the help of the wise man (6-9) who "adorns the hillside garden" in order to correct his people who are indulging in superficial adornment and luxurious activities that lack moral substance. In the welcoming ceremony for the wise man, the ruler honors him by awarding him five bundles of silk. This may seem too small and parsimonious, but it will result in good fortune because it is to be blessed that the ruler attempts to set a good example to curtail extravagance and encourage moral integrity. The most valuable thing in life is not a material thing but the simple and sincere mind of a person.

Divination Direction

Welcome any help that is offered with sincerity. Be businesslike and press on with your undertaking with a firm conviction, and you will have good fortune.

Line 6-9: This yang line is at the top of the Ornamental hexagram, denoting that the progression of adornment has reached its mature stage in which white and simple (true substance without exterior decoration) become the adornment.

The images signify that when there is the pure substance of perfect grace without any extravagance of adornment (wealth, fame, or status), the substance is free of error. It is the stage in which he achieved his goal of attaining happiness by being true to himself.

Divination Direction

Though you feel materially deprived, put your sincere and diligent efforts to cultivate your intellectual and spiritual fortitude. Avoid being greedy for material wealth.

23. The Splitting Apart 剥 (Po) Hexagram

Key attributes: Splitting apart, collapse, the symbol of dispersion

Judgment

"*Po* indicates that (in the state which it symbolizes) it will not be advantageous to make a movement in any direction whatever." (James Legge, *The I Ching*, 105.)

Essence of Hexagram

This hexagram explains the *Tao* of patience as the paradigm for correct conduct in dealing with difficult situations in unfavorable times, especially in times of moral corruption.

Hexagram Image(s)

Mountain attached to Earth stands for the images of the Splitting apart hexagram. It means that, in the time of splitting apart, the ruler retains the security of his dwelling (status) by treating the governed with generosity, like the Mountain (ruler) that rests its base on the Earth (the people).

Hexagram Analysis

This hexagram consists of the lower trigram Earth that symbolizes compliance or obedience, and the upper trigram Mountain, halt or restraint. The lead line of this hexagram, 6-9, is the only yang line of the hexagram; there are five yin lines below the lead line. The hexagram name, "splitting apart" or "collapse," is derived from the image of the hexagram in which Mountain loses its soil, which is sliding down to Earth. The five yin lines and the sole yang line at the top present the image of the petty man in ascendancy, starting at the bottom and pushing the noble man out of the way one step at a time until it reaches the apex. The Splitting-apart hexagram represents the lunar calendar month of September.

6-9 is the sole lead line of the hexagram.

Interpretation of Judgment

The soft (yin) pushing the strong (yang) out of the way stands for the images of the Splitting-apart hexagram. In the era of "splitting apart" or moral corruption, it will be disadvantageous to make any active move. Since the petty man is advancing with great force, it is not advisable for the great man to engage in any ill-prepared move. It is the time for the great man to be compliant with the sign of the time and wait for the good opportunity that is certain to come. It is the time for the noble man to accept the natural cycle in which what goes up will come down and vice versa.

Divination Direction

It augurs ill. Practically everything is on a declining trend, especially in the financial market. Beware of the collapse due to the doings of your inner circle. If you are already in a desperate situation, a better time will follow soon. It is time for you to secure what you have, instead of taking initiatives for new undertakings. Be patient in waiting for the new opportunity coming to you. Guard against accidents and health problems.

Individual Lines: Analysis, Interpretation, and Divination Direction

Line 1-6: This yin line is improperly positioned at the beginning of the Splitting-apart hexagram, correlating with no line. The bedstead mentioned below symbolizes the noble man.

The images signify that the intent of the petty man is to destroy the noble man by destroying his virtues. He begins the task by first destroying the legs of the bedstead (the staff who are serving the noble man). This is a sign of misfortune.

Divination Direction

It augurs ill. Be extremely careful and discreet in any move. Be on guard against any possibility of someone trying to hurt you.

Line 2-6: This yin line is properly positioned, correlating with no line. The petty man's destruction has progressed to the second stage with more serious and imminent damages.

The images signify that the petty man destroys the frame of the bedstead, getting rid of the noble man's close staff to destroy the virtues of the noble man's rectitude. Under the circumstances, one must make a prompt move to escape the danger, instead of putting up a stubborn resistance against the petty man. There is no one who can intervene to make this petty man change his course of action. There will be misfortune.

Divination Direction

It augurs ill. There are ominous signs of imminent dangers. Reflect upon the situation to understand its implications on you. Be extremely careful in any move you make. Do not place a high expectation on other people to help you out of the danger. Maintain your modesty and discreetness in any move.

Line 3-6: This yin line is at the top of the lower trigram and correlates with 6-9, sandwiched between the yin lines, two above and two below it.

The images signify that this petty man, who has had good influence of the noble man, refrains from the progressive destruction of the noble man (the bedstead) because he respects the great man (6-9). This man, though petty, separates himself from others of his own kind. He will incur no blame.

Divination Direction

Your desperate situation will begin to improve. Dissociate yourself from people of bad influence so that you do not get drawn into their chicaneries. Steadfastly maintain your conscientious stand, and you will be rewarded in the end.

Line 4-6: This yin line is properly positioned with no correlating line.

The images signify that the destructive progression of the petty man has reached the bedclothes or "the skin of the noble man." It means that disaster is imminent. There will be misfortune.

Divination Direction

It augurs ill. You are faced with an inevitable misfortune. You must bear with it and wait for a better time, which will come slowly but surely.

Line 5-6: This yin line is improperly positioned and correlates with no line. In this hexagram, 5-6 is the ruler's queen consort. 6-9 represents the position of ruler or the light-giving great man, which is an exception to the usual rule of the fifth line for the ruler.

The images signify that the ruler (great man) can check the ascendancy of petty men with the assistance of his loyal followers. The leader of the loyal subjects acts like the queen consort who leads the court ladies (the four yin lines below her) as though she carries a string of fish to follow the ruler's guidance. In the era of the petty man's ascendancy, the timely action is essential to deal with the situation in order to attain advantageous results.

Divination Direction

You will be highly regarded by your superiors. You will have an opportunity to prove your ability. Maintain your modesty and sincerity, lest your peers become jealous of you.

Line 6-9: This line is the only yang line of the hexagram at its topmost location and the sole lead line. It represents the position of ruler. It symbolizes the last stronghold of the ruler (great man), and he is likened to the shelter that provides protection to the common people of the state.

The images signify that the ruler (great man) is like the biggest fruit at the top of a tree that remains uneaten; it will fall to the earth, and the seeds (the seeds of the good) will sprout anew. Sooner or later, the ruler will restore the respect of the common people who will put him on the carriage (the lower trigram Earth is the symbol of carriage) of honor. To lose the benefits of the great man is likened to the petty man who takes the roof off his own humble hut, rendering it unusable. Evil cannot destroy the good without destroying itself first.

Divination Direction

You must exert your best efforts without being aggressive or confrontational in order to tide yourself over the crisis that will end sooner than you think. It is not the proper time for you to launch any ambitious undertaking.

24. The Returning 復 (Fu) Hexagram

Key attributes: Returning, the symbol of reversal

Judgment

"*Fu* indicates that there will be free course and progress (in what it denotes). (The subject of it) finds no one to distress him in his exits and entrances; friends come to him, and no error is committed. He will return and repeat his (proper) course. In seven days comes his return. There will be advantage in whatever direction movement is made." (James Legge, *The I Ching*, 107.)

Essence of Hexagram

This hexagram explains the *Tao* of recurring cycle in nature as the paradigm for every thing to move at its own natural pace and rest in order to build up the strength to meet the demands of a new cycle.

Hexagram Image(s)

Thunder in Earth stands for the images of the Returning hexagram. Taking the idea from the images represented in this hexagram to strengthen one's energy through respite and tender care, former kings closed the border gates on the day of winter solstice, the shortest daylight in the year, which falls in November (lunar calendar). During this period, the merchants and travelers were not allowed to pass through the gates, and the rulers did not make inspection tours of their domains. This is the time of perfect stillness, because the yin force becomes quiescent with the return of the yang.

Hexagram Analysis

This hexagram consists of the lower trigram Thunder symbolizing movement, and the upper trigram Earth, compliance. The yang energy of Thunder is hiding under Earth, and one yang line has returned to the bottom to begin its ascendancy. It is the reverse of Hexagram #23 Splitting-apart, in which the yin energy progressively gained prevalence over the yang energy except for one yang line at the top. When Thunder roars, it awakens myriad things on Earth to action.

The progression of the months clearly reflects the movement of the yin and yang energies. The Splitting-apart hexagram represents the lunar calendar month of September. In October, all six lines of the hexagram are yin lines. In November, one yang line returns to the bottom of the hexagram, from which hexagram #24 derives its name, Returning. From this point, the yang energy progressively gains its prevalence over yin energy. In this beginning stage of recovery, everything must be nurtured tenderly to strengthen the energy in the recovery. As there are six lines in a hexagram, it takes six stages to complete one cycle before returning to the beginning stage on the seventh stage. This beginning of the yang energy cycle in the Returning hexagram symbolizes the winter solstice, the day with the shortest daylight in the year.

1-9 is the sole lead line of this hexagram.

Interpretation of Judgment

The Returning hexagram means that the yang energy is returning to prevail. This is indicated in the hexagram with the lower trigram Thunder, hidden under the upper trigram Earth. It is yet time to rest and to build up strength before the lower trigram Thunder begins its movement, and the upper trigram Earth complies. The yang energy (1-9) is free to make its exits and entrances with nothing to hinder its movements because its movements are in compliance with the natural law of wax and wane.

In human analogy, the yang line is the friend (the great man) who has returned without violating the law of Heaven. He will continue his upward course in the next five stages until the cycle is completed, and he returns to the beginning stage (the seventh stage) in seven days. This time of friends in ascendancy is an opportune time for one to set out to do something enterprising. By observing the yang energy (or yin energy) returning to begin a new cycle, one can understand how a new cycle begins when one cycle ends, which is the *Tao* of Heaven and Earth.

Divination Direction

It augurs well for restoring what you have lost in the past in your business dealings, human relationships, and health, and returning home after a journey. Try again what failed in the past. You will have progressively more successful results with many friends helping you. Proceed with the plans that you have been working for, and implement them one at a time at a deliberate pace. You will be able to regain your good health, or a healthy person may experience a relapse on a past health problem. An expectant mother will give birth to a girl.

Individual Lines: Analysis, Interpretation, and Divination Direction

Note: Its distance from 1-9 determines the interpretation of each individual line of this hexagram. 1-9 is the only yang line and the lead line. Therefore, the judgment of 1-9 is fundamental good fortune.

Line 1-9: This yang line is properly positioned as the first line of the low trigram Thunder that symbolizes movement. It is the sole lead line of this hexagram.

The images signify that the return movement has begun. Because of his self-discipline, this man returns before he has gone too far; he remedies his error before it reaches the point of regret. There will be fundamental good fortune.

Divination Direction

It augurs well. You will enjoy good fortune each step of the way if you proceed at a slow but steady pace, continually assessing the situation to correct any mistake that might thwart your progress. You will succeed.

Line 2-6: This yin line is properly positioned at the center of the lower trigram. This person is weak in his resolve and goes astray for awhile, going along with others when they move (lower trigram Thunder, movement), but his virtues of the Mean motivates him to return to the proper conduct of *Tao*.

The images signify that this virtuous man is deeply moved to see the great man (1-9) returning to the right course and follows him; there will be good fortune.

Divination Direction

A right human connection holds the key to your success. Cooperate with friends whom you trust, and you will be successful.

Line 3-6: This yin line is improperly positioned at the top of the lower trigram Thunder (movement). The Return that began with the first yang line serves as the praiseworthy role model for the other lines of the hexagram.

The images signify that his repeated conduct of going astray and returning to the right path is precarious, but he will make no error because he returns to the right path each time.

Divination Direction

You will make repeated errors, only to regret it each time. For successful results, you must develop workable plans and cultivate your self-discipline so that you can proceed without deviating from your proper course.

Line 4-6: This yin line is properly positioned, sandwiched between the yin lines, two below and two above it, and correlates with the lead line (1-9).

The images signify that this man followed other men of his kind (the other four yin lines), but midway, he realized his error. He parted with his friends who were going the wrong way to return alone to follow the correct *Tao* of 1-9.

Divination Direction

You will experience difficulty and loneliness, since you pursue your conviction with which your friends do not agree. Nonetheless, it is important for you to nurture sufficient physical and moral strength and follow the right path.

Line 5-6: This yin line is improperly positioned at the center of the upper trigram Earth that symbolizes nurturing.

The images signify that this virtuous man of the Mean sincerely nurtures his strong desire to return to the correct *Tao*, and he will have no regret. He is far from the good role model (1-9), but he can achieve his goal independently, as he practices the virtues of the Mean.

Divination Direction

Although you face difficulty or hindrance, renew your efforts to attain your goal. Have the moral courage to admit your errors and correct them, and try out new ways. Work to achieve the goal without expecting help from others.

Line 6-6: This yin line is at the top of both the Returning hexagram and the upper trigram Earth that symbolizes the multitude or army. It is located farthest from the lead line that serves as the praiseworthy role model in this hexagram.

The images signify that this man has strayed, becoming greedy and stubborn (lacking the Mean). He does not know how to return to the correct *Tao* because he has strayed too far from the righteous path and is too removed from the good role model (1-9) to follow him in the correct *Tao*. Consequently, he will experience natural calamities and human sufferings. There will be misfortune. If he takes military action in this manner, he will suffer a great defeat, and the misfortune will extend to the ruler of his state. Even after the passage of many years, the disastrous aftermath of the defeat will remain.

Divination Direction

It augurs ill. Change the way you have been conducting yourself, and take a new direction with the right attitude, based on an accurate assessment. However, you will find it extremely difficult to be successful.

25. The Freedom from Error 无妄 (Wu Wang) Hexagram

Key attributes: Freedom from error, the symbol of innocence

Judgment

"*Wu Wang* indicates great progress and success, while there will be advantage in being firm and correct. If (its subject and his action) be not correct, he will fall into errors, and it will not be advantageous for him to move in any direction." (James Legge, *The I Ching*, 109.)

Essence of Hexagram

This hexagram explains the *Tao* of innocence as the paradigm for upholding one's sincerity by being true to one's natural self by cultivating virtues in dealing with the vicissitudes in life.

Hexagram Image(s)

Thunder under Heaven stands for the images of the Freedom from Error hexagram. The images symbolize that Thunder or movement brings forth sprouting and growth in a myriad of things without deviation from the way of nature. The former king used the images of this hexagram on how nature works to govern his state. He brought about prosperity by nurturing everything in a timely and natural manner.

Hexagram Analysis

This hexagram consists of the lower trigram Thunder that symbolizes movement or sprouting, and the upper trigram Heaven, the firm, sincere *Tao*. This hexagram is the capsized form of Hexagram #26 Major Restraint. 6-9 has become 1-9 in the Freedom from Error hexagram and the lead line of its lower trigram Thunder, as well as the directive lead line of the hexagram.

Freedom from Error means conducting oneself with sincerity and being true to oneself without any pretense. It also symbolizes the vicissitudes or unpredictability in life, like thunder that brings rain at times and lightning at other times. 5-9 is the structural lead line of this hexagram, and it is properly positioned at the center of the upper trigram Heaven. It correlates with 2-6 at the center of the lower trigram Thunder that complies with the will of Heaven, or *Tao*, the virtue of the Mean.

1-9, directive, and 5-9, structural, are the lead lines of the hexagram.

Interpretation of Judgment

The hexagram images indicate that, in order to stay free from error, one has to exercise the fundamental principles of *Tao* and stay firm and correct by being true to oneself. In the hexagram, the strong (1-9) comes from without (outer trigram) and becomes the leader within (inner trigram). The movement of the lower trigram is commensurate with the will of the upper trigram Heaven, and the virtuous and competent ruler in the upper trigram (5-9) resonates with 2-6, the virtuous loyal subject in the lower trigram.

The practice of correct *Tao* will bring the good fortune of great progress and success, for this is the way to follow the will of Heaven. On the other hand, if one fails to follow correct *Tao* and has unsavory desires, it will result in misfortune, irrespective of whichever way he moves. Beware of this time of Freedom from Error, for Heaven will not render its help to those who tread the erroneous course of action. It would not be fitting for one to set out to engage in an ambitious enterprise.

Divination Direction

You feel insecure with your present situation, but you will not be able to solve your problem through your strong-willed actions. You will have better luck if you make efforts to improve your reputation rather than to realize material gains. Your steady and sincere efforts will lead to good fortune in attaining your goals.

Individual Lines: Analysis, Interpretation, and Divination Direction

Line 1-9: This yang line is properly positioned at the bottom of the hexagram, correlating with no line. The outer trigram Wind of the primary nuclear hexagram symbolizes the heavenly command, and its inner trigram Mountain, halt or holding. The combined images mean that movement (Thunder) or holding (Mountain) is done in compliance with the heavenly command (Heaven, Wind).

The images signify that this man is true to himself, and is both competent and virtuous, conducting himself in compliance with the will of Heaven. His actions will result in good fortune, and he will fulfill his ambitions.

Divination Direction

Follow the natural and conscientious course of action with sincerity for successful results. Greedy or dishonest efforts will result in disaster.

Line 2-6: This yin line is properly positioned at the center of the lower trigram Thunder and correlates with 5-9. Since 1-9 is the lead line of the lower trigram Thunder as well as the directive lead line of the Freedom from Error hexagram, the benefits it receives from 1-9 are greater than those that come from its correlative relationship with 5-9.

The images signify that he reaps the harvest of crops without having plowed the fields himself. He also acquired new land that is already productive, although it has not been cultivated for three years. He has had good fortune without any effort on his part. One's good fortune is beyond human calculation. Therefore, what he can do is to work diligently without idling, in order for him to see measurable results from his efforts.

This attitude of doing one's best on any task will result in good fortune in whatever one does.

Divination Direction

It augurs well. You will have unexpected good fortune. However, if you do not continue your efforts to carry out your plans, the good fortune will not last long.

Line 3-6: This yin line is improperly positioned at the top of the lower trigram Thunder, indicating a precarious, immodest movement. The lower trigram Thunder symbolizes road or foot, thus a traveler. The upper trigram Wind of the primary nuclear hexagram symbolizes string or town, while its lower trigram Mountain, halt or hand.

The images signify that there are times when unexpected or undeserved misfortune occurs, as in the case of the traveler who carries off (steals) someone's cow by cutting loose its tether. The traveler gained a cow, but the loss will cause distress to the town's people, as they will suffer as a result of the investigation of the theft. Nonetheless, one should not lose one's virtue. One needs to be cautious and prepared to accommodate an unexpected or undeserved misfortune in life.

Divination Direction

It augurs ill. You may experience totally unexpected misfortune. It is not the right time for you to actively pursue your goal. Go slowly and wait for a good opportunity that is bound to come.

Line 4-9: This yang line is improperly positioned at the bottom of the upper trigram Heaven. The upper trigram Wind of the primary nuclear hexagram symbolizes the heavenly command, and its lower trigram Mountain, halt.

The images signify that one should practice correct *Tao* firmly in order not to make an error. His impulsive conduct (yang in yin position) will cause problems, and he must realize that he can be free from blame by being true to himself.

Divination Direction

Be considerate of others by being honest in your actions. It is the time for you to consolidate what you already possess, instead of moving ahead actively on your goal.

Line 5-9: This yang line is properly positioned at the center of the upper trigram Heaven and correlates with 2-6, denoting the most ideal ruler in the era of perfect sincerity or Freedom from Error.

The images signify that an unexpected illness strikes him without cause, or a good person may suffer from an undeserved malice. He should refrain from using a medicine (try to defend against the malice), as he will have a natural recovery. If the illness was not caused by one's own fault, using medicine can worsen it. It is better to wait for a natural cure.

Divination Direction

You feel stagnated in your efforts, which is causing you some anxiety and headache. If you try to correct the situation in haste, you will end up further complicating and worsening it. Assess the situation carefully and take action at a natural pace to remedy the situation one step at a time.

Line 6-9: This yang line is improperly positioned at the top of both the hexagram and the upper trigram Heaven, indicating that the progression of the Freedom from Error hexagram has reached its apogee. The lower trigram Thunder symbolizes movement or to initiate an action, and the upper trigram Heaven, to practice *Tao* correctly and firmly.

The images signify that the era of Freedom from Error is about to end. If one initiates a thoughtless action against the sign of time, it will result in a disaster without any benefit.

Divination Direction

It augurs ill. Preserve your resources for the good opportunity that is to come. Do not initiate a move, or you will experience a disastrous misfortune.

26. The Major Restraint 大畜 (Ta Khu or Ta Ch'u) Hexagram

Key attributes: Major restraint, the symbol of great taming force, and the symbol of great accumulation

Judgment

"Under the conditions of *Ta Khu* it will be advantageous to be firm and correct. (If its subject does not seek to) enjoy his revenues in his own family (without taking service at court), there will be good fortune. It will be advantageous for him to cross the great stream." (James Legge, *The I Ching*, 112.)

Essence of Hexagram

This hexagram explains the *Tao* of the major restraint as the paradigm for holding firmly to creative powers through constant self-renewal of one's character with virtuous conduct.

Hexagram Image(s)

The mighty yang force of Heaven that is checked (stored) by the stable force of Mountain stands for the images of the Major Restraint (Great Accumulation) hexagram. The wise and noble uses the images as his model in his efforts to acquire knowledge about the deeds and sayings of the great men of the past in order to cultivate his virtues and strengthen his character by applying this accumulated knowledge in his life.

Hexagram Analysis

This hexagram consists of the lower trigram Heaven that symbolizes the yang force (the great and strong), and the upper trigram Mountain, which is also a yang force with the meaning of halt or restraint. 6-9 of this hexagram is a yang line from which this hexagram gets its name "Major Restraint." The hexagram has four yang lines restrained by two yin lines, in contrast to Hexagram #9 Minor Restraint, in which five yang lines are restrained by a single yin line. The great yang force of the lower trigram Heaven is restrained by the upper trigram Mountain so that the great yang energy is stored in the Mountain. In human terms, the yang energy of Heaven that is stored in the Mountain means accumulating knowledge and virtues within oneself until the time when one is called into public service. In addition, the upper trigram Mountain symbolizes gate, and the upper trigram Lake of the primary nuclear hexagram, mouth. The combined images indicate that one who has accumulated knowledge and virtues should not eat at home, but he should share his knowledge and virtues by eating at court (serving the public). Furthermore, the upper trigram Lake of the primary nuclear hexagram and its lower trigram Thunder that symbolizes wood or boat present the images of crossing the great stream or venturing out for a greater undertaking.

5-6, structural and 6-9, directive, are the lead lines of this hexagram.

Interpretation of Judgment

The "Major Restraint" or the 'Great Accumulation' that is represented in this hexagram explains the advantage one derives from the firm practice of the fundamentals of *Tao*. "Major Restraint" symbolizes holding moral strength and knowledge of truth in storage. The mighty and constant energy (attributes) of Heaven and the sincere, stable energy of Mountain make up the attributes of Great Restraint, which result in great accumulation of various forms of energies. A person can make his accumulated knowledge radiate gloriously by applying this knowledge in his daily practice of virtuous living. It is not proper for such a person to be homebound and eat at the family table; instead, he should be serving the state under the virtuous ruler (5-6) who honors the wise and worthy person or the sage (6-9).

It is the act of righteousness on a grand scale to check (restrain) the strong from using force excessively. A person who can restrain from the excessive use of force will have good fortune. It is the proper time for the man with such virtues to risk the perils of crossing the great river or to move forward to serve the state as the ruler (5-6). The virtuous ruler will be able to receive loyal support from his competent subject (2-9), who is capable of rendering great services to the state.

Divination Direction

It augurs well in practically all matters, especially marriage, financial, and business deals. There is no need to conclude a business dealing in haste, as time is in your side. The longer you wait, the better the deal will be. Work for your goal with patience and persistence; you will succeed. You should set your goal high, preferably in public service. Financial market will start an uptrend soon.

Individual Lines: Analysis, Interpretation, and Divination Direction

Line 1-9: This yang line is properly positioned as the beginning line of the hexagram and correlates with 4-6 of the upper trigram Mountain.

The images signify that, though low in status and inexperienced, this man, who is over-confident about his own strength, has a strong urge to move forward. It will be to his advantage to resist the urge to advance, for he will face perils. It is the time for him to cultivate self-discipline and accumulate virtues and knowledge. If he dares to move ahead, his move will be checked by one in higher status (4-6 of the upper trigram Mountain that symbolizes halt).

Divination Direction

This is not the right time for you to initiate a move. Instead, you should direct all your efforts to preparing yourself for future opportunities. Refrain from becoming overconfident.

Line 2-9: This yang line is at the center of the lower trigram Heaven and correlates with 5-6 of the upper trigram Mountain.

The images signify that this strong and competent man has the urge to advance forcefully in this era of Major Restraint. Owing to his practice of the Mean and the beneficent ruler (5-6) that advises him to halt (Mountain) the advance, he is able to desist from his blind urge to move ahead, as if a wagon has had its strap removed and the body separated from the axle, rendering it immovable.

Divination Direction

You are well prepared and ready to go ahead, but the timing is not right for you to initiate an action. Be patient and wait for the right opportunity that is bound to come.

Line 3-9: This yang line is properly positioned at the top of the lower trigram Heaven, which here symbolizes a fine horse and carriage. The upper trigram Thunder of the primary nuclear hexagram symbolizes movement, and Heaven represents the driving horse.

The images signify that the era of Major Restraint has reached the point of reversal. The first and second yang lines of the lower trigram were checked in their advance by the yin lines of the upper trigram Mountain (halt). The time has come for this well-prepared, competent man to advance, like a fine driving horse following another, especially on the strength of the like-minded benefactor in a high position (6-9). However, he must be mindful of the fact that the era of Major Restraint is not completely over. There are many obstacles to overcome in order to succeed in his efforts. He must firmly tread the correct course of *Tao*. Furthermore, he should not neglect practicing charioteering and self-defense daily to keep fit to advance and accomplish his goal.

Divination Direction

It augurs well. You are well prepared to initiate your move. Nonetheless, refrain from being too hasty. Examine yourself once again to see if there is more to do in your preparation. You will achieve your goal successfully.

Line 4-6: This yin line is properly positioned as the first line of the upper trigram Mountain, correlating with 1-9, whose premature advance is beneficently checked by this line.

The images signify that the timely restraint of 1-9 by 4-6 is analogous to putting a wooden horn cover on a young bull for the time being to prevent the unrestrained growth of the horn that can gore and harm. Owing to the virtuous persuasion of 4-6, the strong and competent 1-9 was able to desist from his urge to make a wrong move and continue to accumulate more resources for a timely advance in the future. The conduct of 4-6 will produce fundamental good fortune for 1-9, who will have a bright future.

Divination Direction

It augurs well. You have both good plans and self-discipline, and you will successfully achieve your goal.

Line 5-6: This yin line is at the center of the upper trigram Mountain and correlates with 2-9, whose premature advance is beneficently checked by this ruler.

The images signify that this virtuous ruler succeeded in persuading 2-9 from making a premature advance and wait for the opportunity to serve the ruler when he is called. The ruler's conduct is analogous to restraining a young boar's wild behavior by gelding him, thus eliminating the cause of unrestrained behavior at the root. In due course, this disciplined and competent subject will serve the ruler well. The ruler will enjoy the blessings from having such a fine subject.

Divination Direction

It augurs well. You understand the importance of timing and self-discipline in implementing your plans. You will achieve your goal.

Line 6-9: This yang line is at the top of the Major Restraint hexagram as the directive lead line, representing the time when the accumulated knowledge and energies, especially the spiritual energy, are put to good use.

The images signify that under the leadership of this enlightened man, the imperative of the era to restrain and accumulate has been successfully achieved. Praising the achievement of this sage, the text of *Ten Wings* states: "How splendid it is to practice the *Tao* as if going the highway of Heaven!" The era of Major Restraint is over, and there is no obstruction to using the accumulated energies. All the wise and competent people can now advance to render great services to the state. There will be success and progress.

Divination Direction

You will have exceptionally good fortune. Now is the time for you to pursue your goal actively and enjoy your success.

27. The Nourishment 頤 (I) Hexagram

Key attributes: Nourishment, the symbol of sustenance

Judgment

"*I* indicates that with firm correctness there will be good fortune (in what is denoted by it). We must look at what we are seeking to nourish, and by the exercise of our thoughts seek for the proper aliment." (James Legge, *The I Ching*, 114.)

Essence of Hexagram

This hexagram explains the *Tao* of nourishment as the paradigm for nourishing both the physical and spiritual well-being for oneself and others through proper food and communication.

Hexagram Image(s)

Mountain above Thunder below stands for the images of the Nourishment hexagram. Thunder (movement) symbolizes the mouth for talking, eating, and drinking, while Mountain symbolizes restraints in eating and drinking (what goes into the mouth), and in using words (what comes out of the mouth), in order to bring beneficial results.

The wise and noble uses the images as his guide in disciplining himself to be prudent in his speech and in what he takes into his mouth for nourishment.

Hexagram Analysis

This hexagram consists of the lower trigram Thunder denoting movement, and the upper trigram Mountain, halt or staying. The two yang lines, one at the bottom and the other at the top of the hexagram and the four yin lines between the two yang lines symbolize mouth. The two yang lines are the upper and lower teeth or upper and lower lips and the four yin lines the mouth cavity or food in the mouth for chewing. The combined image denotes the mouth with the lower jaw in motion (Thunder), and the upper jaw staying still (Mountain) with food in the mouth, from which the hexagram name "Nourishment" is derived. The upper trigram represents the quiet inner quality of spiritual strength that provides leadership or influences other people, while the lower trigram represents the movement of chewing and speaking in everyday living.

5-6, structural, and 6-9, directive, are the lead lines of this hexagram.

Interpretation of Judgment

The Nourishment hexagram means that one who practices *Tao* correctly will have good fortune because of proper nurturing. "Look at what we are seeking to nourish" in the judgment text means a leader must select the right people to provide nourishment of the mind or training. One must also pay attention to what one puts in the mouth to nourish oneself to maintain good health. Modeling after the way Heaven and Earth nourish the myriad things, sages train the wise and noble to work for the benefit of all the people. It is a matter of great importance to observe the principles of Nourishment.

Divination Direction

Beware of health problems related to eating, and be prudent in expressing your opinions, especially about other people. It is the time to prepare well and proceed step-by-step to implement your business plans. It is an auspicious time to seek employment and a harmonious marital relationship. Be honest and friendly with people. Pay attention to what you are doing for your physical and spiritual health.

Individual Lines: Analysis, Interpretation, and Divination Direction

Line 1-9: This yang line is at the beginning of this hexagram and properly positioned, correlating with 4-6. 6-9 is the directive lead line and exerts strong influence over the other lines of the hexagram.

The images signify that this man, competent but low in status, will benefit by serving the high official (6-9) as a trustworthy assistant. However, he has too strong an urge to move ahead, as he is envious of the emolument that the high official (6-9) is earning. The high official laments, "You set aside your potential that is like what the mysterious and efficacious tortoise that lives on air embodies; instead, you look at me with your lower jaw hanging down and your mouth watering over my emolument." The priority in his mind is materialistic gains, not the sincerity to provide good service. His conduct is disrespectful; therefore, there will be misfortune.

Divination Direction

Reflect on your conduct and change your error promptly. Maintain your sincerity, and concentrate on the pursuit of your goal without becoming greedy or envious of other people, especially of those who are more fortunate than you are.

Line 2-6: This yin line is properly positioned at the center of the lower trigram, correlating with no line. The two yang lines of this hexagram extend their nourishment to other lines.

The images signify that one must not shirk the responsibility of self-support. When inevitable circumstances force one to seek nourishment from others, one must be careful to seek it from the right person. This man, virtuous but weak, needs someone to help him obtain necessary nourishment. Although he lacks the ability to support himself, it is not proper or natural for him to continue seeking support from other people. Being close to 1-9, he can get the nourishment from him. However, it is extraordinary and improper for a person of higher status to seek nourishment from someone of a lower status. Instead, he looks higher above him (looks up a high hill) for another nourishing source (6-9). If he decides to seek nourishment from 6-9, it will bring misfortune, as he has no correlative relationship with it. He may end up losing even the friendly nourishment of 1-9.

Divination Direction

You are in a predicament. There is no easy way to get out of it. You should exercise special caution not to covet other people's possessions. Wait patiently for a better time.

Line 3-6: This yin line is improperly positioned at the top of the lower trigram Thunder and correlates with the directive lead line, 6-9. This incompetent man is audacious enough to impose himself in the yang position without practicing the Mean.

The images signify improper nourishment as in the case of this audacious man who is sycophantic to the official in the high position (6-9) in order to gratify his need for physical nourishment and sensual gratification. He will have misfortune. The judgment text states, "One should not use such nourishment for ten years" ("for ten years" means a complete cycle of time or permanently), as such improper nourishment is a great violation of the *Tao* principle. There will be no advantage.

Divination Direction

It augurs ill. You will suffer a financial loss. Your greed will lead you to dire poverty.

Line 4-6: This yin line is properly positioned at the beginning of the upper trigram in the high status of the prime minister and correlates with 1-9. He is virtuous and needs competent assistants to carry out the important responsibilities he has to perform. The nourishment that 3-6 is seeking is for the selfish, sensual gratification. In contrast, 4-6 seeks nourishment to manage the state affairs correctly.

The images signify that this virtuous prime minister has a strong desire to find competent assistants who can help him manage state affairs. Though low in status, 1-9 is the right man. The intense desire (hunger) of this prime minister to obtain the right helper is likened to the unblinking stare of a tiger that is persistent and unceasing to hunt and kill only what he needs to obtain necessary nourishment. It will result in no error.

Divination Direction

Be patient and persistent in trying to overcome the obstacles you face in achieving your goal, and you will succeed. Be generous to your subordinates whose cooperation with you will bring benefits to many.

Line 5-6: This yin line is improperly positioned at the center of the upper trigram, contiguous to the top line and correlating with no line.

The images signify that this ruler is virtuous but weak in his governing ability and must rely heavily on the help of his competent senior advisor (6-9). This is contrary to the order of the nourishing principle, which starts at the top. Nonetheless, this virtuous ruler understands the weakness in his governing ability and diligently follows the recommendations of his advisor, which conform to the principles of the correct practice of the Mean. The ruler's conduct will result in good fortune. However, it is not proper for the ruler to rely on the abilities of other officials to initiate a great enterprise. The line judgment text refers to this as "crossing the great river," and it portends peril for the ruler.

Divination Direction

Listen attentively to the advice you get from the experienced, and be prudent in taking actions to achieve your goal. Now is not a proper time for you to initiate a new move or action.

Line 6-9: This yang line is at the top of the hexagram as the directive lead line, contiguous to 5-6. This man is responsible for providing physical, moral, and mental nourishment to everyone (four yin lines) below him.

The images signify that everyone (the four yin lines) depends on him (6-9) for nourishment. This great man is competent in carrying out the responsibilities, which include the important duty of royal tutor (contiguous relationship) to the ruler. Though his high position holds many perils, he is well qualified and competent; there will be good fortune. It is a proper time for him to launch a great enterprise to bring wealth and happiness to everyone in the state, braving all the perils that accompany crossing a great river. There will be great blessings.

Divination Direction

You are in the position that enables you to help others and, in turn, receive help from other people when you need it. You need to work hard, but you will be amply rewarded for your efforts.

28. The Large Excess 大過 (Ta Kwo) Hexagram

Key attributes: Large excess, the symbol of major preponderance

Judgment

"*Ta Kwo* suggests to us a beam that is weak. There will be advantage in moving (under its conditions) in any direction whatever; there will be success." (James Legge, *The I Ching*, 116.)

Essence of Hexagram

This hexagram explains the *Tao* of balance as the paradigm for a centered life. The centered life requires virtuous integrity in character and good intelligence in order to make judgments to remedy an excess without resorting to an extreme measure.

Hexagram Image(s)

Wind blowing below Lake stands for the images of the Large Excess hexagram. Since Wind symbolizes wood, it presents an image of a tree submerged in the lake. The wise and noble uses the images as his guide to cultivate his virtue of moral integrity that helps him maintain an independent mind without fear of criticism and the courage to withdraw from the world in the era of Large Excess. He is like the tree that is standing upright, although submerged in water.

Hexagram Analysis

This hexagram consists of the lower trigram Wind that symbolizes wood or compliance and the upper trigram Lake, symbolizing joy or lake. 4-9 is the directive lead line, and 2-9 the structural lead line. The four yang lines between the two yin lines symbolize excessive strength in the middle against one weak yin line at each end of the hexagram, presenting the image of a sagging ridgepole. This image of too many strong ones (yang lines) gathered together against two scattered weak ones (yin lines) gives the hexagram its name, "Large Excess."

2-9, structural, and 4-9, directive, are the lead lines of this hexagram.

Interpretation of Judgment

The "Large Excess" denotes the ridgepole sagging in the middle because the strong force is concentrated there, while both ends of the pole are weak. It is analogous to the state that has too much power in the hands of a few, making both the government and the common folk weak and creating an extraordinary situation or a crisis, which calls for immediate remedial action. Another example of excess is too much indulgence in wealth and power and the lack of moral and spiritual discipline.

The statement in the judgment text that "there will be advantage in moving" refers to a situation that cannot be maintained. Fortunately, among the strong, there are two (2-9 and 5-9) who practice the virtues of the Mean. Through their virtues of compliance, modesty (the lower trigram Wind) and inner happiness (upper trigram Lake), they will exert counterbalancing influence against the excessive force. Therefore, appropriate remedial action taken now will be successful. The time of the "Large Excess" calls for appropriate measures to counter it.

Divination Direction

It augurs ill. You will encounter unexpected situations one after another, each demanding your immediate action. Maintain your equanimity, and be deliberate in each action that you take, in order to avoid making any serious error. Once the stormy period is over, you will be successful and prosperous.

Individual Lines: Analysis, Interpretation, and Divination Direction

Line 1-6: This yin line is improperly positioned as the beginning line of the hexagram, contiguous to 2-9 and correlating with 4-9. The white lawn grass cited below is quitch grass, soft and flexible, which bends when wind blows over it or a mat is placed on it, but springs back when such a force is removed.

The images signify that this man is low in status, but humble and prudent in his attitude and approaches in dealing with overwhelming force. It is analogous to placing a mat on white lawn (quitch) grass[27] before placing objects or sacrifice on it, a sign of religious respect by being reverent in his attitude as well as a measure to prevent objects from breaking. He has a pious heart and serves those in higher positions with respect and humility without losing his flexibility and strength, like the quitch grass. He will make no error.

Divination Direction

Your tenacious efforts will bear fruits. Maintain harmonious relationships with other people, and be prudent in your efforts to achieve your goal. Only then will you overcome the hurdles you are dealing with.

Line 2-9: This yang line is improperly positioned, contiguous to 1-6 at the center of the lower trigram Wind that symbolizes tree; it represents dryness. The combined images of the lower trigram Wind (tree) and the upper trigram Lake signify old or decayed trees, such as the willow trees. As the structural lead line of this hexagram, this line has the potential to save the sagging ridgepole from total collapse.

The images symbolize that extraordinary measures are needed to counter extraordinary circumstances when favorable conditions are indicated for such a measure. The old, decayed willow tree near water growing shoots (1-6), or the old man who is competent and virtuous of the Mean (2-9) marrying a young woman is such a case. His conduct in marrying a young woman may seem excessive, but this union will produce every advantage for them. They have a contiguous, mutually harmonious relationship, as 2-9 is physically strong and 1 6 is emotionally strong, and they will produce children.

Divination Direction

Someone who is young and friendly will come forth to help you. Be prudent and creative in pursuing your goal, and you will succeed.

Line 3-9: This yang line is properly positioned at the top of the lower trigram Wind, correlating with 6-6.

The images signify that this yang line in the yang position is the source of the excessive force that creates the weight responsible for the sagging of the ridgepole. There is nothing that can help to shore it up; there will be misfortune. Though this line correlates with 6-6, the top yin line is too weak to be of help. In human terms, this man has become overconfident about his power and ability to the point of arrogance, declining advice or help from other people. He will have misfortune.

Divination Direction

It augurs ill. You are hardheaded and overconfident. You are not respectful and refuse to consider and accept the opinions or advice of other people. Unless you can change your mind-set and attitude, you will experience failures.

Line 4-9: This yang line is improperly positioned as the beginning line of the upper trigram Lake and correlates with 1-6. The lower trigram with 3-9 at the top and 1-6 at the bottom indicates that the lower trigram is top-heavy, while the upper trigram with 4-9 at the bottom and 6-6 at the top indicates that the top is light in weight.

The images signify that this ridgepole is curving upward. This means good fortune, as this line is not sagging by the weight of one below (1-6). To be overconfident like the one below (3-9), which arrogantly refuses any help, will invite cause for regret. Although 4-9 is a yang line, it retains the soft quality, as it is in the yin position; it is willing to join 1-6 for mutual help to carry out its task successfully, not for selfish gain but for the good of all.

Divination Direction

It is the time to establish a goal and the plan to achieve it. In order to overcome the urgent situation you are faced with, keep up your efforts with an open mind and a cooperative attitude toward other people, and you will succeed.

Line 5-9: This yang line is properly positioned at the center of the upper trigram Lake and correlates with no line.

The images signify that a mismatched arrangement in extraordinary times does not last for long, like a withering willow tree producing blossoms, or "an old woman getting a young man as husband." 5-9 is a young, strong man who has no correlative relationship. He enters into a matrimonial alliance with 6-6 (6-6 is above 5-9, indicating she is older), as 2-9 did with 1-6. The old wife cannot produce children for the family lineage. Like the blossoms of the withering willow that will dissipate its energy, how long will this marriage last without new shoots? By itself this marriage is not a situation for blame or praise. This alliance is not a productive one, as it will exhaust the energy of the old woman like the old willow and will hasten her end. Therefore, the marriage can be considered a misfit.

Divination Direction

Your good fortune and prosperity are temporary and will not last long. For the time being, you will be successful in small things, but you will experience difficulties in attaining your long-range goals.

Line 6-6: This yin line is at the top of the Large Excess hexagram and correlates with 3-9, which is responsible for the major portion of the weight that makes the ridgepole sag. 6-6 is too weak to be of help to shore up the sagging ridgepole.

The images signify that the extraordinary situation has reached a climax, but this man is too strongly determined to "cross the river" and carry out his lofty goal of saving the people in this era of the Large Excess. He ends up getting his head submerged in the water, resulting in misfortune. This man is not strong enough to deal with tidal waves, like the crises in the era of the Large Excess, and he becomes a victim of the time. When the four yang lines are bound together into one yang line, the hexagram become the trigram Water; thus the reference to "crossing the river" in the text. It means misfortune, but 6-6 cannot be blamed for it entirely, as the misfortune is due largely to the omen of the time, and his lofty motive of self-sacrifice is judged noble and important.

Divination Direction

It augurs ill. Maintain your moral fortitude in order to escape the criticism coming from other people. Proceed cautiously to achieve your goal. There will be better opportunities for you later.

29. The Abysmal 坎 (Khan or K'an) Hexagram

Key attributes: Abysmal, the symbol of sinking

Judgment

"*Khan*, here repeated, shows the possession of sincerity, through which the mind is penetrating. Action (in accordance with this) will be of high value." (James Legge, *The I Ching*, 118.)

Essence of Hexagram

This hexagram explains the *Tao* of survival as the paradigm for overcoming an overwhelming adversity by maintaining a soft and flexible but strong internal integrity, like the qualities of water.

Hexagram Image(s)

The unceasing flow of Water stands for the images of the Abysmal hexagram.

The wise and noble uses the images as his guide to be consistently virtuous in his conduct and for engaging in continuous self-education and teaching.

Hexagram Analysis

This hexagram consists of the double trigram Water or repetition of danger, the lower representing terrestrial perils such as mountains, rivers and hills, and the upper trigram, the celestial perils of unfathomable height beyond reach. The trigram Water is made up of one yang line that represents Heaven (rain comes from heaven) sandwiched by two yin lines that represent Earth (the river flowing between two shores). Each of the two yang lines in the hexagram is positioned at the center of each trigram and symbolizes the integrity and sincerity of the virtuous man who practices the Mean. Each yang line also symbolizes the soul (spiritual light) confined by two yin lines of physical greed (darkness), a sign of peril.

2-9 and 5-9 are the lead lines of this hexagram.

Interpretation of Judgment

The double trigram Water denotes the requisite integrity and sincerity in the era of numerous perils. Water reaches its destination by flowing unceasingly (the doubling of the trigram), filling all the places in its path without regard to hazards or difficulties of the task, and yet it always remains true to its own nature. Likewise, the one who is true to him and braves perils like water will only strengthen his penetrating mind by the experience. One who practices the virtues of the Mean with sincerity in his heart with the thoroughness and consistency of water will prevail and enjoy the respect of others (two yang lines).

Celestial perils, which are beyond one's control, are rain, snow, storm, tornadoes, and the height of heaven. The numerous perils on the earth include mountains, rivers, ravines and small and large hills. When perils are properly utilized, they become useful as a means of protection. Taking cues from the celestial and terrestrial perils, kings and dukes protected their states against attacks by setting up strategic barriers such as castles, moats, and fortresses. What a matter of great importance it is to make strategic use of the barriers in times of crises!

Divination Direction

It augurs ill. You will face many hurdles in the pursuit of your goal. Be alert against unexpected disasters, especially from flood, theft, bankruptcy, substance abuse, and health problems. Maintain your moral integrity with patience and a flexible attitude in order to pull yourself through the difficult period.

Individual Lines: Analysis, Interpretations, and Divination Direction

Line 1-6: This yin line is improperly positioned at the beginning of the hexagram, correlating with no line.

The images signify that the one who faces constant pitfalls and becomes accustomed to them will fall to the bottom of the pit. One who becomes used to evil ways will lose the correct *Tao* (this improperly positioned weak line is not at the center of the lower trigram) and will have misfortune.

Divination Direction

It augurs ill. You have problems all around you and cannot get out of them. It is as though you are struggling in quicksand. You must wait until a better time arrives.

Line 2-9: This yang line is improperly positioned at the center of the lower trigram Water, contiguous to 1-6 and with no correlating line.

The images signify that this man faces more perils (the upper trigram Water) and cannot expect to overcome the perils all at once. Owing to his practice of the Mean and his contiguous relationship with 1-6 and 3-6, he will be able to alleviate the hardship somewhat if he can get even a small bit of help from them, but he cannot escape the perils altogether. It means that if he is content with small gains in the beginning, the small gains can accumulate and become a strong force that will eventually help him get out of the perils.

Divination Direction

You are not out of the woods yet, as more difficulties are coming your way. Solicit different friends for help. You must work to overcome difficulties one at a time with diligence and patience. The result will be some gains and some losses.

Line 3-6: This yin line is improperly positioned at the top of the lower trigram Water and borders with the upper trigram Water.

The images signify that this man is faced with extreme perils, regardless of whether he stays put or ascends, as if manacles and stocks restrain his freedom. This yin line represents one who is weak and incompetent, yet arrogant to place him in the yang position away from the center of the lower trigram. This line precariously borders the upper trigram Water. This man is about to move from a perilous situation to a new kind of peril. No matter what efforts he makes, there will not be a satisfactory result. It will be better if he waits for a clear opportunity to escape, instead of making efforts to attack the danger directly, which will bog him down deeper in the danger.

Divination Direction

It augurs extremely ill. Now is the time to reflect upon yourself to understand how you are contributing to this dilemma. You have no option but to wait for a better time to come.

Line 4-6: This yin line is properly positioned, contiguous to the ruler, correlating with no line.

The images signify that in times of peril what counts is sincerity, not formalities. This virtuous and loyal prime minister is prudent and frugal in the era of perils, and he enjoys the full trust of the ruler. He cultivates with unostentatious sincerity a close relationship with the ruler. This minister shows his gratitude by sending the ruler meager gifts of a barrel of spirits and several bowls of millet in plain earthenware through the palace window (symbolizes light entering into the ruler's mind to dispel the darkness of peril), instead of using the formal entrance. The mutual understanding and trust between the ruler and the minister in the era of perils will result in no error.

Divination Direction

The hardship you are experiencing will improve gradually. Be sincere and practical in dealing with the hardship you are undergoing, and you will successfully overcome it in the end.

Line 5-9: This yang line is properly positioned, contiguous to 4-6 and correlating with no line.

The images signify that the overambitious invites danger. This competent ruler who practices the virtues of the Mean enjoys a trusting relationship with his prime minister in the era of perils. The virtuous, trusting mutual relationship is analogous to flowing water that reaches its own level at the rim but does not flow over the levee, and some sand mounds and the banks remain dry. Overly ambitious efforts to overcome perils will worsen the situation like overflowing water that breaks up riverbanks. The virtues of the Mean that the ruler practices in the era of Abysmal (perils) has not as yet spread among the ruled to a great extent. The era of perils is not over yet, but the ruler will have no blame.

Divination Direction

Better days are dawning for you, and you will harvest the fruits of your labor. Be patient and continue your sincere efforts.

Line 6-6: This yin line is at the apogee of the Abysmal hexagram, correlating with no line. The ruler, 5-9, has already established a strong, trusting relationship with 4-6 and finds this weak, incompetent high-ranking official (6-6) with a dark and stubborn mind of little use at the height of the perilous era.

The images signify that an extraordinarily difficult situation is created because this man is hopelessly ignorant and stubborn. His situation is analogous to the man who is confined in a prison made of brambly thickets bound with strong black cords for a felony that he committed. His maximum term is three years, after which he will be executed, for he has failed to rehabilitate himself and return to the proper conduct of *Tao* during the three-year term. There will be misfortune.

Divination Direction

It augurs ill. You will fail in every attempt that you make. It is time for you to reflect upon yourself to improve your conduct and not repeat your past mistakes.

30. The Clinging 離 (Li) Hexagram

Key attributes: Clinging, brightness, the symbol of adherence, symbol of fire and light

Judgment

"*Li* indicates that (in regard to what it denotes), it will be advantageous to be firm and correct, and that thus there will be free course and success. Let (its subject) also nourish (a docility like that of) the cow, and there will be good fortune." (James Legge, *The I Ching*, 120.)

Essence of Hexagram

This hexagram explains the *Tao* of integrity as the paradigm for maintaining one's inner tranquillity with clarity of mind throughout the different phases of life.

Hexagram Image(s)

The two Light trigrams stand for images of the Clinging hexagram. The wise and noble uses the images as his guide to spread the influence of his illustrious virtues in all directions unceasingly, like the double lights that symbolize ceaseless brightness.

Hexagram Analysis

This hexagram consists of the double trigram Light, with a yin line occupying the center position of each trigram. The trigram Light represents such attributes as light, fire, sun, and brightness, as well as intelligence, civilization, and adherence. The trigram has one yin line that is sandwiched by two yang lines, and the attribute of adherence or clinging is derived from this. Fire is bright on the outside with a dark, hollow center (yin line), symbolizing dark and light clinging together. Fire needs to attach (cling) itself to something in order to produce light or to burn. The yin line in the center also represents a docile cow that is nurtured in an enclosure. The two Light trigrams represent the progression of the sun in the course of a day and the illustrious virtues of both the ruler and the subjects.

2-6 and 5-6 are the lead lines of this hexagram.

Interpretation of Judgment

The Clinging or Adherence denotes that one will prevail by firmly practicing the correct *Tao*. The sun and the moon cling to heaven, and the myriad of things on the earth like grains, plants, and trees cling to the earth. In the same way, the illustrious virtues of the ruler and his subjects who adhere (cling) to the correct practice of *Tao* will transform the world into an ideal state. Through the practice of the Mean and with modest conduct complying with nature's way, one will prevail in his endeavors, like the cow that is docile in its nature and brings good fortune.

Divination Direction

It augurs well. Your business is thriving and your projects are proceeding well. Pay close attention to the ever-changing circumstances, and act flexibly to meet the changing demands, but maintain your integrity of virtues and principles with a warm and understanding heart for other people. Pay special attention to your health problems.

Individual Lines: Analysis, Interpretation, and Divination Direction

Line 1-9: This yang line is at the bottom of the lower trigram Fire. One of the attributes of fire is to burn upward or to ascend. The bottom line symbolizes the foot taking steps, the beginning of a new day or the rising sun.

The images signify that the beginning is important as it affects what is to follow, like in the case of this man who is ready to step forward (yang line) in the morning. The beginning of the day can be confusing because there are many things ahead of him to consider and do. He has a tendency to move hurriedly (the yang line of trigram Fire) in different directions. If he treads cautiously with the attitude of reverence and an attentive mind, he will be able to avoid making an error.

Divination Direction

Think carefully before acting. Move cautiously to implement your plans. Rushing into action may produce a favorable result, but it will not last long.

Line 2-6: This yin line is one of the structural lead lines and is properly positioned at the center of the lower trigram, which is yellow in color. The color of both the center and the earth is yellow, representing such attributes as emotional balance and the youthful stage in life and symbolizes the midday sun.

The images signify that it is midday or the youthful stage in life. The one who adheres to the yellow color (center) is the one who practices the virtues of the Mean and will have fundamental good fortune. This man has attained the acme of the virtues of the Mean (by being properly positioned at the center) and commands the highest respect of the people. He will succeed in achieving all of his goals.

Divination Direction

It augurs extremely well. Your dreams will be realized fully. You will be successful beyond your expectations in achieving your goals.

Line 3-9: This yang line is the last of the lower trigram Light and symbolizes the setting sun. The hexagram name "Clinging" refers to the setting sun, which will set before long. Here, it serves as the metaphor for a very old man[28] of eighty.

The images signify that one who practices *Tao* maintains his integrity by continuing to cultivate his virtues to the end. There is the old person who bemoans being old (symbolism of clinging) and is jealous of the young, or the one who wastes his remaining days engaging in such pleasurable activities as singing in rhythm while tapping the earthenware pot. How long can he bemoan? One who cannot accept the natural laws will have regrets and wail of his old age. One who wastes his remaining days overindulging in pleasurable activities will face misfortune.

Divination Direction

It augurs ill. The time has come for you to clean up your affairs that are not going well, and to prepare yourself to accept the failure calmly before you plan a new start.

Line 4-9: This yang line is improperly positioned at the bottom of the upper trigram Light, indicating that the fire from the lower trigram has spread to the upper trigram. The yang line in the yin position represents the fierce (aggressive) burning of the fire.

The images signify that a person can consume his energy quickly like fire that consumes wood. In this case, the fire has suddenly spread to the upper trigram (it symbolizes a person who consumes himself too rapidly through misuse of his mind), and he cannot find a place to escape. He is burned to death, and the burnt corpse is abandoned. This fate befell him because he did not practice virtues of the Mean and spent his energy like a falling meteor.

Divination Direction

It augurs ill. You think that you are smarter than others are and behave arrogantly and hastily. Your friends will leave you, and you will have to deal with unexpected disasters alone. It is time for you to understand your weaknesses and remedy them.

Line 5-6: This yin line is improperly positioned at the center of the upper trigram and correlates with no line, indicating that this man is in the place of honor but is weak in his ability.

The images signify that it is late afternoon and there are not many hours of light left. In this late stage of his life, he looks back on his life and bemoans the mistakes he made in his life. This reflection causes him regret and sorrow, and tears stream down in torrents. If he is truly remorseful and uses his life experience to help others during the remaining hours of light, there will be good fortune.

Divination Direction

You are not capable of dealing alone with the distressful situation that occurs too often, and you need good friends who can help you. Examine what you have been doing to find out if you need to change your attitude or the way in which you have been handling each situation. If you do so, your persistent efforts will bring satisfactory results.

Line 6-9: This yang line is at the apogee of the Clinging hexagram, indicating the highest degree of this man's intelligence. This yang line occupies the yin position, indicating the gentle and lenient nature of this intelligent man.

The images signify that proper discipline should be the objective, not punishment, in eliminating evil, like the ruler who employs this man for the expedition to quell the rebellion (symbolizes the control of greedy desires) and restore normalcy in the state. This man is praiseworthy, for he killed the rebel chief to eliminate the root of evil but took the rebel chief's followers as prisoners, sparing their lives. For his victorious and appropriate conduct, he will get no blame.

Divination Direction

It augurs well. The time has come for you to eliminate the root causes of your problems, which will bring fruitful results to you. You will be successful.

31. The Influence 咸 (Hsien) Hexagram

Key attributes: Influence, wooing, the symbol of mutual influence

Judgment

"*Hsien* indicates that (on the fulfillment of the conditions implied in it), there will be free course and success. Its advantageousness will depend on the being firm and correct, (as) in marrying a young lady. There will be good fortune." (James Legge, *The I Ching*, 123.)

Essence of Hexagram

This hexagram explains the principle of attaining harmonious mutual relationships by being understanding of each other's feelings without coercion or possessiveness.

Hexagram Image(s)

Lake above Mountain stands for the images of the Influence hexagram. The wise and noble uses the images as his guide to learn how to bring about harmonious relationships, by emptying one's own mind to accept other opinions so that one's greed and selfishness will not interfere in understanding others, or by being humble and receptive to others.

Hexagram Analysis

The upper section of the sixty-four hexagram series, which deals primarily with natural forces, begins with the Heaven hexagram as the originator of all things in the universe. The lower section of *I Ching*, which deals primarily with human and social forces, begins with the Influence hexagram, with courtship or marital relationship as the foundation of all social relationships. The principle of human conduct for each hexagram in the lower section derives from the social relationships that the images of the hexagram present.

Each line of this hexagram has the correlative relationship, giving the hexagram its name Influence. This hexagram consists of the lower trigram Mountain that symbolizes a young man (youngest son) and the upper trigram Lake, a young lady (youngest daughter). When the strong (yang line) places himself lower than the weak (yin line), it is the sincere posture of the strong wooing the weak. The attributes of Mountain are its passivity, receptivity, and keeping still, and the attribute of the upper trigram Lake is joy, which can fill every nook and corner of the mountain with its water. The stronger (lower trigram) influences the gentle (upper trigram) by quiet but persistent courtship, and the gentle responds joyously. The relationship between the two is the metaphor for harmonious mutual influence between two persons and touching each other's hearts or the communion of spirits. The influence must come from one's impartial attitude without any selfish motivation.

4-9, directive, and 5-9, structural, are the lead lines of the hexagram.

Interpretation of Judgment

When harmonious influence prevails, two people impress favorably upon each other. The young man (yang) places himself below the young lady (yin) by taking the initiative in the courtship, resulting in harmonious reciprocity between two different energies. The young man checks (Mountain, halt) his forceful emotion, and the young lady responds joyfully (Lake, joy). The young man's humble attitude that places him lower than the young lady impresses her favorably. Owing to his correct approach, he will enjoy the good fortune of matrimonial success with the young lady.

The energies of Heaven and Earth work in the same way to mutually influence each other to produce myriads of things and transform them. So do the sages influence the hearts and minds of the people to bring peace to the world by being humble and receptive to the ideas of the people. By observing the mutual influence and the reciprocity of stimulation and response, we come to understand the innate attributes of Heaven and Earth, as well as those of the myriad things they produce.

Divination Direction

It augurs well, especially in courtship and marriage. Pursue your goal with honesty and sincerity, following your intuition; you will succeed. You will benefit from cooperative efforts with other people.

Individual Lines: Analysis, Interpretation, and Divination Direction

Note: Parts of the human body are used metaphorically to describe the degree of influence in touching another's heart or in one's readiness to receive influence. For instance, moving the toes cannot of itself make a person walk; walking requires moving the calves and thighs. Therefore, the influence of the toes in walking is shallow.

Line 1-6: This yin line is at the bottom of the Influence hexagram and correlates with 4-9. The bottom position symbolizes the big toes.

The images signify that, although 1-6 has a relationship with 4-9, the degree of mutual influence remains shallow as if it is limited to his (1-6's) big toes, symbolizing the wishful stage of mutual influence, and he cannot walk toward 4-9. Although he wants to be closer to the high official, it is a shallow relationship because the desire of 1-6 to gain influence is centered on his own needs.

Divination Direction

Your success depends on how well you are prepared for your move. Make each step in your move prudently within your means and ability.

Line 2-6: This yin line is properly positioned at the center of the lower trigram, contiguous to 3-9 (the thigh) and correlating with 5-9. Influence moves from the big toe (1-6) up to the calf of the leg (2-6).

The images signify that the influence is felt in the calves of his legs. As with the influence of the big toe, the calf's influence is limited only to itself. Instead of waiting for the call from the ruler (5-9), if this man aligns himself with the official in the lower status (3-9), it will result in misfortune. Since this man practices the virtues of the Mean, it will be better for him to wait quietly and live by the principles of *Tao*; no harm will come to him, and in the end, he will garner good fortune.

Divination Direction

Refrain from plunging into an action impetuously. Set your goal high and proceed with a well-thought-out plan and implement it one step at a time. You are blessed with many human resources that you can utilize to carry out your plans.

Line 3-9: This yang line is at the top of the lower trigram Mountain (halt), contiguous to 2-6 and correlating with 6-6. The yang line indicates an urge to move aggressively. The influence has reached its third level, the thigh. The thighs move along with the calves and the toes, but it is strongly influenced by 4-9.

The images signify that the influence is felt in the thighs. The metaphor means that this man has too strong an urge to influence others with every desire of his heart, which will lead him to humiliation. He must be able to hold back his desires so that he can appropriately differentiate as to whom to influence (1-6, 2-6, and 6-6) or by whom to be influenced by (4-9). Any capricious move to act at this time is inauspicious and will cause him regret.

Divination Direction

In pursuing the high goal for which you have been planning, beware of temptations that come to your attention, especially sexual intimacy. Maintain your secure, routine lifestyle until you have an opportunity that you perceive as suitable.

Line 4-9: This yang line is improperly positioned at the beginning line of the upper trigram, correlating with 1-6. Influence has reached the heart, but the heart lacks virtuous integrity, as it is improperly positioned. This man paces back and forth between 1-9 and himself.

The images signify that the influence has reached one's heart. If he stays on the firm practice of the correct *Tao*, he will be able to influence others and have no cause for remorse. Love and affection grow in the heart but should affect a relationship naturally without manipulation.[29] A restrained heart is unnatural, making him feel unsettled and pace back and forth. With a restraining heart, his influence will be limited only to the one in his mind (1-6) or the small number of people in his circle, and he will not be able to achieve the magnanimity of bringing benefits to a large number of people.

Divination Direction

You could end up losing bigger gains while you are dwelling on petty attractions. Guard against becoming selfish and greedy. Take the course that will bring benefits to all the parties. If you stay on the unselfish course, you will succeed.

Line 5-9: This yang line is properly positioned at the center of the upper trigram, correlating with 2-6. Influence has reached the back of the neck, which is rigid and firm and ineffective in influencing, but touching one's back is a friendly gesture with no selfish motive.

The images signify that the influence has reached the back of one's neck, which lacks the flexibility of a big forward or backward movement. This man is rigid and his chance to influence other people or being influenced by others will be trivial. He realizes his error of rigidity in his thinking and makes efforts to correct it. He will have no cause for remorse.

Divination Direction

Be selective and do not fall into a temptation coming from other people, since you may get hurt. Refrain from an undertaking that is beyond your means. Success may appear to be around the corner, but it will be hard to attain.

Line 6-6: This yin line is at the top of the Influence hexagram, correlating with 3-9. Influence has reached the jowls, cheeks, and tongue (mouth), all of which are employed in making speeches.

The images signify that Influence is at a point where it is felt in the jowls, cheeks, and tongue. This influence involves much talking without substance in an attempt to influence others, and it produces negative results. This man feels that he is at the height of his joy (the top line of the upper trigram Lake that symbolizes joy). However, this man has become too excited, overtalkative, and given to flattery.

Divination Direction

Watch your speech so that it will not bring harm to you and other people. Guard yourself against being cajoled into doing something that you are not sure about.

32. The Constancy 恒 (Hang) Hexagram

Key attributes: Constancy, duration, the symbol of perseverance

Judgment

"*Hang* indicates successful progress and no error (in what it denotes). But the advantage will come from being firm and correct; and movement in any direction whatever will be advantageous." (James Legge, *The I Ching.*)

Essence of Hexagram

This hexagram explains the principle of enduring union by maintaining the virtuous integrity of principles based on *Tao* and perseverance in the constantly changing world.

Hexagram Image(s)

Thunder above Wind stands for the images of the Constancy hexagram. The wise and noble uses the images as his guide in upholding his moral integrity when taking a stand and never deviating from it.

Hexagram Analysis

This hexagram is the inverse of Hexagram #31 Influence, and it symbolizes the constancy in the union that exists between thunder and wind. This hexagram consists of the inner trigram Wind that symbolizes the eldest daughter, wife, or compliance, and the outer trigram Thunder, the eldest son, husband, or movement. All six lines of the hexagram are in perfect harmony, with each line forming a correlating pair: 1-6 with 4-9, 2-9 with 5-6 and 3-9 with 6-6. The hexagram name "Constancy" denotes the principle of dependability without rigidity, keeping abreast of the times and changing according to the needs of the times, such as the enduring relationship between husband and wife and the perpetual cycles of day and night and the four seasons.

2-9 is the sole lead line of this hexagram.

Interpretation of Judgment

One will prevail by observing the principle of Constancy. Constancy exists between husband and wife when they have harmonious roles and relationship. The husband works outside to support the family, and the wife stays at home (the inner trigram) to raise children; the husband is active and directing (the outer trigram Thunder) and the wife, compliant (the inner trigram Wind). When the relationship is harmonious and orderly, it will be enduring, and they commit no error.

The Constancy principle is represented in this hexagram with the hard line, 4-9 (yang line, man) above, and the soft, 1-6 (yin line, woman) below. Thunder above and Wind below collaborate; when Thunder makes its loud sound, Wind responds by dissipating the pent-up energies in the atmosphere. Such harmonious transactions occur among all the yang and yin energies following the principle of Constancy. Advantages result when the principle of Constancy is observed correctly and firmly at all times. It is the principle of Heaven and Earth that is perpetual and never-ending.

It is the time to initiate action to carry out a plan. In the principle of Constancy, the constancy of cycles exists in the ever-changing movement of everything in the universe; each has a self-renewing beginning when one cycle comes to an end. The sun and moon have their places in Heaven to shine forever. The four seasons change from one into another in a perpetual cycle. In the same way, the sages observe the principle of Constancy by practicing *Tao* at all times to transform the world into a better place. By observing how the principle of Constancy works, we come to understand the nature of Heaven and Earth and the myriad of things in them.

Divination Direction

It augurs well if you are content with the present situation without being greedy or too ambitious. First, build your daily life and business activities on sound moral principles, and do not deviate from them. Make steady efforts to attain your goal without haste or waste, and you will succeed. Your health problem may require prolonged attention.

Individual Lines: Analysis, Interpretation, and Divination Direction

Line 1-6: This yin line is improperly positioned at the bottom of the hexagram, correlating with 4-9. This yin line is the lead line of the lower trigram Wind and represents wife, while the correlating line, 4-9, represents husband. The trigram Wind symbolizes dredging.

The images signify constant dredging. It denotes the newlywed wife (1-6) who has become overconfident and arrogant (yin line in yang position) and "digs" into her husband's affairs without knowledge or understanding, believing that her way is correct. Her deep involvement in her husband's affairs from the beginning of their marriage and her insistence on her correctness will bring misfortune, and no advantage is gained.

This first line represents the beginning stage of a task. One needs to fully understand what should be done and how before he undertakes the task. If one is intrusive and obstinate like the newlywed wife described above, no harmonious relationship can be developed. If one presses hard to accomplish too much in a hurry, he will experience a failure.

Divination Direction

It is important to understand that there are different layers in what appears to be simple. Assess your ability and resources accurately, and stay within your means. Haste and greed will bring failure.

Line 2-9: This yang line is improperly positioned at the center of the lower trigram, correlating with 5-6.

The images signify that this man discovers that a matter of regret goes away. His improper positioning can be a cause of regret if he is intemperate in the use of his strength. However, his constant practice of the virtues of the Mean, which enables him to control an excessive use of his strength, and the supportive relationship with the virtuous ruler will leave him with nothing further to regret.

Divination Direction

Go slow, one step at a time. It is not a proper time for you to initiate a new enterprise. It will be better to stay with what you have been doing.

Line 3-9: This yang line is properly positioned at the top of the lower trigram, correlating with 6-6. Bordering with the upper trigram, this yang line has a proclivity to become aggressive and unsettling.

The images signify that this man does not always maintain his virtue of Constancy and is not trustworthy, as his mood and conduct are changed by outside influences (6-6). Some will impute this as a disgrace, and he no longer has the trust or acceptance of others. Even when he behaves correctly, he will not be accepted.

Divination Direction

You keep changing your stand, and your attitude is unsettled. Your credibility with other people is hurt. Be prudent in your actions; become trustworthy with other people. Maintain your well-thought-out original plan of action.

Line 4-9: This yang line is improperly positioned at the position of the prime minister (this line also represents mind), away from the center of the upper trigram.

The images signify that there is no game to hunt in the field, which is the metaphor of the prime minister who lacks the virtuous integrity (in his mind-set) but attempts to influence others. He is like a hunter who persists in pursuing game in wrong places, not utilizing correct information or a proper hunting method. His efforts will not bring any gain.

Divination Direction

Since your current efforts give you little satisfaction, now is the time for you to change your method and direction.

Line 5-6: This yin line is at the center of the upper trigram, correlating with 2-9. Line 2-9 represents the virtuous man, and this yin line represents the virtuous woman who practices the constancy of the Mean and follows one husband to the end.

The images signify a person who practices the virtue of Constancy correctly. The woman should follow her husband all her life. For a woman, such a practice of Constancy will bring good fortune, as the Constancy required of her is to follow her husband to the end. The husband firmly observes Constancy of the virtuous relationship that exists between husband and wife. However, a man has to deal with many new and changing situations in his social activities and has to act progressively and assertively to meet the demands of new circumstances, instead of trying to conform to his wife all the time. If he behaves rigidly like a woman and does not change direction when called for, misfortune will result.

Divination Direction

For the woman, this is good fortune.

For the man, a hard time is around the corner. He needs to be flexible in order to meet a new situation, and at the same time, he needs determination and preparation to overcome the difficulty he faces.

Line 6-6: This yin line is at the top of both the Constancy hexagram and the upper trigram Thunder that symbolizes movement.

The images signify lack of Constancy with an ever-vacillating, unsettled stance. This person is going against the principle of Constancy that requires one to be more settled and to persevere. Instead, this man constantly moves around making changes (trigram Thunder), for he is too weak (yin line) to occupy the apogee position of the Constancy era. He will face misfortune with serious failures in his pursuits.

Divination Direction

It augurs ill. You will experience serious failures in your endeavors. Learn from your failures, and get a new start following good preparation.

33. The Retreat 遯 (Thun) Hexagram

Key attributes: Retreat, the symbol of regression

Judgment

"*Thun* indicates successful progress (in its circumstances). To a small extent it will (still) be advantageous to be firm and correct." (James Legge, *The I Ching*, 127.)

Essence of Hexagram

This hexagram explains the principle of proper and timely retreat or retirement when there are natural signs calling for such an action.

Hexagram Image(s)

Mountain under Heaven stands for the images of the Retreat hexagram. The wise and noble uses the images as his guide in his conduct of retreating, advancing, or staying still. He keeps the petty and unprincipled at a distance, not because of his hatred or avoidance, but to maintain his strict self-discipline.

Hexagram Analysis

This hexagram consists of the lower trigram Mountain that, in this hexagram, symbolizes the petty or unprincipled man, and the upper trigram Heaven, the wise and noble, or the great man. The Mountain stands high arrogantly, but it is no match to Heaven with its unfathomable height. The gradual advance of the yin energy characterizes this hexagram, with the two yin lines at the bottom of the lower trigram pushing upward. It is the era in favor of the petty man pushing the great men out of the way. In the lunar calendar, this hexagram represents the sixth month or June. The yin energy keeps moving upward as the year advances. In the era of the advancing petty men, the wise and noble (5-9) maintains a correlative relationship with the advancing 2-6 (the advancing yin energy), who practices the virtues of the Mean. Although the noble man recognizes the merits of this particular petty man (yin) who practices the virtues, the sign of the time (the cycle of change in which the petty men are advancing) calls for the wise and noble to retreat as the way to maintain strength and success, but not as flight from the advancing petty men.

There are three lead lines in this hexagram; 1-6 and 2-6 are directive lead lines, and 5-9, the structural lead line.

Interpretation of Judgment

It is the time to retreat in order to prevail. Retreat is different from flight; the former is a sign of strength, and the latter, weakness. What distinguishes the wise from the foolish is to know when to advance and when to retreat or retire, according to the sign of the time. The wise and noble, 5-9, and the advancing petty man, 2-6, share a mutual understanding on how to conduct themselves in accordance with the sign of the time. In the era of Retreat, great achievements based on the rectitude of *Tao* cannot be attained, but the practice of rectitude on small matters is still fitting. What a great, important meaning the time of Retreat carries with it!

Divination Direction

You are in the midst of declining fortune and will experience many disturbing obstructions. Your opinions and ideas, though sound, will be rejected. The sooner you take your hands off matters that are not going well, the better it will be. Auspicious for people engaged in entertainment and service businesses.

Individual Lines: Analysis, Interpretation, and Divination Direction

Line 1-6: This yin line is at the bottom of the Retreat hexagram, which means that it will be the last one to retreat.

The images signify that this man poses himself at the tail end of the retreat from pursuing enemies. He delayed his retreat because he was indecisive, and he exposes himself to higher risks than others. He is in a more perilous position than those ahead of him because he is in the direct line of the pursuing enemies. It is not the proper time for him to take other actions. If he refrains from doing so, he will not suffer calamity.

Divination Direction

You must keep your mind open to catch up with changing realities. It is the time to refrain from your activities as quickly as possible before the matter deteriorates even further.

Line 2-6: This yin line is at the center of the lower trigram and correlates with 5-9. Both 2-6 and 5-9, the correlating lines, represent practicing the Mean in the era of Retreat.

The images signify that the will of this petty man with noble aspiration to follow the great man (5-9) is as strong and firm as if his will is attached firmly to him with a strip of yellow (the color of center) ox hide. The great man is unable to separate this man from him, and this man finally succeeds. The conduct of this petty man is in compliance with the correct practice of the Mean, which is to retreat in order to preserve his virtuous integrity in the era when the small and unprincipled gain favor to advance.

Divination Direction

When you obtain this line in divination, it is time for you to examine if you should take decisive and immediate action to stop your activity and retire, the sooner the better. Otherwise, you may suffer a disastrous consequence.

Line 3-9: This yang line is at the top of the lower trigram and the last of the four yang lines, tarrying behind other yang lines in the era of Retreat. It has a contiguous relationship with 2-6.

The images signify that this man understands that it is the time to Retreat, but he lingers on because of his attachment to 2-6. Such an attachment to wealth, fame, or friendship is not only perilous, but it also wears him out. In the era of Retreat, he will be better off not to engage in public dealings. He will enjoy the good fortune of no harm if he stays home and looks after his servants who have served him with dedication and sincerity.

Divination Direction

It augurs ill. An imminent disaster is looming. Remove yourself from important matters immediately. Limit your activities to small family affairs.

Line 4-9: This yang line that correlates with 1-6 is the first line of the upper trigram Heaven that symbolizes strength.

The images signify that the wise and noble who retreats willingly despite his attachment to 1-6 will enjoy good fortune. The small and unprincipled (1-6) is not disciplined enough to detach himself and follow the wise and noble in retreat. Such conduct distinguishes the wise and noble from the petty and unprincipled.

Divination Direction

The time has come for you to cut yourself off completely from any dishonest practice or bad friends, and to start over with new determination.

Line 5-9: This yang line is at the center of the upper trigram, correlating with 2-6. It represents the person of fame and wealth who practices the virtues of the Mean.

The images signify that this is a man of great determination (firm inwardly) who practices the rectitude of the Mean and recognizes that the time has come for him to retreat. He carries out his retreat (retirement) in a harmonious, praiseworthy way (soft outwardly). He will enjoy good fortune.

Divination Direction

If you detect a sign that you should remove yourself from a matter or situation, you should do so, rather than linger on.

Line 6-9: This yang line is at the top of the Retreat hexagram, correlating with no line. It denotes that this man has no attachment to be concerned about and can retire with a free and happy frame of mind.

The images signify that this man retires freely without doubt or attachment and with many blessings; there is nothing that is disadvantageous to him. It is the most ideal retirement.

Divination Direction

Relax and enjoy; more good fortune will be forthcoming.

34. The Great Strength 大 壯 (Ta Kwang) Hexagram

Key attributes: Great strength, the symbol of major power

Judgment

"*Ta Kwang* indicates that (under the conditions which it symbolizes) it will be advantageous to be firm and correct." (James Legge, *The I Ching*, 129.)

Essence of Hexagram

This hexagram explains the principle of regulating the use of strength to be in harmony with correct *Tao*.

Hexagram Image(s)

Thunder above Heaven stands for the images of the Great Strength hexagram. The great strength lies in nature's way. The wise and noble uses the images as a guide for regulating his conduct so that he will not tread a course of action unless it conforms to the proper way of *Tao* that conforms to nature's way.

Hexagram Analysis

This hexagram consists of the lower trigram Heaven that denotes strength, and the upper trigram Thunder, movement or action. There are four yang lines that move forward together forcefully and in harmony. The upper trigram Thunder (action) activated the lower trigram Heaven (strength) to move with great force; hence, the derivation of the hexagram name, "Great Strength." This hexagram represents February in the lunar calendar. The yang energy will reach its apex in April with the entire six lines yang. The lower trigram Heaven also symbolizes decorum or correct manner, while the upper trigram Thunder, foot or the act of treading.

4-9 is the sole lead line of this hexagram.

Interpretation of Judgment

The "Great Strength" that this hexagram stands for refers to the strength of the yang energy, represented by the four yang lines moving upward (the upper trigram Thunder), taking over the positions of the petty unprincipled (yin lines). When one gains great strength, he often becomes arrogant. Therefore, great strength must be accompanied by the practice of rectitude in *Tao* in order to bring about great achievement. The one who achieves greatness through the practice of the rectitude understands and follows the natural attributes of Heaven and Earth.

Divination Direction

You are riding on a strong upswing trend, especially favorable for business expansion and investments. You must watch for becoming overly self-confident, as you have strong urges to move ahead, even when the result of your efforts may fall short of your expectations. First, calm yourself and then map out your action plans carefully. Restrain yourself from becoming overconfident and arrogant. If you do this, you will achieve your goal, since you are competent and resourceful.

Individual Lines: Analysis, Interpretation, and Divination Direction

Line 1-9: This yang line is at the bottom of the hexagram, antagonistically correlating with 4-9.

The images signify that he has the strength in his toes. This is the metaphor for the beginning stage of an event and low in status, with no one of higher status to help him. He will experience misfortune if he moves aggressively to achieve his goal and will be thoroughly frustrated with many obstacles to overcome.

Divination Direction

It augurs ill for you to actively seek to attain your goal at this time. Your misjudgment of timing will result in failures. Conserve your strength and wait for a good opportunity.

Line 2-9: This yang line is at the center of the lower trigram, correlating with 5-6.

The images signify that the opportunity for this man to advance has opened up, and he stays on the course of rectitude of the Mean and exerts self-restraint in using his strength. He will have good fortune.

Divination Direction

A good time is approaching. Maintain your modest attitude and sound approaches in your activities, and you will be successful.

Line 3-9: This yang line is at the top of the lower trigram, and borders the upper trigram. It possesses excessive strength and makes its move aggressively.

The images signify that the strong, petty, and unprincipled (1-9) fails to conserve his strength by yielding to the temptation to display his power; the wise and noble (2-9) uses restraints and does not abuse his power. Even for one (3-9) in the correct position who follows the example of 1-9, using excessive power will entangle and endanger him. The situation is analogous to the goat that butts his head against a hedge and gets his horns entangled in it.

Divination Direction

Beware! Your move may put you in a predicament. Be modest and sincere in your conduct, and proceed slowly and deliberately in your actions.

Line 4-9: This yang line is improperly positioned as the first line of the upper trigram Thunder. The yang in the yin position indicates vigorous movement. This is the leader of the three yang lines below.

The images signify that the one who stays in the rectitude of *Tao* will have good fortune with nothing to regret. This situation is analogous to the goat that works diligently with great perseverance and finds an opening in the hedge to avoid the entanglement and continues advancing. This wise man's use of his internal strength in cooperation with others (lower three yang lines) is likened to the way in which the axle of a big cart works with the combined force.

Divination Direction

It augurs well. You will soon have a good payoff if you persevere in your efforts.

Line 5-6: This yin line is improperly positioned at the center of the upper trigram and correlates with 2-9. This yin line in the yang position moderates its strength, representing this man who practices the virtues of the Mean and lends his support to 2-9.

The images signify that the way in which this virtuous man moderates his strength is analogous to losing his goat (the symbol of untamed strength with outward hardness and inward weakness) that went beyond his field boundaries. His goat is now in the field that belongs to someone else, so he gives up the chase, which means that now he is free with no more resistance. In this era of Great Strength, the moderation of strength shown by this man with the virtues of the Mean will result in no regret. (The rectitude of the Mean or peaceful and persuasive means is superior to the uncontrolled use of strength or confrontation.)

Divination Direction

Work on developing your self-discipline and refrain from actively pursuing your materialistic goal at this time.

Line 6-6: This yin line is properly positioned at the top of the Great Strength hexagram, correlating with 3-9. The Great Strength has reached its apogee.

The images signify that the era of Great Strength has reached its apogee, which is analogous to the goat that can neither retreat nor advance from his entanglement in the hedge that resulted from his reckless butting. This is unfortunate, because nothing beneficial can be achieved under such a circumstance. If one understands the obstacles (learn from the experience) and has endurance to overcome them with prudent behavior, the damnable situation will not last long and will result in good fortune.

Divination Direction

It is not a proper time to move ahead to achieve your goal. Assess the situation you are in thoroughly, and be extremely prudent in your conduct.

35. The Advance 晋 (Zin) Hexagram

Key attributes: Advance, the symbol of progress

Judgment

"In *Zin* we see a prince who secures the tranquillity (of the people) presented on that account with numerous horses (by the king), and three times in a day received at interviews." (James Legge, *The I Ching*, 131.)

Essence of Hexagram

This hexagram explains the principle of making progressive advance in one's virtues through self-cultivation, enabling him to serve the higher (power) obediently without being self-centered.

Hexagram Image(s)

Light (sun) over Earth stands for the images of the Advance hexagram. The wise and noble uses the images as his guide in his efforts to adhere to the brightness of *Tao* so that his virtues shine forth.

Hexagram Analysis

This hexagram consists of the lower trigram Earth that symbolizes the earth, obedience, multitude, and mare, and the upper trigram Light that represents the sun, brightness, and the sovereignty. The upper trigram Water of the primary nuclear hexagram symbolizes the fine horse.

5-6 is the sole lead line of this hexagram.

Interpretation of Judgment

The Advance hexagram represents the time of brilliance, as when the sun ascends over the earth. The people of the state are loyal and obedient to the sovereign whose virtues shine illustriously; the governed serve him with great admiration. The feudal lord in charge of the justice system is so popular among the people that he is called by the honorific name of "the Lord of Peace." The sovereign has conferred a great many horses to him and has allowed him personal audiences three times a day (three yin lines of the lower trigram). This demonstrates how the mutual trust and harmony that exist between the ruler and the feudal lord bring about great progress.[30]

Divination Direction

It augurs very well. Your good fortune is on the rise. Every aspect of your life is bright and gives you happiness and contentment. In order to prolong this favorable situation, you must maintain your sincere and cooperative efforts without becoming arrogant. You will reap both success and popularity.

Individual Lines: Analysis, Interpretation, and Divination Direction

Line 1-6: This yin line is improperly positioned at the beginning of the hexagram, correlating with 4-9. Since this person (1-6) does not have the virtue of being in the center or in the proper position, 4-9, despite their correlative relationship, thwarts his advance.

The images signify that this man is low in status, and others (4-9) do not recognize his efforts in the beginning stage. He has to walk alone in his righteousness. Staying on the righteous course will lead him to good fortune. He has neither a trusting relationship with anyone in his lowly status (no contiguous relationship with 2-6) nor an appointment to serve the high in status. Nonetheless, if he remains collected and confident and cultivates his virtues, there will be no error.

Divination Direction

It is not the proper time for you to make a move to achieve your goal, as there are too many obstacles in your way. Keep composed and get ready for the approaching opportunity that will come before long.

Line 2-6: This yin line is properly positioned at the center of the lower trigram, correlating with no line.

The images signify that this man wants to advance, and he is saddened that he did not receive a response from the one higher in status or power. However, his practice of the virtues of the Mean will lead him to good fortune, and he will eventually receive the blessings of the great spiritual mother. He is like the one who, being harmonious and obedient, receives happy blessings from Mother Nature.

Divination Direction

Though you may not see it now, a bright future is ahead of you. Do not be in a rush to achieve your goal. Instead, maintain your high vision and steady efforts, and you will succeed with some unexpected good fortune.

Line 3-6: This yin line is improperly positioned at the top of the lower trigram Earth as one of the three yin lines.

The images signify that this man has the trust and support of his friends (1-6, 2-6), as all three have a desire to advance in harmony (Earth). There will be no regret.

Divination Direction

Good fortune is dawning on you. It is the right time to make a move. If you maintain your trustworthiness, your friends will help you when you need it.

Line 4-9: This yang line is improperly positioned at the beginning of the upper trigram. The yang line denotes bigness in size, and the lower trigram Mountain of the primary nuclear hexagram a rat, creating the combined symbol of a big rat.

The images signify that this prime minister occupies the high position improperly with a wily personality that lacks in the virtues of the Mean, in the era when virtuous Advance is called for. He feels insecure, as he knows he is occupying the position improperly, amassing material possessions like a big rat and thwarting other people in the lower status (the three yin lines below) from advancing. It is dangerous for him to remain obstinate in that state of mind.

Divination Direction

It is time for self-examination to see if you are engaged in an illegal or dishonest activity that may bring benefits to you now but become the source of serious troubles in the future. It's the time that requires your strong determination to cut yourself off from such a practice or an improper relationship.

Line 5-6: This yin line is at the center of the upper trigram Light, representing the lenient ruler who practices the illustrious virtues of the Mean.

The images signify that this ruler has nothing to regret in the high status he occupies. Although he is improperly positioned with a gentle disposition, he possesses the illustrious virtues of the Mean. He does not need to worry about the ups and downs (success or failure) of his daily activities. What is the more important is that his gentle disposition and virtuous conduct brought him the loyal and virtuous subjects (the three yin lines of the lower trigram) to help him. They will serve him well and receive the blessings of good fortune. This ruler will have advantages in every way.

Divination Direction

Your obstacles are giving way for you to advance; the time of good fortune is at hand. You need not hesitate over the obstacles you face. Move ahead forcefully, and you will succeed.

Line 6-9: This yang line is one of the two yang lines in the hexagram and improperly positioned at the top of the hexagram. The yang stands for aggressive force, which is contrary to the principles of Advance that represent the peaceful advance of the yin force.

The images signify that this man has advanced to the apex of the horn (of the ram) with a very aggressive use of force to quell the rebellious people (4-9) in his city (the upper trigram). In this situation, his use of great force is justified, and he has avoided a serious error. There are times when power needs to be used aggressively to advance an objective. However, if he obstinately continues to use his power in this manner, he will get a remorseful result. Continual aggressive use of power is not an illustrious virtue.

Divination Direction

Correct your tendency to be stubborn and obstinate, which will lead you to difficulties and failures. Cultivate your ability to listen to reasonable opinions and advice of other people before you start with a new plan.

36. The Darkening of the Light 明夷 (Ming I) Hexagram

Key attributes: Darkening of the light, the symbol of lack of appreciation

Judgment

"*Ming I* indicates that (in the circumstances which it denotes) it will be advantageous to realize the difficulty (of the position), and maintain firm correctness." (James Legge, *The I Ching*, 134.)

Essence of Hexagram

This hexagram explains the principle of survival in a Dark Age by practicing perseverance as an expedient measure and concealing one's outstanding virtues and intelligence.

Hexagram Image(s)

Light below Earth stands for the images of the Darkening of the Light hexagram. The wise and noble uses the images as his guide for governing without revealing his high intelligence and virtues, which might be intimidating to the people.

Hexagram Analysis

This hexagram consists of the lower trigram Light that symbolizes sun, brightness, or intelligence, and the upper trigram Earth, the earth, or obedience. As the era of the Advance ends, the Dark Age begins. The hexagram image, the sun beneath the earth, represents the era of darkness when the weak, foolish ruler afflicts the wise and loyal subjects with trouble for staying on the correct course of *Tao*.

There are three lead lines; 6-6 as the directive, and 2-6 and 5-6 as the structural lead lines.

Interpretation of Judgment

The "Darkening of the Light" in this hexagram describes the time when the brightness of the sun set under the earth and darkened it. It is the metaphor for the person who, during a time of great adversities, cultivates illustrious virtues within himself while being obedient and yielding outside, in order to survive. It describes what King *Wan*, the founder of *Chou* dynasty, did to endure great adversity.[31] He turned the adversity he was under to his advantage by maintaining his course of rectitude while not revealing his illustrious virtues to avoid being seen as a threat by the tyrannical king *Zhou* of the *Yin* dynasty. Viscount *Ji*, king *Zhou*'s uncle, endured the threat of persecution and being put to death by his nephew by pretending to have lost his mind, while he maintained the rectitude of *Tao*.

Divination Direction

It augurs ill. Darkness prevails ahead, and you are already plagued with many unjustified adversities, especially in your business, financial dealings, litigation, and human relationships. The financial market will have a sharp decline. Make efforts to safeguard your internal and external resources. Diligently maintain your conservative, planned course of action at a slow pace, waiting for a better time to come. Guard against health problems.

Individual Lines: Analysis, Interpretation, and Divination Direction

Line 1-9: This yang line is properly positioned at the bottom of the hexagram, farthest from the directive lead line 6-6 that represents the darkest point in the dark age. It stands for the wise and noble in the era of the Darkening of the Light.

The images signify that in the dark age, the wise and noble takes flight to avoid the torments of the age, like the bird that flies with its wings drooping low to evade being noticed. He keeps going for three days (many days) without eating. In the dark age, one who maintains the correct course, abiding by his principles, suffers deprivation. This man looks to 2-6 (one of the lead lines) for understanding and friendship, but he finds the host speaking ill of him. One must be cautious in asking favors from others.

Divination Direction

It augurs ill. Nothing works out smoothly, and you have no one to turn to for help. Avoid any competitive situation or argument with other people. Endure and wait out this difficult time for a better time.

Line 2-6: This yin line is properly positioned at the center of the lower trigram.

The images signify that this righteous man (good force or light) was wounded in the left thigh (1-9 for foot, 2-6, thigh) by the evil force (darkness), which restricts his movement, but he is not seriously disabled. It is urgent to save others who are also endangered by the evil force. He needs to act with all his strength as swiftly as the fast horse to save others from the pursuer before it becomes too late (before it gets dark). It is possible to attain his goal when he observes the principles of the Mean, and there will be good fortune.

Divination Direction

Although in a trickling way, the time of good fortune is approaching. You will do well in small matters for the time being. Before long, opportunities will open up for you to actively seek to attain your important goal.

Line 3-9: This yang line is properly positioned at the top of the lower trigram Light, the one who is strong and bright. It correlates with the directive lead line 6-6 that represents the most foolish and wicked ruler (darkness). The correlative relationship here represents 3-9's efforts to restore righteousness. The trigram Light stands for south in direction.

The images signify that in the era of the Darkening of the Light, this strong and wise man goes hunting in the south (light). It is the metaphor for the powerful and wise man going on an expedition to subdue the enemies (darkness) in order to restore the era of brightness. He captures their great chief (6-6), resulting in great victory. Although his intention is commendable, he should not undertake such a drastic corrective action hastily unless there is a pressing need. He must first dispel the darkness within himself.

Divination Direction

The time of good fortune is at hand; take a planned and decisive action to win over your competitor and achieve your goal.

Line 4-6: This yin line is at the bottom of the upper trigram Earth that symbolizes compliance.

The images signify that in the era of Darkening of Light, this man, who is the older brother of the king, enters the left side of the belly of the ruler (6-6) who darkens the state, in order to learn what is in the heart and mind of this ruler. This is the metaphor of the man getting close to the ruler in a compliant manner in order to try to understand the ruler's feelings and intent. He concludes that there is no hope for change and leaves the ruler's courtyard through the gate to run from harm's way.

Divination Direction

There is no improvement in your situation, and you need to discover the underlying cause of the problem. Take decisive action, either to pursue the matter more actively or to give it up entirely.

Line 5-6: This yin line is properly positioned at the center of the upper trigram Earth. Usually, this is the ruler's position, but in the Darkening of the Light era, 6-6 takes over this position, indicating that this foolish ruler has neither the proper status nor loyal followers.

The images represent the experiences of Viscount *Ji* in the era of Darkening the Light. Adhering to the rectitude of *Tao*, he succeeded in preserving the light in the Dark Age and proved that the practice of the rectitude is advantageous. This is the anecdotal reference on how Viscount *Ji* was able to escape the persecution of his nephew, the despotic ruler *Zhou* and the last king of *Shang* (later, called *Yin*), by hiding his brilliance and feigning insanity.

Divination Direction

It augurs ill. There are too many obstructions in your way for you to achieve your goal. Be creative and flexible in dealing with the obstructions. Be patient and go slowly.

Line 6-6: This yin line is properly positioned at the apex of the Darkening the Light hexagram as the directive lead line, taking over the ruler's status in the dark age.

The images signify that this is a foolish ruler lacking in virtues. First, he climbs to 'heaven' by becoming the ruler and casting the darkness of his power over the four corners of his feudal state (hurting many people), only to fall into the earth, or be driven to ruin by losing the *Tao* in his governance.

Divination Direction

It augurs ill. It is the time of declining fortune. It may appear that everything is going well, but before long you will find the situation deteriorating. The earlier you withdraw from it, the better it will be.

37. The Members of a Family 家人 (Kia Zan or Jiaren) Hexagram

Key attributes: Members of a family, the symbol of the family

Judgment

"For (the realization of what is taught in) *Kia Zan*, (or for the regulation of the family), what is most advantageous is that the wife be firm and correct." (James Legge, *The I Ching*, 136.)

Essence of Hexagram

This hexagram explains the principle of harmonious family life as the basis of harmonious society through the balanced exercise of roles and responsibilities by each family member.

Hexagram Image(s)

Fire burning upward to generate Wind stands for the images of the Members of a Family hexagram. What the hexagram images delineate, with the inner trigram Fire generating the outer trigram Wind, is the principle of education, which must first begin in the family before spreading its benefits to people outside of the family.

The wise and noble uses the images as his guide to communicate with sincere heart and mind and to conduct himself with consistency.

Hexagram Analysis

This hexagram consists of the lower trigram Fire (Light), which generates the upper trigram Wind. The Fire and Wind together symbolize the essential ingredients of a family: fire that generates warmth and the wind or breeze, the gentleness. Thus, this hexagram represents a harmonious family. The harmonious relationships are represented in the lines of the hexagram: 6-9 represents father with yang in the yin line, indicating strong leadership in the family; 1-9 represents son. The correlative relationship between 5-9 and 2-6 represents that of husband and wife. Sibling relationships are represented by 5-9 and 3-9 and by 4-6 and 2-6, with the younger siblings obedient to the older.

In dealing with family conflicts, two primary nuclear hexagrams, Water and Fire, symbolize a proper and balanced use of the opposite energies.

2-6 and 5-9 are the lead lines of the hexagram.

Interpretation of Judgment

In the family, it is most important and advantageous that the women practice the rectitude of *Tao*. The woman's proper place (2-6) is inside of the house, while man's (5-9) is outside of the house. Men and women should keep their proper places as expressed in the great principle of Heaven and Earth. The family has the strict regnant, who are called father and mother (5-9, 2-6). The *Tao* of the family is correctly observed when family members conduct themselves properly with mutual understanding. The father conducts himself properly as father, the son as son, the elder brother as elder brother, the younger brother as younger brother, the husband as husband and the wife as wife, and they influence each other through affection and in the appropriate manner. When the family is maintained properly, all the social relationships in the entire world will be in order.

Divination Direction

It augurs well for marriage, harmonious family life, and business transactions. It is not a proper time to launch an ambitious enterprise. Be content with the activities that help keep your family in harmony.

Individual Lines: Analysis, Interpretation, and Divination Direction

Line 1-9: This yang line is properly positioned at the beginning of the Family hexagram. The images signify that the family, or a child, is at its beginning stage in which strict family rules are established while the members are in the formative period. When order and controls are established from the beginning, family discords will be prevented later, and there will not be occasions for regret.

Divination Direction

Make careful and sincere efforts to develop your plan in the beginning so that you do not need to change your mind in the middle of the course.

Line 2-6: This yin line is properly positioned at the center of the lower trigram, correlating with 5-9.

The images signify that this virtuous wife does not deviate from her duty to stay at home and prepare meals or do other household tasks for the family. Being humble and compliant, she has the virtues of the Mean and serves as the unifying force in the family. She carries out the duties of a wife correctly, and the family will have good fortune.

Divination Direction

If you can successfully resist the temptations to try out what appears to be expedient and carry out your assignments faithfully, you will be successful.

Line 3-9: This yang line is properly positioned at the top of the lower trigram Fire. As the top line of the lower trigram, it represents the influence of the father who is so severe (not positioned at the center of the trigram) that he loses control of his temper, and the family feels that they are in the midst of a flame of fire.

The images signify that family members need correct discipline. This father governs his family too strictly, although it serves to maintain order in the family. It is desirable to balance severity (control) and laxity (freedom). However, if a father needs to choose between severity and laxity, the severity in discipline better serves maintaining family order than laxity that leads to weaken the order. If the wife and children overindulge in laughter and merriment resulting from the laxity, it can lead to disorder in the family, with remorseful results.

Divination Direction

You have a tendency to be either too harsh in dealing with other people, inviting their criticism, or overly timid in pursuing your goals, resulting in failure. You need to cultivate emotional moderation and stability, which will open up a smooth and auspicious road before you.

Line 4-6: This yin line is properly positioned as the beginning line of the upper trigram. This line represents the wife's influence in the house.

The images signify that the wife enriches family life by carrying out her duty to manage the family's internal affairs properly, complying with the principles of the Mean. There will be great good fortune.

Divination Direction

It augurs very well. You will succeed in attaining all of your goals (financial and career) as long as you are honest and faithful in your pursuits.

Line 5-9: This yang line is properly positioned at the center of the upper trigram Wind, correlating with 2-6. This line symbolizes the king of a state or the father in a family. Since this line is at the center, the virtues of the Mean temper the aggressive use of his authority with moderation.

The images signify that the king (father) extends his influence to bring harmony among the family members through mutual love and affection. There will be no worry, only good fortune.

Divination Direction

You will find it difficult to accomplish much alone. Other people will help you to attain your goal. Foster harmonious relationships among the people you deal with. It is to your advantage to engage in small family matters rather than in an ambitious enterprise.

Line 6-9: This yang line is improperly positioned at the top of the Members of a Family hexagram. The *Tao* of Family has reached its full maturity, or the final stage.

The images signify that this man manages his family with inspiring sincerity and constant self-reflection, so that he does not deviate from the correct practice of *Tao*. In the end, there will be good fortune.

Divination Direction

You have successfully attained your goal. Now is the time to evaluate if you need to establish a higher goal. Pursue your new goal with sincerity and self-discipline, and you will succeed.

38. The Division and Disunion 睽 (Khwei) Hexagram

Key attributes: Division and disunion, the symbol of opposition

Judgment

"*Khwei* indicates that (notwithstanding the condition of things which it denotes), in small matters there will (still) be good success." (James Legge, *The I Ching*, 139.)

Essence of Hexagram

This hexagram explains the principle of creating harmony through integration of differences among individuals, and yet allowing each to retain his individuality.

Hexagram Image(s)

Fire above Lake stands for the images of thc Division and Disunion hexagram. The wise and noble uses the images as his guide to act properly to bring about harmony among people by employing common denominators in their differences, yet allowing each to retain his individuality.

Hexagram Analysis

This hexagram consists of the lower trigram Lake from where water flows downward and the upper trigram Fire that burns upward. The lower trigram represents the youngest daughter and the upper trigram the second daughter. They belong to different trigrams, denoting that each has a different personality and is not able to get along with the other, although they are in the same family. (Except for 1-9, all the other lines are improperly positioned.) The contrasting characteristics of the two trigrams and the improperly positioned lines in the hexagram give this hexagram its name, "Division and Disunion." A further symbol of the lower trigram Lake is joy, and the upper trigram Light (Fire), brightness or civilization. Although both 2-9 and 5-6 are improperly positioned, they have correlative relationship as the lead lines, representing the main theme of this hexagram, which is "harmony out of disunion."

2-9 and 5-6 are the lead lines of this hexagram.

Interpretation of Judgment

The Division and Disunion hexagram denotes opposition, as characterized by the contrary movements of Fire and Lake: fire moves upward, while lake water moves downward. This opposition is seen in the two women who reside in the same family, each with different ideas. However, if each is virtuous, they can work together and have success in small things, one at a time.

The dynamics working in each trigram denote the principle of working together in spite of their opposite characteristics. The soft 5-6 in the center of the upper trigram can work closely (correlate) with 2-9 in the center of the lower trigram, as both cling to the bright virtues of the upper trigram Light with the joy of the lower trigram Lake. When contrasting virtues of yin and yang (5-6 and 2-9) respond to each other, the result is good fortune in many small matters that are achieved at a gradual pace.

When opposites are reconciled through their similarities in purpose, they become useful in achieving a task. This is shown in how Heaven and Earth, though opposite in nature (one yang, the other yin), work to accomplish the same objectives. Male and female, though different, share aspirations. The myriad of things in the universe, each unique and different, all function to carry out their assigned tasks naturally. What a matter of great importance it is to have the proper application of this principle!

Divination Direction

It augurs ill. You are likely to get involved in conflicting relationships with other people. You will face many obstacles in obtaining your goal. Try to maintain harmony among family members, and be courteous and understanding in dealing with other people to bring about a harmonious relationship. Your financial holdings are on a declining trend.

Individual Lines: Analysis, Interpretation, and Divination Direction

Line 1-9: This yang line is properly positioned at the beginning of the hexagram, antagonistically correlating with 4-9 that stands for the evil-minded man in this hexagram.

The images signify that this man conducts himself properly without using force to accomplish unity in the beginning stage of the Division and Disunion era. He has nothing to regret. Even if the one whom he trusts leaves him, like the horse that provides him transportation runs away, he will not use force to bring him back. The horse knows the master is friendly, and if it is left alone without chasing after it, it will return on its own. Likewise, even if he does not seek after the one who has left him, in due course of time, the man who left will regret having left and will return on his own. There is no need to use force to bring him back, as their trustful relationship will resolve the situation naturally. When the evil-minded person (4-9) requests a meeting, this virtuous man grants it in the spirit of generosity, but he is cautious not to make mistakes. By avoiding hostile confrontation in this communication, this virtuous man can escape blame that the evil-minded man may bring against him.

Divination Direction

You are having a hard time, and nothing seems to work for you. Someone may try to hurt you by putting you in a distressful situation. It will be to your advantage to conduct yourself in the spirit of accommodation, even with your opponent. Endure the hard time with patience and friendliness, for a better time will come.

Line 2-9: This yang line is improperly positioned at the center of the lower trigram, correlating with 5-6.

The images signify that unusual circumstances prevent this virtuous and competent man from meeting his lord (5-6) in the courtyard. He meets his lord casually on a byway without following official decorum. Not observing official decorum in order to accommodate the needs of the time of Division and Disunion will not be cause for blame because it is not due to the subject losing the *Tao*. What is more important in this time of Division and Disunion is to promote a mutually harmonious relationship between the ruler and the subject.

Divination Direction

Your greedy conduct will cause disputes with other people, and you will fail in your endeavor. Your efforts to work with others with sincerity and accommodation will bring you benefits.

Line 3-6: This improperly positioned yin line is sandwiched between two yang lines and correlates with 6-9. It is not able to form a beneficial relationship with 2-9, 4-9, or 6-9, as all of them are improperly positioned. This is especially true for 4-9, who is jealous of 3-6, because he is confused and thinks that 2-9 is pushing 3-6 to take over his (4-9) position.

The images signify that this man feels everyone is against him, as though the carriage he is riding is being pushed back downhill, and the oxen pulling it thrusts its horns upward, straining to correct the course and advance. This person's predicament is due to improperly placing himself in the position of power and his neighbors obstructing his advance. The misunderstanding he is faced with is likened to the case of an alleged criminal whose forehead was tattooed and his nose cut off, although he is not a criminal. Misfortune has befallen on him (improperly positioned) in the era of Division and Disunion, and he has to endure the suffering until the misunderstanding is resolved. His suffering will eventually end, and he will be able to restore his beneficial relationship with 6-9.

Divination Direction

Due to misunderstanding, you will encounter some obstructions in your efforts. It is not the proper time to initiate a new enterprise. If you already have, maintain your sincere and consistent efforts to overcome the difficulties.

Line 4-9: This yang line is improperly positioned, correlating with no line. He is close to 5-6, the ruler, but he fails to form a close relationship, as 5-6 has already established a correlative relationship with 2-9. Neither can he form a relationship with 3-6, which is correlating with 6-9. This man feels isolated and all alone. He reflects upon himself and repents for his insincere and arrogant conduct. He knows that 1-9 is a competent man of integrity, and he exerts special efforts to form a sincere, trustful relationship with him.

The images signify that isolation and separation create division and disunion. But strong desire with sincerity in his heart and good communication is powerful enough to overcome the barriers to form a mutually trusting relationship between the two independent-minded people. Such a union is precarious (1-9 and 4-9 correlate antagonistically), and continuous efforts to maintain the relationship will produce no error.

Divination Direction

Your friends are leaving you because you are selfish and obstinate. Make efforts to form a trusting relationship with other people through your cooperation and friendly attitude.

Line 5-6: This yin line is improperly positioned at the center of the upper trigram, correlating with 2-9.

The images signify that gentle virtue is the key to good relationships, and there is nothing to regret about this virtuous ruler's lack of power (yin in yang position). He has the competent relative (2-9) who will eventually recognize his sincerity and assist him. When the time comes, establishing an understanding relationship between the ruler and the relative is as easy and pleasing as biting through a piece of soft skin; it will result in blessings without error.

Divination Direction

Find an able and trustful person to help you weather the hard time you are in.

Line 6-9: This yang line is improperly positioned at the top of both the upper trigram Fire and the Division and Disunion hexagram. It correlates with 3-6, who is riding in the carriage. 6-9 mistakenly sees 3-6 as a pig covered with mud, as 6-9 has a suspicious mind toward others. When 6-9 and 3-6 achieve mutual understanding, all the suspicion that 6-9 has for 3-6 will be dispelled, as when yin and yang come together to produce rain.

The images signify that in the era of the Division and Disunion, the suspicions he harbored against the wrong person made him become isolated. In his mistaken, suspicious mind, his friend in the carriage (3-6) looked as filthy as a pig covered with mud and the carriage looked as if it were loaded with demons. He draws his bow and aims at the person in the carriage. (Division and Disunion has reached its climax.) Once he clears up his suspicions and realizes that this person is not his enemy, he establishes a mutually friendly relationship with this person over drinks. When a suspicious mind is cleared, tension is relieved. Like the harmonious union of yin and yang that produces rain, with all the suspicions gone, the trusting relationship between the two (6-9 and 3-6) develops to the point of a marriage between the two families; there will be good fortune.

Divination Direction

Your suspicious mind causes you to distrust people who have no intent to hurt you, leading you to lose friends. If you are having a hard time, examine yourself and open your mind so that you make yourself receptive to understanding and trusting other people. If you can do this, it will result in blessings.

39. The Inhibition 蹇 (Kien) Hexagram

Key attributes: Inhibition, obstruction, the symbol of difficulty

Judgment

"In (the state indicated by) *Kien* advantage will be found in the southwest, and the contrary in the north-east. It will be advantageous (also) to meet with the great man. (In these circumstances), with firmness and correctness, there will be good fortune." (James Legge, *The I Ching*, 141.)

Essence of Hexagram

This hexagram explains the principle of overcoming obstacles through clear-cut choice that conforms to *Tao,* to avoid or minimize a difficulty and to use adversity for self-cultivation.

Hexagram Image(s)

Water above Mountain stands for the images of the Inhibition hexagram and for the time of adversity with perils ahead. When the wise and noble meets an obstacle, he uses the images as his guide and withdraws and cultivates his virtues through self-reflection, like the way in which water flows down the mountain, meandering through the difficult but destined routes. Likewise, in the time of Inhibition, the wise and noble does not rush ahead recklessly to achieve his ambitions or blame others for the difficulties, but chooses the virtuous and proper course in making his moves.

Hexagram Analysis

This hexagram consists of the lower trigram Mountain that denotes halt and the upper trigram Water, peril. It explains the principles of proper conduct in the time of adversity. The act of halting in the time of peril is analogous to the person whose feet are crippled, making walking difficult. The lower trigram Mountain that represents the northeast in direction symbolizes rugged passage and difficulties, while the southwest direction that is represented by the trigram Earth symbolizes level ground and smooth passage. The major characteristic of this hexagram is that every line except the first line is properly positioned, denoting that a person with strong determination and wise choice of direction can overcome the obstacles. Hence, the state can be stabilized in an orderly way in the time of the Inhibition (adversity) if the ruler (5-9) practices the rectitude of *Tao*.

5-9 is the sole lead line of this hexagram.

Interpretation of Judgment

The Inhibition hexagram denotes adversity with perils ahead. Wisdom enables one to halt or withdraw in the face of danger to study the situation and prepare adequately to overcome the difficulty; such disciplined conduct is possible only by the wise. The southwest is level ground and represents safe and smooth passage. It is advantageous to choose such a route in the time of adversity by finding the right ruler who practices the constancy of the Mean (5-9). It is disadvantageous to take the northeast route that represents a difficult, rugged passage, where one (3-9) finds high mountains to be conquered and deep water to be crossed; in the end, the passage will be blocked. This is analogous to the practice of *Tao* being blocked. In the time of adversity, there is a definite advantage, even if one has to brave the perils with strong determination, to find a great man (5-9) for proper advice, which will be a meritorious achievement. If the ruler and those in high positions practice the rectitude of *Tao*, there will be good fortune, and the state will be governed properly. What a matter of great importance it is to have proper management in the time of Inhibition!

Divination Direction

It augurs ill. You are besieged with difficult problems that include death and health problems with no trustworthy person to ask for help. Take decisive action on business or financial dealings to minimize your loss, and beware of chicaneries and a romantic involvement. Though difficult, you must maintain your emotional stability to avoid mistakes caused by your rash actions. Proceed cautiously and take care of one thing at a time. If you maintain your sincerity and friendliness with other people, you will have a satisfying ending.

Individual Lines: Analysis, Interpretation, and Divination Direction

Line 1-6: This yin line is improperly positioned at the bottom of the Inhibition hexagram, correlating with no line.

The images signify that faced with obstacles, this weak person in the lowest status will face more difficulties if he makes a reckless move to achieve his goal. On the other hand, he will be rewarded if he retracts his planned move or stays put, waiting for a right moment to advance, which only the wise can do.

Divination Direction

You are struggling with one difficult problem after another. You must resist your strong urges to take some rash actions. Assess each situation carefully and weed out inappropriate actions before taking any action. You need patience to endure this difficult time and to wait it out until a more favorable time comes.

Line 2-6: This yin line is properly positioned at the center of the lower trigram, correlating with 5-9.

The images signify that one must face up to a difficulty and exert all the efforts he can muster to overcome it when this is called for in serving a higher cause. This virtuous minister of the king (5-9) is having a hard time. He is dealing with one knotty problem after another, serving the king with devotion and loyalty in the time of Inhibition, not seeking personal gains. The hard time may continue, but in the end, the king will recognize the minister's loyalty and will not place any blame on him.

Divination Direction

Your hard time still continues. Any obstacle or misunderstanding will disappear if you handle the situation with sincerity and devotion. You must have patience to endure it without taking any rash action to solve your problem.

Line 3-9: This yang line is properly positioned at the top of the lower trigram Mountain, correlating with 6-6, which is too weak to be of any help.

The images signify that, although this man is competent, he will suffer if he makes moves to face and overcome the perils. He must weigh this risk in view of his family responsibilities. The official in high status (6-6) is too weak to give him help for his advance in the time of Inhibition. He returns home to stay (lower trigram Mountain, halt) with his family. His family members (1-6 and 2-6) welcome him.

Divination Direction

The hard time is still continuing. The wise way to manage the continuing hard time is for you to foster harmonious relationships among your friends and subordinates for mutual cooperation and benefits.

Line 4-6: This yin line is properly positioned at the beginning of the upper trigram, correlating with no line.

The images signify that this virtuous prime minister will have more difficult problems if he initiates his project to solve the state problems by himself. It will be to his advantage if he holds back and seeks the cooperation of his competent subordinate (3-9) and wait for the right time to act.

Divination Direction

In this time of Inhibition, you begin to see a light at the end of the tunnel. However, you will not be able to survive the hard time alone; seek the help of those who have the resources to help you.

Line 5-9: This yang line is properly positioned at the center of the upper trigram Water, correlating with 2-6.

The images signify that in dealing with state affairs, the virtuous and competent ruler is mired with difficult problems in the time of Inhibition, which he must resolve. This ruler practices the virtues of the Mean with moral integrity. The friendly forces in his state (2-6, 3-9, and 4-6) will come to help him.

Divination Direction

Although you are in deep trouble, you are not completely helpless. You will be able to overcome it if you can get help from your friends. Do not go alone, but seek the help of your friends to solve your problem. Make consistent, sincere efforts to maintain your trustful relationship with other people.

Line 6-6: This yin line is properly positioned at the top of the hexagram Inhibition, correlating with 3-9. The time of adversity has reached its apex. This man is gentle and virtuous, but he needs competent assistants to manage the difficulties.

The images signify that this man will get in deeper trouble if he leaves the scene of perils to avoid them and save himself. The adverse time requires that he utilize his experience and obtain help from the one in the inner circle (3-9 in the inner trigram) to help the ruler (5-9) overcome the quagmire he is in. This is the venerable way of serving a great man (5-9) to overcome perils in the time of adversity.

Divination Direction

The hard time is about to end, although you are not completely out of the woods yet. You must be discreet in your conduct and seek advice of those you trust before you take an important action.

40. The Loosening 解 (Kieh) Hexagram

Key attributes: Loosening, the symbol of deliverance

Judgment

"In (the state indicated by) *Kieh* advantage will be found in the southwest. If no (further) operations be called for, there will be good fortune in coming back (to the old conditions). If some operations be called for, there will be good fortune in the early conducting of them." (James Legge, *The I Ching*, 144.)

Essence of Hexagram

This hexagram explains the principle of restoring one's normative living by eliminating the psychological problems of one's own making to resolve one's problems and being lenient and forgiving to others.

Hexagram Image(s)

Thunder above Water stands for the images of the Loosening hexagram, or the era of deliverance, which follows the era of Inhibition. The wise and noble uses the images as his guide to forgive people who commit misdemeanors and pardon criminals, and give them opportunities for rehabilitation, like the thunder and rain that come together to release the pent-up dismal atmosphere.

Hexagram Analysis

This hexagram consists of the lower trigram Water that denotes peril, and the upper trigram Thunder, movement. Movement in a perilous situation represents deliverance from the peril, or unraveling a complication, like the thunder in the spring that delivers rain, which melts frozen water. Each line of the hexagram represents the various steps in the deliverance or removal of the obstacles previously encountered.

Imagine that this hexagram started with two Earth trigrams. A yang line moves in to take a position in each trigram. A yang line takes the yin position at the bottom line of the upper trigram Earth, which represents the southwest direction, the multitude of people, and the position of the prime minister. When the yang line returns to the lower trigram, it takes the yin position at the center of the trigram. The upper trigram Water of the primary nuclear hexagram symbolizes meritorious achievement. Thunder in the sky (upper trigram) and rain below (lower trigram Water) symbolize the interaction, which activates all the plants and trees on the earth to grow and release their buds.

2-9 and 5-6 are the lead lines of this hexagram.

Interpretation of Judgment

The Loosening hexagram stands for movement (upper trigram Thunder) to bring deliverance from a peril (lower trigram Water). The enemy has been defeated, and the war is over. The perils and obstacles have been eliminated. It is the time for the ruler to focus on efforts to protect the well-being of the masses and for individuals to feel relaxed and free of tensions. The direction of the earth is southwest, and this symbolizes level and smooth passage, as in peacetime. The prime minister (4-9) administers the state affairs efficiently and gains the trust of the people in the state. Peace and stability are restored without worry about perils, as the competent and loyal (2-9) practices the virtues of the Mean. If there are any remaining perils (upper trigram Water of the primary nuclear hexagram), handling them speedily to restore the normal state of living will bring meritorious achievements. The deliverance is like the interactions between Heaven and Earth that bring thunder (upper trigram) and rain (lower trigram), which make grasses grow and trees sprout and produce fruits. What a matter of great importance it is to have proper management of the restorative principles in the time of Loosening!

Divination Direction

Following the long, drawn-out period of hardship, the good time has finally arrived. If you still have some unresolved problem, you must act quickly to find the cause and fix it; this is the best time to do this. Your financial situation is improving, and investments are on an uptrend. It augurs well for you to travel or move.

Individual Lines: Analysis, Interpretation, and Divination Direction

Line 1-6: This yin line is improperly positioned at the beginning of the Loosening hexagram, contiguous to 2-9 and correlating with 4-9.

The images signify that in the beginning of the deliverance era, this man is in respite and needs to prepare for a future move. Owing to his relationships with the virtuous 2-9 and the competent 4-9 who are men in higher positions, he can look forward without concern for blame.

Divination Direction

Your hardship is diminishing, but you are not completely out of the woods. Find out what is thwarting your progress, and get the help of those with the resources to help you eliminate the cause.

Line 2-9: This yang line is improperly positioned at the center of the lower trigram, correlating with 5-6. The three foxes in the text below refer to the three yin lines (1-6, 3-6, and 6-6) in the hexagram; they denote the unworthy elements in the state.

The images signify that this competent man who enjoys the full trust of the ruler (5-9) carries out the task of rounding up the unworthy people in the state, as if he were capturing three foxes in the spring hunting season using yellow arrows. The color yellow represents the center or the Mean, and the arrow represents the straight course, a metaphor for administering justice to the people fairly with devotion and rectitude. His virtues of rectitude will bring good fortune.

Divination Direction

It augurs well. The time has come for you to make an active move to attain your goal. Careful planning and prudent conduct will lead you to successful results.

Line 3-6: This yin line is improperly positioned at the top of the lower trigram, contiguous to 4-9, sandwiched between two yang lines and correlating with no line.

The images signify that ill prepared deliverance can be dangerous and cause problems. This man has neither the virtue of the Mean or the competence for the position. He ingratiates himself with the prime minister (4-9) to hold the high position for which he is not well qualified. His conduct is like that of a poor man who usually carries a heavy burden on his back. When his lot suddenly improves, he dares to ride in the carriage meant for high officials. His conduct does not fit his status and will result in attracting robbers to himself. If he is robbed, whom should he blame? He may insist that his conduct is correct, but there will be cause for regret.

Divination Direction

You tend to be arrogant and try to usurp the position for which you are not well qualified. Such inappropriate ambition will only lead you to frustrations and failures. Be humble and patient to be successful.

Line 4-9: This yang line is improperly positioned. It is contiguous to 3-6 and correlates with 1-6, who is in respite.

The images signify that this competent prime minister is befriending the flatterer (3-6). He should deliver himself from this man by cutting off the relationship, like removing the aching toe, although it is hard to do. (The aching toe refers to the unqualified person 3-6 occupying the high office.) Once the unsavory relationship is cut off, the prime minister will be able to have a mutually trusting relationship with the competent and virtuous friend (2-9).

Divination Direction

The emotional relationship you now enjoy is hampering your progress. Examine the relationship carefully and cut it off, in order to attain the goal that you value more than the relationship.

Line 5-6: This yin line is improperly positioned at the center of the upper trigram, correlating with 2-9.

The images signify that this virtuous ruler has competent and loyal subjects (2-9 and 4-9) who help him solve state problems by removing unworthy people. When the ruler is clear in his own mind with firm inner resolve, the petty man (3-6) will comprehend this resolve and resign from his unqualified position. Such resolve of the great man has an effect on the petty man's mind, and the petty man restores his faith and trust in the wise and noble.

Divination Direction

Assess your relationships and avoid the people who lack sincerity and trustworthiness. Listen to the advice of your trusted friends in your efforts to attain your goal, and you will be successful.

Line 6-6: This yin line is properly positioned at the top of both the Loosening hexagram and the upper trigram Thunder, denoting the zenith of movement for deliverance. This line represents the duke who bears the important responsibility of assuring peace and safety in the state. This line correlates antagonistically with 3-6. 3-6 is the powerful unworthy person in high position (referred to as the hawk), the foe of the state who is agile and dangerous like a hawk. 3-6 is at the top of the lower trigram and represents the hawk sitting on the top of a high wall.

The images signify that when use of force is necessary to bring about deliverance from wicked and hardened criminals, special preparations and clear objectives are required. At the zenith of the deliverance era, the duke successfully puts down the revolt against the state by 3-6 and protects the state and the ruler. His action is analogous to the duke who shoots (well prepared for action with adequate means) the hawk that is perched on the top of a high wall and successfully captures it. There is nothing disadvantageous in his action.

Divination Direction

You have an enemy who is trying to hurt you, and you must prevent him from succeeding. Maintain your virtuous integrity with sincere and persistent efforts, and you will be successful.

41. The Decrease 損 (Sun) Hexagram

Key attributes: Decrease, lessening, the symbol of diminution

Judgment

"In (what is denoted by) *Sun*, if there be sincerity (in him who employs it), there will be great good fortune: freedom from error; firmness and correctness that can be maintained; and advantage in every movement that shall be made. In what shall this (sincerity in the exercise of Sun) be employed? (Even) in sacrifice two baskets of grain, (though there be nothing else), may be presented." (James Legge, *The I Ching*, 146.)

Essence of Hexagram

This hexagram explains the principle of beneficial use of resources in the time of decrease. One example is to bring about the balance by taking from excess and adding to less, as illustrated by government taxation in tandem with the signs of the time of Decrease to bring the least suffering to the governed. Another example is to bring about the decrease in one's pretense and severe emotional outburst through cultivation of one's inner strength.

Hexagram Image(s)

Lake below Mountain stands for the images of the Decrease hexagram. The wise and noble uses the images as his guide to cultivate his virtues in conduct by restraining his anger and suppressing his greed, like the firmly standing mountain (virtue), although it is being eroded by lake water. Lake water evaporates and becomes rain and falls on the mountain to make vegetation grow.

Hexagram Analysis

This hexagram consists of the lower trigram Lake and the upper trigram Mountain. The deeper the lake, the higher the mountain. The active energy of lake water causes the passive mountain to lose its soil to the lake, which in turn is offset by the lake water through its evaporation, bringing rain to the mountain for the growth of its vegetation.

Yang denotes fullness or increase, and yin, emptiness or decrease. This hexagram is a derivative form of Hexagram #11 Peace, in which the lower trigram is full with three yang lines, and the upper trigram is empty with three yin lines. The Decrease hexagram is obtained by decreasing the top line (3-9) of the lower trigram of the Peace hexagram from a yang line to a yin line and replacing the top yin line (6-6) with the yang line. This replacement symbolizes losing lake water through evaporation and bringing rain to add vegetation to the mountain.

This hexagram has three lead lines; 3-6 and 6-9 as the directive and 5-6 as the structural.

Interpretation of Judgment

The Decrease hexagram portrays a decrease in the lower trigram and an increase in the upper trigram. The principle represented by the Decrease hexagram is to obtain a balance in benefits by reducing what is in excess and adding to what is lacking. In governing, it is to make fair and sincere efforts to bring the least amount of suffering to the people during a period of decrease in prosperity. As an example, when the government collects taxes from the people, it must exercise fairness and sincerity in order to bring the least suffering to the governed. When the taxation is done in this manner, it will result in fundamental good fortune for the governed and the state with no error. The one who maintains the rectitude of *Tao* and acts in accordance with this principle will have the advantage.

In the era of Decrease, this principle should be employed even in religious ceremonies. The offerings should be limited to only two bowls (the lower trigram Thunder of the primary nuclear hexagram represents a bowl) of grain in a plain container, instead of plentiful sacrificial offerings in large decorative containers that are made in the time of abundance. The integrity of sincerity in one's mind is more important than pretense and formality. The frugal religious ceremonial offering of two bowls of grain is being responsive to the signs of the diminution era, which demand that one take from the strong and add to the weak. This decrease and increase must take place in response to the needs of the time.

Divination Direction

It augurs your willing self-sacrifice, which will result to your advantage in the long run. In business, sincere and consistent efforts with a long-range goal will bring you good fortune. Act quickly in financial dealings, as a downtrend will begin before long. It is especially auspicious for marriage. Make efforts to maintain your good health.

Individual Lines: Analysis, Interpretation, and Divination Direction

Line 1-9: This yang line is properly positioned at the bottom of the hexagram and correlates with 4-6, the incompetent prime minister.

The images signify that this competent and unselfish man responds quickly to help his friend, the sick prime minister (4-6). There will be no error. He must provide help without bragging or calculating the benefit, once his own emergency is taken care of; in return, his friend in the higher status should carefully assess how much help he should accept without causing the helper undue harm. There should be a meeting of the minds between the two.

Divination Direction

To sacrifice yourself for a good cause is to increase your real value. You may get requests to help other people, at times at your own expense. Assess the situation and do it without hesitation, if it is for a good cause.

Line 2-9: This yang line is improperly positioned at the center of the lower trigram, correlating with 5-6, the ruler.

The images signify that one has to be able to help others without diminishing one's own dignity. This virtuous man should not make a move to help the ruler at this time, as such a move means diminishing his virtuous integrity if it is derived from his selfish motive. Instead, it will be beneficial if he can maintain the rectitude of the Mean, which will result in lasting benefit to the ruler. Misfortune will result if he moves away from the rectitude.

Divination Direction

It increases your real value if you always maintain your integrity, as you can use what you have for a right cause at the right time. Do not follow blindly what other people are doing. Maintain your proper position and avoid being drawn into temptations.

Line 3-6: This yin line is improperly positioned at the top of the lower trigram, correlating with 6-9. In the text below, this line is referred to as one man, and the three lines of the lower trigram as three men. This line explains the principle of fostering harmonious relationships among people.

The images signify that a good, harmonious result can be obtained best between two people. Three or more people can bring up too many different opinions and upset the balance of energy working among them, causing disharmony in achieving a goal. It is likened to three men traveling together. One of them is separated because his opinion (3-6) is different (yin line) from the other two (yang lines). The two who have similar opinions will pair off and exclude the other because the difference creates suspicion between them. If 3-6 travels alone, he has a strong need for a companion. He will find a friend (6-9); although both men are improperly positioned, they share common understanding and friendship.

Divination Direction

It is the time to implement your plans. Concentrate all your efforts on a single goal without being distracted by too many things and opinions. If you try to do too many things at the same time, you cannot succeed even in one. Establish your priority and concentrate your efforts on one thing at a time.

Line 4-6: This yin line is properly positioned, sandwiched between two yin lines, and correlates with 1-9.

The images signify that, in order for the prime minister to diminish the suffering from his ailments (defects in the mind, which he acknowledges), he must seek help. The prime minister's ailments symbolize not only his own weakness and incompetence, but also those of the ruler above him and those of his subordinate. To remedy the situation, he must act quickly to invite the help of the strong and competent 1-9. His acknowledgment and quick action will bring him happiness; it is better not to have an ailment to begin with, but a quick recovery will be the cause for happiness.

Divination Direction

The correction begins with admission of a defect. You must first acknowledge that you have a problem and act quickly to get help. If you vacillate, you will lose the opportunity for success.

Line 5-6: This yin line is improperly positioned, correlating with 2-9. The "ten groupings of tortoises" in the text below refers to the ancient practice of turtle divination. In ancient China, shells were used for money; ten groupings of tortoises equaled one hundred shells, making turtle divination using the ten groupings very expensive.

The images signify that good fortune from Heaven never fails in its delivery. In the era of the Decrease hexagram, this ruler practices the virtues of the Mean and is receptive to the help from every competent subject (2-9, 6-9) who is happy and willing to serve the ruler. The ruler's benefits are so assured (his good fortune is predestined) that there is no need to resort to the expensive turtle divination that costs as much as ten groupings of tortoises to find this out. There will be fundamental good fortune blessed by Heaven (the tortoise is an earthly creature used in divination, representing Heaven).

Divination Direction

It augurs very well. Humility is a way of opening oneself to receive blessings of Heaven and Earth. Because of your humble and friendly attitude, you will receive help from many people, some unexpected.

Line 6-9: This yang line is improperly positioned at the top of the Decrease hexagram, contiguous to 5-6 and correlating with 3-6. So far, the diminishing of the lower trigram has brought about the increase of the upper trigram. The time has now come for this official to help others who need help for an increase in blessings (benefits). The era of Decrease is about to turn into the era of Increase.

The images signify that there are ways to share benefits for the good of all. This competent high official brings benefits to the ruler (5-6) and his subjects without diminishing his virtuous prestige. He (6-9) received the largest increase in benefits, and his great aspiration is to enrich the governed through good administration. The time is right for him to go ahead to achieve his goal, as he will get the help of the loyal minister (3-6) who is willing to forego increasing his family wealth and serve for the benefit of other people in the state who need help. In this way, the interest of both the government and the families in the state can come together for mutual benefits. If the high officials can maintain the rectitude of *Tao*, there will be good fortune.

Divination Direction

It augurs well. Your long suffering from the adverse situation will end soon, and you will succeed in attaining your goal, not only for your own benefit but also helping others. Maintain your conscientious course of action to the end.

42. The Increase 益 (Yi) Hexagram

Key attributes: Increase, the symbol of addition

Judgment

"*Yi* indicates that (in the state, which it denotes) there will be advantage in every movement which shall be undertaken, that it will be advantageous (even) to cross the great stream." (James Legge, *The I Ching*, 149.)

Essence of Hexagram

This hexagram explains the principle of realizing increased benefits through sharing, the stronger aiding the weak by sharing resources, which will bring about an increase in one's virtues and advance mutual collaboration for great achievement.

Hexagram Image(s)

Wind above Thunder stands for the images of the Increase hexagram. The wise and noble uses the images as his guide to increase his virtues by changing to the good swiftly like the wind when he sees it in others and by correcting his errors with great strength and determination like thunder.

Hexagram Analysis

This hexagram is the capsized form of Hexagram #41 Decrease. It consists of the lower trigram Thunder that denotes wood as well as movement, and the upper trigram Wind, also representing wood as well as compliance. This hexagram is a derivative form of Hexagram #12 Retrogression. While Hexagram #41 represents the principles of taxation in which the governed (lower trigram) decrease their resources to help the ruler (upper trigram), hexagram #42 explains the principle of increasing the wealth of the governed by the ruler. The Increase hexagram symbolizes this by replacing the bottom yang line of the upper trigram (government) of hexagram #12 with the bottom yin line of the lower trigram (the governed). Wind and Thunder are synergistic; when the wind blows harder, it carries the sound of thunder further; when thunder roars louder, it stirs up the wind more turbulently. Thus, they mutually reinforce each other. Both wind and thunder represent wood, symbolizing here the boat and oar that are used in crossing the perilous great river.

There are four lead lines in this hexagram: 1-9 and 4-6, directive; 2-6 and 5-9, structural.

Interpretation of Judgment

The Increase hexagram represents enrichment of the governed. It is the proper time to go ahead to achieve great goals for the state. The ruler in the upper trigram shares his wealth for the benefit of the people under his rule, and the joy of the people is boundless. Such an act of benevolence from above for the people below is the great and glorious *Tao*. Both the ruler (5-9) and the people (lower trigram, especially 2-6) enjoy the harmonious relationship and the blessings of happiness that come from practicing the virtues of the Mean.

It is the advantageous time to undertake ambitious enterprises even though there are dangers, like crossing the great river utilizing the aid of a boat and oar. When the ruler acts to increase the wealth of the governed, the people will see daily progress in their benefits. It is like Heaven that sets in motion such things as the four seasons, rain and wind, and Earth that begets a myriad of things, resulting in limitless benefits for the people. The principle of the Increase hexagram should be implemented in accordance with the needs of the time.

Divination Direction

It augurs well, especially for marriage, farming, construction and other business operations, and legal matters. Now is the time for you to pursue your goal. If you come across hurdles along the way, take advantage of the available resources to overcome them. Guard against a physical injury.

Individual Lines: Analysis, Interpretation, and Divination Direction

Line 1-9: This yang line is properly positioned at the beginning of this hexagram, correlating with 4-6.

The images signify that he has the advantage if he undertakes important work. Although he is low in status, he will have fundamental good fortune because he receives the help of the high official (4-6), and he maintains a humble attitude and does not overrate what he is doing, even though it is important. There will be no error.

Divination Direction

It augurs well. Your problems are about to be solved. Concentrate your efforts in areas with which you are familiar. You will have many opportunities to expand what you are doing and to achieve your goal.

Line 2-6: This yin line is properly positioned at the center of the lower trigram, correlating with 5-9. Since this hexagram is the capsized form of the preceding Decrease hexagram (hexagram #41), this line is similar to 5-6 of the preceding hexagram.

The images signify that this man practices the virtues of the Mean with an uncluttered state of mind and accepts other people as they are. He enjoys an increase in benefits coming from Heaven (5-9) or an unexpected source (unexpected because 1-9 came from 4-9 of the outer trigram of Hexagram #12 Stagnation). Because of his virtues, his blessings of increase are so well assured that even the expensive divination with ten groupings of turtle shells will not be able to deny it. (Refer to the comments on Line 5-9 of hexagram #41.)

As long as he stays on the rectitude of *Tao*, he will be blessed. It is the kind of virtuous mind-set that the king should practice when he makes offerings to god; there will be good fortune.

Divination Direction

It augurs well. Keep your mind humble and open. Many will cooperate with you in your endeavor. With sincerity and persistence, continue your good efforts, and you will succeed.

Line 3-6: This yin line is improperly positioned at the top of the lower trigram, correlating with 6-9. Improperly positioned in this precarious position, with greed as the motive and correlating with 6-9, there will be no benefit of Increase coming from above.

The images signify that at times a difficult situation or misfortune hides good fortune in it. In the era of Increase, this person does not receive any benefit of Increase from above. He has to accept his unfortunate situation that is derived from his position and make efforts to increase his benefits working through his hardship. The wealth accumulated in this way may lead him to indolence or cause suspicion in people's minds. He should use his increased wealth to help those who are in need, demonstrating his credibility and trustworthiness. He can then report to the duke in all sincerity; this is like presenting a jade object[32] as proof of sincerity.

Divination Direction

Your success needs more than your own efforts. Goodwill comes from your appreciation of help from others. Otherwise, you will experience an unexpected misfortune. Sincere and persistent efforts to remedy your mind-set will lead you to better days.

Line 4-6: This yin line is properly positioned, contiguous to 5-9 and correlating with 1-9. This prime minister is loyal to the ruler and has a sincere desire to bring Increase to the governed. He is worthy to be called one with the virtues of the Mean.

The images signify that the one who mediates distribution of benefits should be fair and reliable. This prime minister who practices the virtues of the Mean advises the ruler about his resolve to bring Increase to the governed, and his recommendations are accepted. This man is so reliable and his recommendations are so beneficial that an important decision such as moving the state capital (state capitals were frequently relocated in ancient China) can be entrusted to him.

Divination Direction

It is the time to put ideas into action. You will get favorable recognition of your superiors and a promotion to a higher position. You will have some changes in your life, such as a move to a new place or a change of job.

Line 5-9: This line is properly positioned at the center of the upper trigram, correlating with 2-6.

The images signify that kind, benevolent hearts bring their own rewards of good fortune. This ruler has a sincere and benevolent heart, and in the era of Increase, he implements his policies of sharing his wealth with the governed. His subjects will appreciate his benevolent virtues as he attains this ambitious goal. Without question, there will be fundamental good fortune.

Divination Direction

It augurs very well. Your sincere efforts will bring an abundant pay-off. Many will cooperate with you in your efforts. It is the proper time for you to seek an important achievement.

Line 6-9: This yang line is improperly positioned at the top of the Increase hexagram, correlating with 3-6. It is a greedy official, the one who has taken over the yin position improperly at the final stage of the Increase era. He reveals his insatiable desire to promote his own ambitions, contrary to the *Tao* in the time of Increase, which is to share the wealth of those in the ruling class (upper trigram) with the ruled under them (lower trigram).

The images signify that this high-ranking official is so prejudiced and self-serving that he does not care about bringing any benefit to others. Some will seek to assail him for his lack of virtuous consistency in his mind and heart. There will be misfortune.

Divination Direction

It augurs ill. Your greedy and self-serving attitude will make many resent you. You need to reflect upon yourself and correct your shortcomings.

43. The Breakthrough 夬 (Kwai) Hexagram

Key attributes: Breakthrough, the symbol of resoluteness

Judgment

"*Kwai* requires (in him who would fulfill its meaning) the exhibition (of the culprit's guilt) in the royal court, and a sincere and earnest appeal (for sympathy and support), with a consciousness of the peril (involved in cutting off the criminal). He should (also) make announcement in his own city, and show that it will not be well to have recourse at once to arms. (In this way) there will be advantage in whatever he shall go forward to." (James Legge, *The I Ching*, 151.)

Essence of Hexagram

This hexagram explains the principle of overcoming a barrier (an evil force) through careful planning with cooperative forces, continuous self-examination, and resolute determination.

Hexagram Image(s)

Lake above Heaven stands for the images of the Breakthrough (Resolution) hexagram. The wise and noble uses the images as his guide for resolute exercise of his virtues in dispensing blessings (remuneration) to those under him. His conduct is like water vapor from the lake that rises up to the sky to bring rain to nourish those below, and he refrains from being stagnated in continuing with his renewal of virtuous deeds.

Hexagram Analysis

This hexagram consists of the lower trigram Heaven that denotes the *Tao*, or the wise and noble, and the upper trigram Lake, joy. The yin line at the top symbolizes the petty official (evil force) who gives bad advice to the ruler with "sweet" words (trigram Lake represents mouth). The five yang lines under the yin line represent the wise and noble in the state whose combined force will eliminate the evil and dangerous one (6-6). In the lunar calendar, this hexagram stands for the month of March when the last remnant of wintry dampness (6-6) is about to be taken over completely (breakthrough) by the force of light (yang) moving into the month of April, when all six lines are yang (hexagram # 1).

This hexagram has three lead lines; 6-6 as directive, and 5-9 and 2-9 as structural.

Interpretation of Judgment

The Breakthrough hexagram refers to the change resulting from the resolute action taken by the positive force to eliminate the negative force, which makes the wise and noble man joyous (upper trigram Lake). He must openly discredit the petty, evil man by disclosing his evil ways to the people in the royal courtyard and making a sincere appeal to invite his many officials and followers (five yang lines) to support the good cause. This undertaking is perilous, but if it is executed with care, keeping the danger in mind, he will reap the glory of victory. Before taking the action, he must assure the people in his city (himself and the people who follow him) how reluctant he is to use force against the evil man and his followers, for such an action will obstruct virtue by raising hatred among the people and bringing harm to everyone. The time has come for the positive force (five yang lines) to advance to successfully achieve its goal.

Divination Direction

You are in a strong position but not for long, especially if you have a stubborn character; many troubles will plague you, some unexpected. Be prudent in every move, and avoid the folly of swimming against the current of the time. The pending litigation for a justifiable cause will result in your favor.

Individual Lines: Analysis, Interpretation, and Divination Direction

Line 1-9: This yang line is properly positioned at the beginning of the hexagram, correlating with no line.

The images signify that a beginning is difficult but important, as it sets the stage for ensuing outcomes. Being overconfident of the strength shown in his toes (the lowest line and the toes symbolize the beginning of advancing), he ventured forth to get rid of the evil man (6-6) and failed. He will incur blame for the error of his premature venture that resulted in his defeat.

Divination Direction

Do not take a rash action out of overconfidence in your ability. Before taking any important action, first examine if your plans are accurate and timely.

Line 2-9: This yang line is improperly positioned at the center of the lower trigram, correlating with no line, and represents mouth.

The images signify that readiness prevents worries and distress, even when there is a cry of alarm against a surprise armed attack at night by 6-6. If he is attacked, he does not need to worry, as he practices the virtues of the Mean and has already prepared well for it.

Divination Direction

It is not the right time for you to implement your plan. Careful planning and preparation is as important as your ability to attain your goal. Discuss your plan with your friend who has experience and knowledge. When all is done, you will succeed.

Line 3-9: This yang line is properly positioned at the top of the lower trigram, correlating with 6-6.

The images signify that a special situation creates unique difficulties. This noble man's strength and vigor are reflected in his cheekbones (a sign of strong determination and readiness for action). Even so, if he engages in a rash action, it will result in misfortune, since he cannot succeed alone, even if he has a resolute determination to remove the evil man. Among all the wise and noble, this man is the only one who has a mutual relationship with the evil man (3-9 correlates with 6-6). This could arouse a little suspicion and invoke ire among his comrades, as if he gets slightly wet while walking alone in the rain. In the end, his comrades will come to appreciate his sincerity, and he will incur no blame.

Divination Direction

Some may disagree with you, making you feel angry, but keep in mind you need their cooperation in order to attain your goal. You may encounter some initial obstacles, but try not to antagonize them and keep up with your unobtrusive planning and preparation for the opportunity to attain your goals.

Line 4-9: This yang line is improperly positioned at the beginning of the upper trigram, correlating with no line.

The images signify that this stubborn man is restless, like a person who has no skin on his buttocks. He walks with difficulty because of the pain, and he does not know what to do with his urge to advance. This is because he occupies the improper position, away from the virtues of the Mean. If he allows himself to be led like sheep by his comrades, there will be no regret. However, he does not trust the advice of his comrades, as his obstinacy prevents him from hearing it.

Divination Direction

You cannot make up your mind and vacillate, creating a predicament. Keep in mind that you need the help of someone who can look at your situation objectively and advise you on a direction. Cultivate your ability to accept the advice of a trustworthy friend, and act decisively once you have worked out your plan carefully.

Line 5-9: This yang line is properly positioned at the center of the upper trigram.

The images signify that the ruler must take a resolute action to cut off the unsavory influence of his advisor (6-6), like uprooting a purslane to kill it for certainty. (The purslane is a weed with tender leaves and deep roots that grows in the shade and is hard to kill.) He does this without resorting to the use of armed force, but by pursuing the course of the Mean. This is an appropriate measure with no blame, but it is short of earning him glorious merit because it would have been better if he had not associated with such an evil-minded man to begin with.

Divination Direction

The disciplined mind can tell what is worth paying for. Cultivate insight into your personality so that you are not easily persuaded by sweet words that lead you in the wrong direction. Set up your priorities and exert your efforts to attain the most important priority, even at the sacrifice of other priorities.

Line 6-6: This yin line is properly positioned at the top of the Breakthrough hexagram, correlating with 3-9. This line represents the petty man whom everyone is determined to remove from his position.

The images signify that there is no one for this evil man to turn to for help. Before long the petty man will be removed from his position. However, if one neglects to guard against the evil force regaining its foothold, there will be misfortune.

Divination Direction

It augurs an extremely ill fortune. You are in despair, for nothing is working in your favor. The sooner you give up your current undertaking, the better it will be.

44. The Meeting 姤 (Kau) Hexagram

Key attributes: Meeting, intercourse, the symbol of coming to meet

Judgment

"*Kau* shows a female who is bold and strong. It will not be good to marry (such) a female." (James Legge, *The I Ching*, 154.)

Essence of Hexagram

This hexagram explains the principle of bringing forces together to successfully encounter a challenge.

Hexagram Image(s)

Wind blowing below Heaven stands for the images of the Meeting hexagram. The wise ruler uses the images as his guide in implementing the principles of good governing by informing and educating his subjects throughout the nation about government policies, and thereby eliminating the negative elements in the state, like the wind that spreads heavenly commands widely.

Note: This hexagram presents the image of wind blowing below heaven, while in Hexagram #20 Observation, the wind is blowing above earth. Both are related to the ruler's governing of the state. In hexagram #20 the ruler governs by gaining understanding of the people's plight through his tour and observation. In this hexagram the ruler governs by issuing edicts to bring improvements in the state, based on understanding he has gained through his tour and observation.

Hexagram Analysis

This hexagram consists of the lower trigram Wind that denotes the eldest daughter and the upper trigram Heaven, man. (There are three men in the upper trigram.) The eldest daughter in the hexagram represents the woman who appears on the scene forcefully and boldly takes on the five men to win them over to her way, creating conflicts among the men.

In April, the yang force reached its apex with all six lines as yang. In May, a yin line forces itself to occupy the bottom line and forms Hexagram #44 Meeting, establishing a base for the progressive advance of yin in the succeeding months. (This is the month of the summer solstice when the dark force or yin begins its ascendance.) The bottom yin line represents a negative force (petty man) returning to the scene to advance.

The meeting of the yang force (light) with the yin force (darkness) upsets the status quo because it symbolizes the wise and noble (yang) encountering the petty man's (yin) advance. Unless the yin force is checked, it will drive all the wise and noble out of power (government).

This hexagram has three lead lines: 1-6, directive, and 5-9 and 2-9, structural.

Interpretation of Judgment

The Meeting hexagram symbolizes the bold woman (with an unsavory hidden motive) who encounters men, or the yin force (petty man) who encounters the yang force (great man). This woman will not be able to maintain harmony in the family. It is not favorable to marry such a woman, for the marriage will not last long. There are more auspicious encounters, like the meeting of Heaven and Earth, through which myriad things in different categories exhibit their attributes. When the yang force occupies the center position (5-9) properly, or the great and noble rules the state through the practice of the Mean, great transformation will take place in the whole world. The concept represented by the Meeting hexagram as to who meets whom, when they meet, for what purpose, and how open they are, is indeed important and great!

Divination Direction

You will unexpectedly encounter personal or business problems, especially in marital affairs. Be patient and wait calmly for a better time.

Individual Lines: Analysis, Interpretation, and Divination Direction

Line 1-6: This yin line is improperly positioned at the beginning of the hexagram, contiguous to 2-9, and correlating with 4-9. The contiguous 2-9, which is one of the structural lead lines, plays a major role to restrain the forceful advance of 1-6, like the metal (sturdy) drag (2-9) that is fastened to a wagon (1-6) to check it from moving.

The images signify that the attempt by the petty man (1-6) to advance must be stopped at once, like a wagon that is fastened to a metal drag (2-9). The petty man wants to take advantage of his relationship with the high official (4-9) and tries to take over the higher positions one by one, filling them with petty men like him. It is a mistake to underestimate the petty man's move at this beginning stage, and 2-9, who is stronger, higher in status, and closest to him, should restrain him. Because of the great restraint, if the petty man stays on the correct course of *Tao* (the natural way), it will result in good fortune. On the other hand, if he is left alone to advance, he will bring misfortune. It is like the misguided situation of a lean sow, which is left alone to gambol and grows up to become wild.

Divination Direction

It augurs ill. You are at the mercy of your impatience that will lead to knotty problems that you are not prepared to deal with. Exercise extreme caution, and do not undertake anything that is not familiar to you, or you will fail.

Line 2-9: This yang line is improperly positioned at the center of the lower trigram as the structural lead line, contiguous to 1-6.

The images signify that the noble man (2-9) restrains the petty man (1-6) from unmerited advance. (Here 1-6 is characterized as fish to represent the weak, smelly character of a petty man.) It is like keeping the fish wrapped, instead of serving it to the guests (4-9), or preventing the lecherous influence of the petty man from reaching the guests (good people). There will be no blame for his action, as one should not feed his guests rotten fish or allow the petty man to exert bad influence over the guests.

Divination Direction

Refrain from associating with a shady character that may trick you into a disaster. Act prudently, especially in dealing with a stranger. Your decisive action to correct your mistakes will bring a favorable result.

Line 3-9: This yang line is properly positioned at the top of the lower trigram, correlating with no line.

The images signify that this man is hesitant in taking an action, as he is tempted to fall into the overture coming from the petty man but cannot meet him. He is acting like the one without any skin on his buttocks; this condition causes pain and makes him falter when he walks. Thus, he is restrained from his desire to advance. He finds out that the noble man (2-9) has already taken decisive action to restrain the petty man, even though the higher authority (4-9) has a mutual relationship with the petty man. His vacillation prevents him from creating a risky situation, and he will incur no great blame for his hesitation.

Divination Direction

You feel uncertain in your predicament. It is not the proper time to initiate any major undertaking. Buy time until you become more self-assured before you initiate a major move.

Line 4-9: This yang line is improperly positioned, correlating with 1-6.

The images signify that everything can become useful at times, and it is wrong to completely isolate even petty men, like the fish in the package kept out of sight. It is like a high official who is out of touch with the people he governs. When he needs them, they are no longer available to him; he finds they are under the firm control of someone else (2-9).

Divination Direction

You will get unexpected interference in your business. It is not a proper time for you to initiate a major undertaking, especially one that requires cooperation with other people. Evaluate your situation and carry out your tasks one at a time.

Line 5-9: This yang line is properly positioned at the center of the upper trigram, correlating with no line. Here, 5-9 represents a medlar tree that has large leaves and grows tall and upright, and 1-6 represents the gourds of the vine that climbs up the medlar tree, which get obscured by the large leaves of the tree. It is a metaphor that portrays how the virtuous conceals his power and brilliance and deals with the petty man's advance with toleration and protectiveness.

The images signify that the virtuous man brings the petty man under control with tolerance and protection, like the leaves of medlar tree that cover the gourds. The ruler (5-9) hides his brilliance, practicing the correct virtues of the Mean. Like the gourd that ripens and falls to the ground naturally of its own weight, the ascendancy cycle of the petty man will end, and he will fall when the cycle reaches its apex. The virtuous maintains his constancy of virtue, like the medlar tree, and he uses his heavenly mandate to intervene at the right time, not rushing prematurely before the matter reaches the natural state for its resolution.

Divination Direction

Someone is obstructing you from being successful. Avoid confrontation, and concentrate on your efforts to overcome the difficulties with sincerity and persistence.

Line 6-9: This yang line is improperly positioned at the top of the hexagram, correlating with no line. This yang line represents the tip of a horn that looks aggressive and poses a menace to others.

The images signify that this official who has retired from his high office counters the petty man's ascendancy brusquely in an arrogant and menacing manner, like an animal that threatens with its horns. As an official who has retired from important responsibilities at the height of the Meeting era, he will incur some resentment for his attitude, but there will be no grave consequence to anyone, and he will receive little blame.

Divination Direction

Examine your attitude in relating with other people. Cultivate a moderate and friendly attitude to improve your relationships.

45. The Gathering-together 萃 (Zhui) Hexagram

Key attributes: Gathering together, the symbol of collection

Judgment

"In (the state denoted by) *Zhui*, the king will repair to his ancestral temple. It will be advantageous (also) to meet with the great man; and then there will be progress and success, though the advantage must come through firm correctness. The use of great victims will conduce to good fortune; and in whatever direction movement is made, it will be advantageous." (James Legge, *The I Ching*, 156.)

Essence of Hexagram

This hexagram explains the principle of successful leadership, bringing positive forces together to achieve virtuous objectives.

Hexagram Image(s)

Lake above Earth stands for the images of the Gathering-together hexagram. The wise and noble uses the images as his guide in bringing his resources together to prepare for an emergency that may arise when a large number of people gather together. He may get his weapons ready for unexpected attacks, or prepare for a disaster when the accumulated lake water breaks loose.

Hexagram Analysis

Two hexagrams, Hexagram #8 Union and the Getting-together (Gathering) hexagram, have similar images of water above the earth. This hexagram presents stronger images of the symbol of collection, with the Lake trigram having two yang lines above the earth, as contrasted to the Union hexagram with the Water trigram that has only one yang line above the earth.

This hexagram consists of the lower trigram Earth that denotes compliance and the upper trigram Lake, joy. The hexagram symbolizes the ruler (5-9) in the upper trigram who gains the loyalty (compliance) of the people (lower trigram), and they in turn follow the ruler joyfully (upper trigram). It presents the image of everyone in the state gathering together for a celebration. Lake above Earth denotes the gathering of lake water; the two yang lines represent the leadership which brings about the gathering together of the people, surrounded by four yin lines which portray the crowd that is gathering. The ruler (5-9) in the upper trigram correlates with the common folk (2-6), and in similar fashion, the high official (4-9) correlates with the people in lower status (1-6).

5-9 is the sole lead line of this hexagram.

Interpretation of Judgment

The Gathering-together hexagram indicates that when everyone comes together (the gathering of family members, clan members, and positive energies symbolize a harmonious union), the affairs of the state run smoothly, and the state is preserved. The ruler is competent and practices the virtues of the Mean, and the people come together and respond compliantly and joyfully to his rule. In this peaceful atmosphere, the sovereign goes to his ancestral temple to worship the souls of his ancestors with his deep respect of filial piety, thus reinforcing perpetuation of the gathering together.

"It will be advantageous (also) to meet with the great man" in the judgment text means that such a joyful gathering happens only when the ruler governs in compliance with the correct *Tao*. The ruler must provide the leadership that will produce a collective moral force in the state that brings people's minds together; this is best brought about through religious practice. It will conduce good fortune if the ruler offers large sacrificial offerings to his ancestral souls in his worship ceremony. It is the advantageous time to proceed to attain his goals, as he complies with the heavenly commands. By observing and understanding various gatherings of people and myriads of other things in nature and classifying them, one can come to understand how nature works through the myriads of things in the heaven and on the earth.

Divination Direction

It augurs very well. The time has come for you to proceed to attain your goal, as long as your intention is sound and your actions will not hurt other people. It is especially auspicious for financial dealings and marital relationships.

Individual Lines: Analysis, Interpretation, and Divination Direction

Line 1-6: This yin line is improperly positioned at the bottom of the hexagram, correlating with 4-9, symbolizing the disorder and confusion in the beginning stage of a gathering.

The images signify that people need good leadership for a gathering, but it is no easy task to identify a correct leader. This petty man has a sincere desire to relate to the high official (4-9), but he fails to carry it through to fruition. There are petty men of his kind nearby (two yin lines above), and he is torn between the gathering with the high official and the petty men. He ends up joining the petty men's gathering because he is confused. If the leader can help him clear up his confusion and responds to his call for help with a handclasp, he will follow the leader joyfully. Even if the high official rejects his request, he should not worry, for such a request would incur no blame.

Divination Direction

You are uncertain about which way to go, and you vacillate in taking action. First assess the situation without a bias and follow the direction of the leader with whom you have a trustful relationship.

Line 2-6: This yin line is properly positioned at the center of the lower trigram, correlating with 5-9.

The images signify that this virtuous man brings the like-minded people together to serve the correct leader with sincerity and loyalty, which will bring good fortune with no error. When there is sincerity in his heart, the frugal offerings that this man is making to his ancestral souls, like the meager offering in the spring season which is the lean time of the year, will be acceptable because the souls will appreciate his sincere dedication more than any offering.

Divination Direction

Your situation will improve in time. Someone in a higher position will help you to get a promotion. Pursue your goal with sincerity and persistence, and you will succeed.

Line 3-6: This yin line is improperly positioned at the top of the lower trigram, contiguous to 4-9, and it has an antagonistic relationship with 6-6. He is left out from the association of other men (1-6 and 2-6) of his kind.

The images signify that this man wishes a union with others of his kind but feels left out from the group (1-6 and 2-6). His union with 4-9 is not proper because both are improperly positioned. He grieves because he is unable to find anyone with whom he can form a union. He decides to seek union with 6-6, who is properly positioned close to the center of the upper trigram, even though there is no correlative relationship. His request is granted, and his desire is fulfilled. There is no error in his approach, only a slight humiliation in the beginning.

Divination Direction

You are having a difficult time, as you do not know whom to turn to for help. Keep up your sincere and persistent efforts toward your goal; eventually, you will overcome the difficulties and succeed.

Line 4-9: This yang line is improperly positioned and correlates with 1-6. Despite its improper positioning, this prime minister has the ability to assist the ruler (5-9) selflessly because he has strength and popularity among the people (three yin lines under him) in the era of Gathering together.

The images signify that he will have great good fortune without incurring any blame for his improper position because he has the ability to bring together the people under him with no selfish motive but only to serve the ruler.

Divination Direction

It augurs well. You enjoy good relationships with people and provide good leadership. However, there is the danger that you may become the target of envy and jealousy.

Line 5-9: This yang is the lead line and is properly positioned at the center of the upper trigram, correlating with 2-6.

The images signify that a high position is not good enough for good leadership. Among the people who gather around him, there are some that do so because of his position and power, not out of loyalty and confidence in the leadership. In order for a leader to reach the level of brilliance in leadership, he must observe the fundamental virtues of *Tao* and firmly maintain the rectitude through his great benevolence; regret will then disappear.

Divination Direction

Your status or wealth is not all that it appears to be. You may be holding an empty bag, while the other person is enjoying the contents. Be practical in your endeavor. Sincere and persistent efforts will lead you to be successful.

Line 6-6: This yin line is properly positioned at the top of the hexagram, correlating with no line.

The images signify that one in a leadership position must have an unselfish motive for the good of all in the gathering. This man wails and weeps because his good motive is misunderstood, and he is not accepted into the gathering. Finally, people come to understand his good intention and his earnest desire and accept him into the gathering. He will incur no blame.

Divination Direction

You feel lost and confused, not knowing which way to turn for a right direction. Without a practical and reasonable plan, you will continue to have difficulties and worries. Wake up from your fantasies and proceed step-by-step to carry out a practical plan.

46. The Rising and Advancing 升 (Shang) Hexagram

Key attributes: Rising and advancing, the symbol of pushing upward

Judgment

"*Shang* indicates that (under its conditions) there will be great progress and success. Seeking by (the qualities implied in it) to meet with the great man, its subject need have no anxiety. Advance to the south will be fortunate." (James Legge, *The I Ching*, 159.)

Essence of Hexagram

This hexagram explains the principle of achieving steady growth through hard work and accumulation of small successes.

Hexagram Image(s)

The Rising and Advancing hexagram with Earth above Wind (wood) stands for the images of the tree growing in the earth. The wise and noble uses the images as his guide in achieving lofty and great virtues through the unceasing accumulation of many modest and compliant virtues, as in nature when the tree begins by sprouting under the earth and grows steadily to become a large tree with many branches and leaves.

Hexagram Analysis

This hexagram consists of the lower trigram Wind (wood) that denotes tree and the virtue of modesty, and the upper trigram Earth, compliance. The hexagram portrays the image of a tree sprout in the earth. In the lower trigram, the bottom line denotes the roots, and the two yang lines the trunk of the tree. The upper trigram Thunder of the primary nuclear hexagram also represents a tree. The combined images of the two trees in the hexagram portray a well-nourished tree sprout in the earth pushing upward, making gentle efforts to adapt to the difficulties it faces. Eventually, tree branches and leaves begin forming and spreading above the ground, from which the hexagram name "Rising and Advancing" derives. The "great man" in the judgment text refers to 2-9, who is great because he is competent and practices the virtues of the Mean and who is fit to rise to the position of ruler, 5-6.

1-6, directive, and 5-6, structural, are the lead lines of the hexagram.

Interpretation of Judgment

The Rising and Advancing hexagram indicates that there will be great progress and success. The gentle (soft) and virtuous man (5-6) occupies the position of ruler. This virtuous ruler desires the state to progress; this desire is in accord with the needs of the time of Rising and Advancing. He calls for a meeting with the great and virtuous (2-9), who responds willingly (5-6 and 2-9 correlate). 2-9 has no reason to worry because his meeting with the ruler will result in joy and blessings. The ruler, who has the virtues of modesty (lower trigram) and compliance (upper trigram), asks the great man to serve under him, and the great man agrees. Thus, the ruler has obtained the right person who will enable him to advance the state affairs to the south. (The south represents brightness and warmth, or honest, good government.) There will be good fortune.

Divination Direction

It augurs well, especially in marriage, occupational promotion, trading, business, travel and financial market. You are riding on the rising wave of good fortune with many friends to work together with you. Move with careful planning, and you will succeed. It is not favorable to make a move to a new house. You will regain your good health. An expectant mother will have an easy delivery of a daughter.

Individual Lines: Analysis, Interpretation, and Divination Direction

Line 1-6: This yin line is improperly positioned at the beginning of this hexagram, correlating with no line. It starts at the bottom with a modest beginning, like the roots of a tree that will assuredly break from the ground as shoots (2-9 and 3-9) and continue to grow steadily to become a large tree by being compliant. The three yin lines of the upper trigram help this yin line move upward.

The images signify that its rise and advance assure great good fortune, for the others above it (the three yin lines of the upper trigram Earth) welcome its gentle and compliant advance.

Divination Direction

It augurs very well. Your fortune is on the rise, but it has a long way to go. What you have now may seem meager, but it will keep growing if you cultivate it through your deliberately paced and steady efforts.

Line 2-9: This yang line is improperly positioned at the center of the lower trigram, correlating with 5-6. It represents a competent and loyal subject who enjoys the full confidence of the ruler (5-6).

The images signify that the man with strong upright character as well as sincerity and piety in his mind is in his beginning stage of advance, and even his frugal offerings as those made in the spring worship ceremony are acceptable, and he will incur no blame. His sincerity will bring the joy of blessings.

Divination Direction

Your sincerity will help you establish trustful relationships with people. Your advantages lie in the field of public service rather than profit-motivated business.

Line 3-9: This yang line is properly positioned at the top of the lower trigram, correlating with 6-6. Its forceful thrust upward (the top yang of the lower trigram) is reinforced by the compliance of the upper trigram Earth and its correlative relationship with 6-6.

The images signify that his rising (thrusting above the earth's surface) is made easily without resistance, like passing through a vacant town where there is nothing to obstruct him. (No obstruction in this man's passage suggests that this man behaves too boldly, and such unobstructed rising may not last for long; there is no judgment of good fortune.)

Divination Direction

Your fortune is on a rising trend, but perhaps too strongly. You will obtain the position that you want with commensurate benefits.

Line 4-6: This yin line is properly positioned, correlating with no line. The king mentioned below refers to the last king of *Shang*. Feudal lord *Wan* continued to hold his religious ceremonial rites[33] at Mount *Khi*,[34] his feudal territory, even though his political power exceeded the King's.

The images signify that the virtue of modesty is an essential ingredient for one's rising and advance. This feudal lord maintained his virtues of modesty as he was rising and advancing. There will only be good fortune with no blame.

Divination Direction

It augurs well, and your goal will be reached. Pursue your goal at your natural pace without becoming greedy or overly ambitious, and you will succeed. Always be reasonable and considerate of other people's feelings.

Line 5-6: This yin line is improperly positioned at the center of the upper trigram, correlating with 2-9.

The images signify that slow but steady progress results in success, and this man who practices the rectitude of the Mean will enjoy the good fortune of rising to the position of ruler, as if he were climbing the stairs to the top. He will have the service of the great and loyal assistant (2-9) and will achieve his goal to govern the state in peace and prosperity.

Divination Direction

Always be sincere and conscientious. Pursue your goal step-by-step with persistent efforts, and you will succeed.

Line 6-6: This yin line is properly positioned at the top of the hexagram, correlating with 3-9. In the era of Rising and Advancing, it is unable to acknowledge that it has reached its apex. It keeps rising recklessly, which will eventually result in a disastrous fall.

The images signify that the foolish high official keeps rising recklessly (blindly), despite having reached the apex, and should now stay on the correct *Tao* of serving others in their advancing. He will end up losing all his gains and get exhausted.

Divination Direction

You must examine yourself to rein in your greed and excessive ambition. Otherwise, you will end up losing much of what you have achieved.

47. The Oppression 困 (Khwan or Kun) Hexagram

Key attributes: Oppression, the symbol of repression, impasse

Judgment

"In (the condition denoted by) *Kwan* there may (yet be) progress and success. For the firm and correct, the (really) great man, there will be good fortune. He will fall into no error. If he make speeches, his words cannot be made good." (James Legge, *The I Ching*, 161.)

Essence of Hexagram

This hexagram explains the principle of prevailing over adversity or oppression (entrapment) by maintaining one's emotional stability and mental clarity, making use of adversity for self-development and success.

Hexagram Image(s)

The Oppression hexagram with Lake above Water stands for the images of the lake drained of its water. The wise and noble uses the images as the guide to his conduct in a time of national crisis to exert his utmost efforts, even at the risk of his life, to follow his will.

Hexagram Analysis

This hexagram consists of the lower trigram Water that denotes peril, and the upper trigram Lake, joy. The graphic images of the hexagram portray the empty lake with the water having drained downward, which characterize the state of deprivation or oppression. It also presents the images of a joyful mind in the face of peril. The three yang lines of the hexagram, two of which are together, are sandwiched by yin lines: 2-9 by 1-6 and 3-6; 4-9 and 5-9 by 3-6 and 6-6. This symbolizes a state in which petty men surround the great, and the influence of the great men is restrained, presenting the image of oppression. The state of oppression is created by external force and, more importantly, by one's mind-set of ignorance, greed, impulsivity, and arrogance.

2-9 and 5-9 are the lead lines of this hexagram.

Interpretation of Judgment

The Oppression hexagram describes the state in which the yang lines are hindered by the yin lines, or great men by petty men. One need not lose his proper conduct even under this Oppression because he can maintain the stability of his mind by being optimistic. Only the wise and noble can do this, and the result will be progress and success. When a great man maintains the correctness of *Tao* by practicing the Mean, he will have good fortune and no error. In the time of Oppression, one's words are not believed, and too many words will only lead one into a more desperate situation. In such a time, one must be strong within—with virtuous integrity, rather than trying to influence others with words. (The emphasis is on action, not on words.)

Divination Direction

It augurs ill. You feel hard-pressed, finding no hope in any direction. It is not the time for you to be in despair; instead, have faith in yourself and carry out your tasks with sincerity and persistence. Wait patiently for a better time to arrive. Refrain from any kind of venture, as it will result in disaster.

Individual Lines: Analysis, Interpretation, and Divination Direction

Line 1-6: This yin line is improperly positioned at the bottom of the hexagram, correlating with 4-9. In the lowest status, its efforts to gain the support of 4-9 were sidetracked by its contiguous 2-9.

The images signify that a person in adversity must have inner strength to endure and overcome the adversity. Having been strained and distressed, this man suffers as though his buttocks are hurting from sitting on a tree stump, and he is uncomfortable and at a loss. His dark (confused), distressed mind feels as though it is groping for direction in a deep secluded valley without having a glimpse of the noble man (4-9) for three years (a long period of time).

Divination Direction

It augurs ill. You feel distressed, as nothing gets achieved as you had planned. Wait patiently for a better time.

Line 2-9: This yang line is improperly positioned at the center of the lower trigram, contiguous to 1-6 and correlating with no line. In the era of Oppression, the three great men (three yang lines of 2-9, 4-9, and 5-9) practice the virtues of the Mean and have developed collaborative relationships to overcome the constraints of the petty men (yin lines).

The images signify that one's inner strength with piety prepares one to overcome adversity. This virtuous great man (2-9) manages his suffering in the era of Oppression with wine and viands (calm and optimistic in the depressing situation) while waiting for his opportunity to serve the state. Since he maintains the practice of the Mean, he will have blessings. In the meantime, the ceremonial, vermilion knee cover[35] (symbolizing the ruler) arrives to inform him that the ruler is looking for him. He must conduct himself as sincerely and respectfully as in the time of sacrificial offering in the worship ceremony. Aggressive behavior without moral and spiritual preparations in seeking the ruler's favor will invite misfortune. Respectful waiting for the ruler's invitation will have no error.

Divination Direction

Do not deviate from your modest way of life. Your hard time will soon be over with some unexpected help. In the meantime, continue with your sincere and persistent efforts without haste.

Line 3-6: This yin line is improperly positioned at the top of the lower trigram, sandwiched between two yang lines, and correlates with no line. In a precarious position without the practice of the Mean, it appeals for the support of 4-9, but it gets a stonehearted response. It turns to 2-9 for support, only to feel the discomfort of sitting on thorny vines.

The images signify that a person who is ignorant, selfish, and lacking in virtues will have adversity of his own making. In the era of Oppression, this man feels as if he is hitting himself against a rock, for he is riding over (oppressing) the great man (2-9). He turns to one of higher status (4-9) for help but receives only a cold response. Feeling disheartened, he returns home, only to find his wife to be nowhere, which means misfortune. (This implies an approaching death, though he is not aware of it.) If one is lacking in inner virtues and tries all kinds of trickery to escape his entrapment, the result is nothing but disgrace to his name.

Divination Direction

It augurs ill. You are struggling to disengage yourself from the distressful situation in vain. Instead, save your energy and resources for a new opportunity.

Line 4-9: This yang line is improperly positioned, correlating with 1-6. "It comes slowly" below refers to 4-9 slowly coming to help 1-6 from its outer trigram.

The images signify that a helping hand must reach the needy in time with correct and speedy means. This feudal lord (4-9) wants to help his distressed subordinate (1-6), but he comes slowly, because his gold carriage (carriages decorated in gold were used by feudal lords of the *Chou* dynasty) has to overcome obstacles (2-9, which is contiguous with 1-6) to reach its destination. This is regrettable. Although the means the feudal lord is using are not proper (not in a proper position), he manages to overcome the obstacles, and in the end he succeeds in helping his subordinate.

Divination Direction

Refrain from becoming overconfident in your ability or resources, since you will experience many obstacles. Do not leave your future to chance. Only sincere persistent efforts with self-restraint will lead you to succeed.

Line 5-9: This yang line is properly positioned at the center of the upper trigram Lake that denotes joy, correlating with no line.

The images signify that the ruler is virtuous and competent but is surrounded by high officials who put obstacles in his way to prevent him from relating with the virtuous and competent subject (2-9). The oppression, which is coming from the high officials who wear the scarlet knee-cover, makes him feel constrained in his conduct, as though his nose and feet are cut off. Nevertheless, this virtuous ruler will not use "an eye for an eye" approach in meting out severe punishment against his oppressors. Instead, the ruler maintains his virtuous integrity with the same sincerity and piety that he has when he makes the sacrificial offering to the spirit for the welfare of his state. Because of his sincere conduct, the day of joy may be slow in coming, but in the end there will be blessings for all.

Divination Direction

You may feel that you are still in the woods, but your sincere and persistent efforts are about to pay off. Continue with them with your positive outlook, and you will succeed.

Line 6-6: This yin line is properly positioned at the top of the hexagram, antagonistically correlating with 3-6. At the apogee of the Oppression era, its position is precarious and dangerous.

The images signify that he must endure the suffering of the Oppression era, as if creeper plants and vines (3-6) bind him. He feels insecure and in peril, as he is too weak and indecisive to change his negative emotional bondage. If he repents his arrogance and pride of the Oppression era and decides to break away from his past mistakes, it will result in good fortune.

Divination Direction

You have had hard luck. Reassess the situation and take decisive action in a new direction to correct past mistakes. Take one step at a time to assure success at each step and not rush into any undertaking.

48. The Well 井 (Zing) Hexagram

Key attributes: Well, the symbol of source

Judgment

"(Looking at) *Zing*, (we think of) how (the site of) a town may be changed, while (the fashion of) its wells undergoes no change. (The water of a well) never disappears and never receives (any great) increase, and those who come and those who go can draw and enjoy the benefit. If (the drawing) have nearly been accomplished, but, before the rope has quite reached the water, the bucket is broken, this is evil." (James Legge, *The I Ching*, 164.)

Essence of Hexagram

This hexagram explains the principle of good governing as the source for well-being of the people and individuals attaining harmonious life. Man must cultivate virtuous integrity (the inexhaustible source of wisdom in living) and put the virtues into practice in one's conduct.

Hexagram Image(s)

Water above Wood stands for the images of the Well hexagram, portraying wood sucking the water upward to nourish the branches and leaves of a tree. The wise and noble uses the images as his guide in his efforts to comfort the common folk in their toil and encourage mutual aid.

Hexagram Analysis

This hexagram consists of the lower trigram Wind that denotes both wood and entering, or the wooden bucket being lowered into a well to draw water, and the upper trigram Water, the well water. The graphic images of the hexagram are made up of the following: 1-6 for the spring that is the source of the well; 2-9 and 3-9 for the well water; 4-6 for the wall of the well; 5-9 for the drawn water; and 6-6 for the well cover. In ancient China, a unit of eight families owned and used the same well.[36] A town was composed of four well units of families. The two yang lines, 2-9 and 5-9, each positioned at the center of each trigram, symbolize the constant moral fortitude of the great men, like the well water that maintains a constant water level.

5-9 is the sole lead line of this hexagram.

Interpretation of Judgment

The Well hexagram with Water above Wind stands for the images of entering into the water to draw it up. The well symbolizes the source of inexhaustible nourishment. The town may be moved to a new location, but the well remains in the same location. It represents the moral fortitude of those who practice the virtues of the Mean (2-9 and 5-9). There is neither a decrease nor increase in the well water. The dependability of the well is a good model to use in governing and in living one's life in the community. All the townspeople, whether they move away from or move into the town, draw water from the well for nourishment. This is analogous to the *Tao* remaining unchanged under the continual changes in society. The process of drawing the well water is not complete if the bucket almost reaches the water. Likewise, one has to carry through to the end to achieve a goal. It is not enough that the government has policies that will benefit the people; they must be carried out. If the drawing bucket (pot) gets broken, or a situation is carelessly handled, there will be misfortune.

Divination Direction

The hard time is still with you, requiring your unswerving motivation and corresponding efforts. You need to make sincere, persistent efforts to achieve your goal. It is favorable to engage in a trading business. It is not favorable to travel, move, or expand your business. Guard against health problems.

Individual Lines: Analysis, Interpretation, and Divination Direction

Line 1-6: This yin line is improperly positioned at the bottom of the hexagram, correlating with no line.

The images signify that a person with a sordid mind is useless, like the well water that is so muddy that it is unfit for drinking. 1-6 represents the bottom of the well. No bird will come to an old well that has been abandoned for a long time. Likewise, unless the virtues of *Tao* are constantly practiced, they will serve no useful purpose.

Divination Direction

Sporadic good deeds or efforts are not good enough to succeed. Examine yourself to see if your arrogance and pride keep you from other people and make you feel isolated and lonely. Cultivate your ability to relate with other people. Wait for a favorable opportunity to initiate a move toward your goal.

Line 2-9: This yang line is improperly positioned at the center of the lower trigram, contiguous to 1-6, correlating with no line. This yang line represents a plentiful supply of well water. However, the water cannot be drawn (no correlating line), and it flows through the cracks in the wall of the well. Therefore, the well benefits only the little fish and creatures (contiguous 1-6).

The images signify that a great talent is wasted unless it is put to good use, like the unutilized well water that benefits only the fish. 2-9 has no great people to relate with (the bucket is broken), and he ends up relating with the petty (little fish). The village people need to maintain the well properly so that they can draw the water for their use; otherwise, the well is like a broken jar that does not hold water.

Divination Direction

It augurs ill. You have a hard time finding someone that recognizes your ability and puts it to good use. Your hardship will last for some time.

Line 3-9: This yang line is properly positioned at the top of the lower trigram and correlates with 6-6, symbolizing the correct and competent mind-set of this man.

The images signify that the well has been dredged clean, but no one drinks water out of it; passersby deplore the waste. It is analogous to a man (3-9) who is well prepared in his mind and heart to serve, but the ruler does not make use of him. 6-6 understands the situation and feels pain and sympathy in his heart for him because the ruler should put this man to good use for state affairs, like the clean well for use by the people. If the sovereign were wise and clear-minded to accept him for service, there would be blessings for everyone: himself, the sovereign, and the people.

Divination Direction

You are well prepared and ready to take on a worthwhile project, but the timing is not right. Continue with your preparation; a good opportunity is not far away.

Line 4-6: This yin line is properly positioned, contiguous to 5-9, correlating with no line. This prime minister is sincere in his heart but without much competence.

The images signify that the well needs repairs and relining with bricks. It is analogous to the prime minister who dedicates himself to improving his deficiencies in order to better serve the people. The people will experience some inconveniences while he is working on self-improvement, but they will benefit from his services later, and he will make no error.

Divination Direction

First, put your personal and family matters in order; then, pursue your goal.

Line 5-9: This yang line is properly positioned at the center of the upper trigram. This well water is far above the muddy section (1-6); it is like fresh, clear well water fed by a spring. It (5-9) represents the virtuous (center) and competent (yang line) sovereign.

The images signify that the well is clean and the water is like the cold spring water that is fit for anyone to drink. A virtuous man is the source of the water of life; only when the sovereign practices the virtues of the Mean and properly governs the state does everyone benefit from it.

Divination Direction

It augurs well. Now is the time for you to actively pursue achieving your goal. Be generous with your resources to help other people, instead of being greedy and selfish.

Line 6-6: This yin line is properly positioned at the top of the hexagram, correlating with 3-9.

The images signify that the water drawn from the well was brought up for use. The well should not be covered so that its benefits are available to anyone who comes to draw water from it. Likewise, the benefits coming from a great man are inexhaustible; the virtuous ruler can bring the boundlessly abundant and benevolent benefits of good government to all the people under his rule. The sincerity of this man (6-6) who serves the ruler and the people will bring fundamental good fortune, like the uncovered well providing an inexhaustible supply of spring water. The result is great achievement of peace and prosperity for the state.

Divination Direction

It augurs very well. It is the time of a bountiful harvest from what you planted in the spring and the hard work you put in throughout the period of growth. Other people will share the benefits of your success as well.

49. The Revolution 革 (Ko) Hexagram

Key attributes: Revolution, the symbol of change

Judgment

(What takes place as indicated by) *Ko* is believed in only after it has been accomplished. There will be great progress and success. Advantage will come from being firm and correct. (In that case) occasion for repentance will disappear." (James Legge, *The I Ching*, 167.)

Essence of Hexagram

This hexagram explains the principle of successful revolution to bring about a change in government or society, based on the need for drastic changes, through careful planning, proper timing, and correct implementation.

Hexagram Image(s)

Lake above Fire stands for the images of the Revolution hexagram, representing the change brought about by the conflict of opposing forces. The wise and noble man helps the people adjust to inevitable and necessary political and social changes by preparing them for the demands of the new time. In the same way, the wise and noble man prepares the people for changes in the seasons of the year by establishing an almanac that the people can use to mark the time in order to prepare for the change of season with its different demands.

Hexagram Analysis

The Chinese character of this hexagram name "Revolution" is the synonym for leather or "the hide of a cow," characterizing both the tenacity and endurance that are essential for successful revolutionary efforts and the ensuing change.

This hexagram consists of the lower trigram Light that denotes fire, the second daughter, and summer, and the upper trigram Lake[37] that denotes lake water, the youngest daughter, and autumn. The hexagram name "Revolution" means radical changes brought about by mutually opposing forces when harmonious mutual adaptation is obstructed. An example of this is the interaction between fire and water (lake), wherein each destroys the other. It is analogous to the interaction between two young sisters living in the same household, wherein the younger sister places herself above her older sister and arouses the latter's animosity, and to the seasonal change from the summer heat that is driven away by the autumn coolness.

The lower trigram Light symbolizes clear, reasoned intelligence, and the upper trigram Lake, joy. The combined images portray that Revolution or radical change is called for only when compelling reasons exist for such a change. There must be an intelligent plan to produce success.

5-9 is the sole lead line of this hexagram.

Interpretation of Judgment

The Revolution hexagram with Lake above Fire portrays the changes brought about by the interaction between water and fire. They destroy each other by water extinguishing fire and fire evaporating water, or by the interaction of two females living together who cannot get along with each other. A radical change in government is called for only when there is an absolute necessity, and only a confident leader whom the people trust can carry it out. When a radical change is carried out with well-defined reasoning (lower trigram Light), the welcome support (upper trigram Lake, joy) of the people, and a correct course of action based on planning and proper timing, the result is great progress and success. When such a change is carried out properly, there will be no regret. Heaven and Earth use such a change to produce the four seasons; so did the kings of *Tang* and *Wu*[38] who changed the government through a revolution to comply with the heavenly mandate, responding to the wishes of the people. What a matter of great importance the time of Revolution is!

Divination Direction

It is the time to reassess your situation and make necessary changes. Although it is difficult to make changes, they are necessary in order to succeed. The time has come to change your job, move, or to bring about other changes you have been planning. You will be successful in a financial venture. Pending litigation will overturn your expectations.

Individual Lines: Analysis, Interpretation, and Divination Direction

Line 1-9: This yang line is properly positioned at the beginning of this hexagram, correlating with no line.

The images signify that it is premature to initiate a radical change. Although he is competent and well prepared, he should not make such a move at this time. He should remain docile with steadfast and virtuous integrity, as though bound by the tough hide of a yellow cow (hide refers to 2-6, ascribing to it the attribute of a docile cow, and yellow, the color of the center). He is too low in his status and has no one from whom he can ask for support (no correlate); he cannot do it alone.

Divination Direction

You see the cause of the current stagnation and feel ready to get rid of the cause. But it is still premature for a change; wait patiently for an opportunity to initiate your move.

Line 2-6: This yin line is properly positioned at the center of the lower trigram, correlating with 5-9. This virtuous subject enjoys the confidence of the ruler, an ideal alliance to bring about a radical change or revolution.

The images signify that one, with both leadership and support of people, must first ensure that the time is ripe for a radical change, having exhausted all the efforts for reforms. He then makes careful preparations, and decides on the date to initiate the move in compliance with the sexgenary cycle. There will be no error, and the action will result in successful blessings.

Divination Direction

You have been plagued with one problem after another. It's the time to take a drastic measure to change your situation. If you do not resort to a rash action but do it with careful planning, you will succeed.

Line 3-9: This yang line is properly positioned at the top of the lower trigram, correlating with 6-6. This line denotes competence (yang line) and high intelligence (the top of the trigram Light), along with a tendency to make an overconfident, reckless move.

The images signify that his move will bring misfortune when it is done prematurely or with too much hesitation. The move is for the right cause, but it is still too perilous to initiate his move. When he hears about the necessity of change three (many) times, he will fully deliberate with friends (6-6) in order to arrive at a convincing decision to make the move to bring about the needed change. The people will then support the move.

Divination Direction

Listen carefully to the opinions of your friends regarding what kind of change is necessary. Once you are convinced that it is the time to make a change, you must plan carefully and act on it with confidence.

Line 4-9: This yang line is improperly positioned at the beginning of the upper trigram, correlating with no line. It is the line where Fire comes into contact with Water (Lake), denoting the right time for a radical change. Timing resonates with the theme of the Revolution hexagram.

The images signify that this competent prime minister has chosen the proper time to implement radical changes under the direction of the competent ruler and with the support of the people. All changes are proceeding as planned, and all the regrets disappear. He is confident in his actions, as he has the trust of both the ruler and the people. His achievements in mandated reform will result in good fortune.

Divination Direction

You are riding on the rising tide of good fortune. Pursue your goal with sincerity and implement the necessary changes to attain your goal.

Line 5-9: This yang line is properly positioned at the center of the upper trigram, correlating with 2-6. The tiger described below refers to the radical changes that the sovereign (5-9) brings about, like the change in the colors of the tiger's stripes to the shinier and more beautiful colors in the fall.

The images signify that the radical changes that the great ruler brings to the state and its people are as brilliant and beautiful (new ordinances are clear and beneficial to the people) as the changed colors of the tiger's stripes in the fall from molting. He has such trust and confidence of the people that there is no need to divine for the outcome.

Divination Direction

It augurs well. You are enjoying the rising tide of great good fortune. All of your plans for changes will have successful results.

Line 6-6: This yin line is properly positioned at the top of the hexagram, correlating with 4-9. The radical changes achieved by the wise and noble in the state are compared to the change in the colors of the panther's spots that are bright and beautiful, but not as much as those of the tiger's stripes.

The images signify that the major changes have been achieved, and the subsequent smaller changes brought about by the wise and noble shine brightly, like the altered colors of the panther's spots in the fall from molting. This also symbolizes the deeper level of the great man's self-realization, as compared to the petty man's superficial conformity because of outside pressures. The petty men in the state change their faces superficially (to please their superiors), like from molting, by observing the new ordinances.

The important objectives of the changes have been achieved, and no further new radical changes should be planned; if they are attempted, it will result in misfortune. It is the time to live in peace and enjoy the good fortune by maintaining the fortitude of constancy.

Divination Direction

You have successfully attained your goal. If you become arrogant and greedy, you will end up losing much of what you have gained. Continue with your efforts to complement and supplement your strengths and weaknesses in order to sustain your attained goal.

50. The Cauldron 鼎 (Ting) Hexagram

Key attributes: Cauldron, the symbol of nourishment

Judgment

"*Ting* gives the intimation of great progress and success." (James Legge, *The I Ching*, 169.)

Essence of Hexagram

This hexagram explains the principle of spiritual nourishment as the foundation of civilization and of a virtuous government that serves the people.

Hexagram Image(s)

Fire above Wood (Wind) stands for the images of the Cauldron hexagram; wood needs to be fed to the fire for the flame to go upward to cook the ingredients in the cauldron. The wise and noble uses the images to guide him in correct conduct in his efforts to rectify positions to match the qualifications of people and thereby promote the stability of the state, in firm compliance with the heavenly mandates. It is like the cauldron that maintains a stable position and carries out its proper function.

Hexagram Analysis

This hexagram consists of the lower trigram Wind that denotes wood, entrance, and compliance, and the upper trigram Light, fire, and enlightenment. The Cauldron hexagram is the capsized form of the preceding hexagram, #49 Revolution. A Revolution is to get rid of bad practices or bad government, while the Cauldron symbolizes cooking or preparing new food (bringing about changes) and nourishing the competent and virtuous who serve in the new government.

The hexagram portrays images of a cauldron with three legs, two ears, and the body that holds the food to be cooked. The first divided line (yin line) represents the three legs, the next three yang lines the body of cauldron, the fifth divided line (yin line) the two ears, and the last yang line the carrying bar. In the Revolution hexagram, 2-6 correlates with 5-9, whereas in the Cauldron hexagram, 2-6 moves up to become 5-6 and correlates with 2-9, reversing their positioning in the Revolution hexagram. The dynamism that is working in the Cauldron hexagram is the wood (lower trigram Wind for wood and entering) going into fire (upper trigram) to produce heat to cook the food in the cauldron.

Hexagram #48 The Well and this hexagram are the only two of the sixty-four hexagrams that are named after man-made objects, and both hexagrams have the theme that is related to nourishment. The former describes the government nourishing its people physically, primarily by agriculture, while the latter describes nourishing its people by cultivating virtues and talents for a civilized life.

This hexagram has two lead lines of 5-6 and 6-9.

Interpretation of Judgment

The Cauldron hexagram represents the images of wood being put into the fire to cook food, which is the function of a cauldron. The sage uses the cauldron to cook the sacrificial offering to present to the Supreme Deity, which represents the act for spiritual nourishment as the culmination of civilization. The cauldron is also used to cook a large amount of food to nourish the wise and noble men (cooking inside the cauldron symbolizes the internal cultivation of virtues and talents among people to promote good government and civilized life). Through the mind-set of compliance (lower trigram) or willingness, one can develop keen ears to hear well (listen) and clear eyes (upper trigram Light) to see well (understand). The gentle and virtuous (2-6 of the Revolution hexagram) who succeeded in his revolutionary efforts has now advanced to become the center of the upper trigram (5-6) in the Cauldron hexagram as the virtuous sovereign. It (5-6) correlates with the yang line of 2-9 that represents the loyal and competent subject. Therefore, the Cauldron hexagram is an intimation of great progress and success.

Divination Direction

It augurs very well. Your position is secure and you are open to accommodate new ideas. You are in a leadership position and must pay attention to the well-being of other people. Your health and financial conditions will improve. You will be successful with many blessings in your sincere efforts.

Individual Lines: Analysis, Interpretation, and Divination Direction

Line 1-6: This yin line is improperly positioned at the bottom of the hexagram, contiguous to 2-9 and correlating with 4-9. It represents the feet of the cauldron. The cauldron is turned upside down with its feet pointing upward (this line correlates with 4-9 above it).

The images signify that when the government is run well, everyone in the state can find a useful role to play, especially with assistance (one of the three legs of cauldron). It is like the cauldron turned upside down with its feet pointing upward. In this position, the cauldron is not completely useless because it can empty itself of the bad residue to ready it to fill with good and nourishing (4-9) ingredients to be cooked. It is like the concubine (low in the social status) who gave birth to a son for the man who does not have a son by his legitimate wife. This situation is not as acceptable as the legitimate wife giving birth to a son, but having this son will incur no blame for the concubine.

Divination Direction

In the beginning, you must overcome some hurdles to attain your goal. Use your mind flexibly, looking for an alternative to your way of doing that is not working. Your sincere and persistent efforts will lead you to success.

Line 2-9: This yang line is improperly positioned at the center of the lower trigram, contiguous to 1-6 and correlating with 5-6. (A yin line symbolizes emptiness, and a yang line, fullness.)

The images signify that one can achieve something important through concentrated efforts for which this man is well balanced with virtues, like the cauldron filled with food to be cooked. This man must decide whose direction (1-6 or 5-6) he should follow in cooking the food. He wants to follow the great man's (5-6), but the petty man (1-6 as foe) tries to interrupt the cooking process by dipping into the food before it is fully cooked. Finally, this man sincerely concentrates on his task and is able to resist the temptation of the enemy (1-6). In the end, there will be good fortune.

Divination Direction

You have a fine personality and good abilities but are hindered by many temptations that stimulate your greed. You need a strong conviction in your action. Continually examine your motive and behavior in order not to deviate from but to focus your activities toward your goal.

Line 3-9: This yang line is properly positioned at the top of the lower trigram without a correlating line. The top of the lower trigram Wind, denoting wood, has antagonistic correlation with 6-9 the top line of the upper trigram Fire, presents the image of a great many pieces of wood feeding a strong fire.

The images signify that the ears of the cauldron have changed and have become too hot to touch and hold because he continued to feed the fire with wood (its antagonistic correlation with 6-9) for too long. The cauldron cannot be used, and it is not possible to serve the feast of delicious, fatty pheasant meat, like the good talents of a man, which will become wasted if he cannot find a proper role in which to use them in the society. When rain comes (in time, the situation will change), the harmonious interaction between yin (5-6, the cauldron ears, or the ruler) and yang (3-9, the prime minister) will cool the ears of the cauldron. The regret will then be diminished, and in the end, there will be good fortune.

Divination Direction

You are overconfident about your ability and have a strong urge to move ahead without careful preparations, which can delay your achieving the goal. Calm down and evaluate to see if there is a different way of handling the situation or a new direction to take to achieve your goal. A rash judgment will lead you to fail.

Line 4-9: This yang line is improperly positioned at the position of prime minister and correlates with 1-6. The improper position that this prime minister occupies and the confidence he places in the weak incompetent man (1-6) are compared to the broken leg of a cauldron.

The images signify that an unfit person or a person ill-prepared for a task causes unexpected problems. The cauldron with a broken leg (1-6) is analogous to the prime minister (4-9) who is ill-fitted for the job and mismanages the state affairs, engaging a weak and incompetent assistant (1-6) to help him. This is likened to the cauldron with broken feet that has overturned, spilling the pottage that was being prepared for the ruler to feed the princes. How can the prime minister be trusted? He will be dealt with a severe punishment.[39] ("Severe punishment" here appears in some other Chinese texts as "made to blush for shame.") There will be misfortune.

Divination Direction

It augurs ill. You are not well qualified for the present position or task and will experience one failure after another. Proceed in a slow but steady pace within your limitations to minimize the damage or failure.

Line 5-6: This yin line is improperly positioned at the center of the upper trigram, contiguous to 6-9 and correlating with 2-9.

The images signify that the ruler who makes the practice of the Mean his guiding principle is like the yellow rings of a cauldron that has golden earrings. The hole in the earring symbolizes the emptied mind and humble attitude of the virtuous ruler who is willing to fill his mind with good advice from his advisors (6-9 and 2-9). The yellow color represents the Mean, or the color of correctness. There will be advantage if the ruler maintains the rectitude.

Divination Direction

It augurs well. Your efforts will produce successful results. Keep your mind open to take in the good advice of those whom you trust. Continue with your sincere efforts, and you will be amply rewarded with successful results.

Line 6-9: This yang line is improperly positioned at the top of the hexagram, contiguous to 5-6, correlating with no line.

The images signify that the ruler's top advisor possesses a gentle personality and firm, virtuous integrity. He performs his advisory duties well by regulating these two qualities and helps the ruler govern the state well by nourishing the worthy for leadership roles. It is analogous to the jade earrings of a cauldron, which have the qualities of the softness of color and the hardness of stone to carry out their function to lift the cauldron. There will be great good fortune with no disadvantage in any action.

Divination Direction

It augurs very well. Your friends are willing to cooperate with you in your undertaking. Your sincere efforts will lead to the successful attainment of your goal.

51. The Shock 震 (Kan or Chen) Hexagram

Key attributes: Shock, the symbol of exciting power

Judgment

"*Kan* gives the intimation of ease and development. When (the time of) movement (which it indicated) comes, (the subject of the hexagram) will be found looking out with apprehension, and yet smiling and talking cheerfully. When the movement (like a crash of thunder) terrifies all within a hundred *li*, he will be (like the sincere worshipper) who is not (startled into) letting go his ladle and (cup of) sacrificial spirits." (James Legge, *The I Ching*, 172.)

Essence of Hexagram

This hexagram explains the principle of maintaining a laudable attitude with inner integrity in a time of a shocking event that can come from within or without.

Hexagram Image(s)

The double trigram Thunder stands for the images of the Shock hexagram. The wise and noble uses the images as his guide for cultivating his noble character by reflecting on his weaknesses that need to be corrected in order to be sincere in his heart and in his deeds.

Hexagram Analysis

This hexagram is composed of two Thunder trigrams. Each trigram has one yang line under two yin lines, symbolizing the movement of the yang force trying to break through the yin forces; this violent movement produces the sound of the clash or thunder. The trigram Thunder also represents the eldest son (symbol of power). Here, he is the crown prince, the heir to the throne. "*Li*" in the judgment text is a unit of distance measurement, about two and a half miles.

1-9 is the sole lead line of this hexagram.

Interpretation of Judgment

The Shock hexagram represents the shock or quake caused by acts of nature (the Deity) or any man-made upheaval, such as revolution that stirs movement in one's mind. When a shock is properly handled, it will bring progress and success. A thunderous threat brings shock to people in faraway places and fear to people nearby within one hundred *li* of the shock. This shock and fear can inspire people to become aware of the powerful nature, making them reverent toward god and examining their inner selves, resulting in blessings for the people. When the thunderous threat is over, people experience joy because they have found a way to cope with such threats by maintaining their composure.

The crown prince (the eldest son) understands the principle of the Shock hexagram. He is confident and concentrates on the important task of religious service he is engaged in. He will not be frightened by thunder into letting go of the ladle while dipping out the oblatory spirits because he is composed and very reverent toward the Deity and his ancestral spirits. He is worthy of succeeding to the throne to protect the state and maintain the ancestral temple as the chief priest.

Divination Direction

You are energetic and competitive. You will prevail if you concentrate on one thing at a time. Your financial investment will fluctuate a great deal. Maintain your sincerity in your speech and conduct without making empty promises or bragging. Move ahead with confidence to achieve your practical goal. Refrain yourself from getting involved in arguments with other people. Pay attention to health problems. It augurs well to travel. An expectant mother will give birth to a boy.

Individual Lines: Analysis, Interpretation, and Divination Direction

Line 1-9: This yang line is properly positioned at the beginning of the hexagram, correlating with no line. Positioned at the beginning, the shock is felt here first. It is the sole lead line of the hexagram.

The images signify that Shock stimulates movement and progress. When a shock (thunder, quake, etc.) comes, people shiver with apprehension, but they will be glad when it is over, as in the time of a natural disaster or human ordeal when one can overcome the odds of survival by acting with caution. Once the thunderous threat has passed, the people feel relieved and become cheery, as they have learned that the threat is transitory and that they can cope with such threats by maintaining calmness in the heart. There will be good fortune.

Divination Direction

Go ahead with your plans to achieve your goal. As you proceed, you will come across some hurdles to overcome, but you will succeed in the end.

Line 2-6: This yin line is properly positioned at the center of the lower trigram, correlating with no line. Being close to 1-9, it is helplessly affected by the fiercely strong shock of 1-9. "In seven days he will regain them" below refers to the progressive movement of a line in the hexagram cycle, which returns to its original position in its seventh movement. It means that the virtuous one (2-6) who practices the Mean returns to safety and repossesses what he had to abandon.

The images signify that one should get out of the shock's way, instead of resisting against it, when a thunderous threat (Shock) arrives fiercely. He (2-6) loses all his possessions and takes refuge by climbing to the high hills. He does not go after the abandoned possessions for, in seven days when the threat is over, he will repossess them.

Divination Direction

You will experience an unexpected event that is shocking. Do not let the shocking event frustrate you to give up your hope for a new effort. First, assess it to find out what small steps need to be taken to control the situation, and then act accordingly.

Line 3-6: This yin line is improperly positioned at the top of the lower trigram; it is far away from the Shock (1-9), correlating with no line.

The images signify that maintaining the alert mind is important in handling any kind of shocking event. This man (3-6) hears a thunderous sound in the distance (1-9) and finds room in his mind to think about the real meaning of such threat. He (3-6) feels fortunate because he is in the position of strength (far away from the shock). Under such a distant threat, by being cautious there will be little suffering.

Divination Direction

The difficulty that you have may seem overwhelming, but be patient. You will soon be able to find the solution to the problem that you are worried about.

Line 4-9: This yang line is improperly positioned, sandwiched by two yin lines, correlating with no line. The lower trigram Mountain and the upper trigram Water of the primary nuclear hexagram symbolize a peril in the mud (sinking). Though this yang line stands for strong and shining achievement, it is mired in the mud.

The images signify that success depends on more than one's ability or preparation, since a shock can come from one's own making or a source beyond one's control. In the era of Shock, the virtues of 4-9 have not been able to shine forth, and he has not experienced a great achievement. The competent person who goes beyond his capabilities (greedy) will sink in the mud, like the thunder that has great force gets buried in the mud and is unable to function.

Divination Direction

Your undertaking is more than you can handle, and you will give it up eventually. Do not be overconfident in your ability, for there are many other factors that contribute to success.

Line 5-6: This yin line is improperly positioned at the center of the upper trigram, correlating with no line. The phrase "thunderous threats go away to return with fierce force" described below refers to 1-9 going away and 4-9 returning.

The images signify that one should maintain the integrity of the Mean even in the midst of repeated shocks. In the era of Shock, even the virtuous ruler has to deal with one tumultuous event after another, as if thunderous threats go away, only to return with fiercer force. The ruler handles everything with appropriate caution, in compliance with the principles of the Mean. He conducts the worship ceremony without letting go of the ladle (refer to Interpretation of Judgment section above). He will suffer no loss, even with repeated shocks.

Divination Direction

You will have one hardship after another, but you must endure them to the end without giving up your goal. Only then will you succeed.

Line 6-6: This yin line is properly positioned at the end of the hexagram with an antagonistic correlationship with 3-6. Thunderous threat has returned (4-9) and intensely affects its neighbor (5-6). Its relationship with 3-6 is like a marital relationship without mutual love.

The images signify that the era of Shock has reached its height, and this man senses thunderous threats coming close around him, making him terrified and distraught. He looks all around, fear-stricken. He behaves in this manner because he has not attained the virtues of the Mean that bring peace of mind. His untimely move will result in misfortune. The thunderous threat is mainly affecting his neighbor (5-6) and has not yet reached him. If he waits to regain his senses without making an untimely move, there will be no error. Nonetheless, he cannot escape the criticisms of his close relatives for failing to help the neighbor.

Divination Direction

It augurs ill. Whatever you do, you will have difficulty succeeding. Reassess the situation and prepare for a new opportunity to appear. You will succeed in your endeavor if you can learn from other people's failures and apply their experiences to your situation. Cultivate your emotional strength so that you can accept friendly advice and criticism without becoming upset.

52. The Resting 艮 (Kan or Gen) Hexagram

Key attributes: Checking, keeping still, the symbol of stability

Judgment

"When one's resting is like that of the back, and he loses all consciousness of self; when he walks in his courtyard, and does not see any (of the persons) in it, there will be no error." (James Legge, *The I Ching,* 175.)

Essence of Hexagram

This hexagram explains the principle of sustaining one's integrity without deviating from the correct principles of *Tao* and having the clarity of mind to correct one's movement when necessary.

Hexagram Image(s)

Mountain above Mountain stands for the images of the Resting hexagram. The wise and noble uses the images as his guide in cultivating his virtues for proper conduct so that he will not deviate from his appropriate station, or his thought will not wander off from the situation he is in.

Hexagram Analysis

This hexagram is composed of the double trigram Mountain, with one mountain on top of another. The trigram Mountain represents halt, keeping still, or being stable. One yang line (active) above two yin lines (passive, stable) denotes the stage in which the yang line has reached its apex and cannot move further, from which the hexagram name "Resting" is derived. All the lines in the hexagram correlate antagonistically, symbolizing the absence of any friendly relationship among the lines. The yang line of the trigram Mountain represents the courtyard gate, and the two yin lines, two persons in the courtyard back to back; the spine of the back stands for a mountain ridge.

6-9 is the sole lead line of this hexagram.

Interpretation of Judgment

The Resting hexagram stands for holding on to the principles of *Tao* to halt when necessary and to act when the time requires it. When one's resting and acting are in accord with the need of the time, one is living up to the essence of *Tao*. "One's resting is like that of the back" in the judgment text means resting firmly on the correct principles without distraction. Since the upper and lower trigram lines of the hexagram correlate antagonistically and do not get along with each other, it follows that one loses his relationship with other people, as though one does not see the other person face-to-face, even in the same courtyard.[40] If he can devote himself to cultivating the virtues of *Tao*, he will make no error. "He loses all consciousness of self"[41] in the judgment text refers to the back as the location of all the nerve fibers. The sentence means that when the back is checked, all the organ senses, those of the eyes, nose, ears, and mouth that stimulate human desires and greed, are in check (balanced or centered and calm). The senses will not influence the person's judgment and conduct improperly.

Divination Direction

It is the time of stagnation. You see no progress in your endeavor and feel frustrated. It is in your favor to engage in an undertaking that requires slow but steady efforts. It will be favorable to involve yourself in real estate dealings. Instead of trying to achieve your goal now, save your money and your energy to prepare for a future opportunity. It is not a good time to move. If you have a health problem, it will improve slowly.

Individual Lines: Analysis, Interpretation, and Divination Direction

Line 1-6: This yin line is improperly positioned at the beginning of the Resting hexagram, correlating with no line. It is the bottom line and is compared to one's toes.

The images signify that this man, by restraining his advance at the beginning to see if he is on the correct course, has not lost the correct way to conduct himself, which is like checking his movement at his toes. The toes must move first for him to advance. His conduct will make no error. It will be to his advantage to stay on the correct course of conduct.

Divination Direction

Move cautiously with a moderate goal. Even though you will have some obstacles along the way, you must adhere to your original goal to be successful.

Line 2-6: This yin line is properly positioned at the center of the lower trigram, contiguous to 3-9 and correlating with no line. This line is compared to the calves of the legs that follow the movement of the thighs (3-9). The upper trigram Thunder of the primary nuclear hexagram denotes movement.

The images signify that this virtuous man who practices the Mean understands his proper place. He is at the mercy of his active master (3-9) who compels him to follow, like his calves that must follow the movement of his thighs. His efforts to stop his master from making the reckless move are ignored. He (2-6) is unhappy because he cannot help his master check his reckless movement and he has to go along. (The calves cannot act separately from the thighs.)

Divination Direction

It augurs ill. Your plans will not work well, not because you are at fault, but because you are in a difficult situation. Do not get involved in a dispute. Make efforts to prepare for a new opportunity.

Line 3-9: This yang line is properly positioned at the top of the lower trigram, bordering with the upper trigram and correlating with no line. It is the lead line of the lower trigram. This line represents the loin, which needs to be flexible for the movement of the upper and lower parts of the body. When the loins lack flexibility, pressure from the movement is applied in the wrong place, resulting in the muscles tearing.

The images signify that the calmness in heart should not be attained by forcible means but through cultivation of the Means or inner composure. The loin holds the pivotal position that connects the upper and lower parts of the body, and when its movement is restricted, it brings rigidity in the movement of the whole body, irritating one's heart to burn with a desire to move. If the restless heart forces the loin to move, it may split the back flesh. Likewise, one must cultivate the virtues of the Mean in order to attain inner composure, and he should not let his excessive ambition bring misfortune to his life. This man (3-9) is both competent and ambitious but lacks in the virtues of the Mean. (He is too ambitious.) Because he is blocked, he is forced to be rigid in his movement. He is in a dangerous situation because if he struggles hard to free himself, he may cause harm to himself or others. He is tormented because he cannot exercise his leadership position (lead line of the lower trigram), which requires proper movements and checks. Exerting his energy and strength to move would cause his back muscles to tear, which is comparable to his movement being checked at the loins.

Divination Direction

Your obstinacy is obstructing your progress. Make efforts to be more flexible in your ambition and attitude, and to understand your weakness as well as your strengths.

Line 4-6: This yin line is properly positioned at the beginning of the upper trigram, correlating with no line. This line represents the trunk of the body.

The images signify that this man is able to maintain calmness in his heart by restraining his torso, although he has not reached the highest virtues, like the back that has no selfish desire at all. This high official (4-6) is gentle but is not able to make strong recommendations to correct the ruler's conduct for fear of the ruler's wrath. The gentle conduct of this high official is like checking the movement of his trunk to avoid immobilizing the whole body, bringing calm to the restless heart. He will incur no blame to himself.

Divination Direction

Feel reassured it is not because of your fault or shortcomings that your goal has not been attained. There is a right time to make a move. Do not take any rash action. Use your time and resources for careful planning to get ready for a new opportunity.

Line 5-6: This yin line is improperly positioned at the center of the upper trigram, correlating with no line. This line represents the jowls of a person.

The images signify that this man practices the virtues of the Mean and exercises proper restraints in his speeches. It is like checking the movement of his jowls to prevent making rash and inappropriate speeches and comments. There will be no regret.

Divination Direction

Be prudent in your actions, especially in your speech.

Line 6-9: This yang line is improperly positioned at the top of the Resting hexagram, correlating with no line.

The images signify that he has attained profound tranquillity and honesty at the apogee of the Resting (restraint) era and has carried out the virtues of restraint to the end with sincere devotion. There will be good fortune.

Divination Direction

It augurs well. Now is the time to achieve your goal. It is payoff time for your investment of time, efforts and many resources.

53. Progressive Advance 漸 (Kien or Jian) Hexagram

Key attributes: Progressive advance, the symbol of gradual progress

Judgment

"*Kien* suggests to us the marriage of a young lady, and the good fortune (attending it). There will be advantage in being firm and correct." (James Legge, *The I Ching*, 178.)

Essence of Hexagram

This hexagram explains the principle of gradual and orderly efforts to attain goals in human relationships, business endeavors, governing, and self-development.

Hexagram Image(s)

The Progressive Advance hexagram with a tree on the mountain presents the images of gradual and progressive advance. The wise and noble uses the images as his guide in his efforts to live by the noble virtues and to influence the social mores for the better, which can only be done at a gradual pace.

Hexagram Analysis

This hexagram consists of the lower trigram Mountain that denotes halt and the upper trigram Wind, wood (tree) or compliance. The name of this hexagram comes from the images of the tree on the mountain growing gradually, or the gradual soaking process of water. "The marriage of a young lady" in the judgment text refers to the six matrimonial steps,[42] a step-by-step procedure to consummate a marriage in ancient China. The first step is the marriage proposal, and the last step is welcoming the bride in the groom's home. The ritual progresses gradually, with the timing of the steps mutually agreed upon by the two families. Hexagram #53 is the capsized form of Hexagram #54 Marrying Maiden; it has a special relationship with hexagram #54, depicting gradual progress to advance to succeeding positions based on merit.

2-6 and 5-9 are the lead lines of this hexagram.

Interpretation of Judgment

The Progressive Advance hexagram denotes gradual progress, like taking all the proper and progressive steps in the marriage of a young lady. Such a prudent approach will result in good fortune. In a similar way, in state affairs, an official has to go through gradual and proper steps in order to advance. (4-6 in hexagram #53 is the official who advanced from 3-6 in hexagram #54.) He abides in the rectitude of *Tao* in his advance and is now in a position to put the state affairs on the right course. He helps the ruler carry out the governance well, in compliance with the moral authority of the Mean (5-9). If one has the inner strength of restraint (lower trigram Mountain) and the outer manner of compliance (upper trigram Wind), the conduct of such a person will not flounder. There will be advantage to one who abides by the principles firmly and correctly.

Divination Direction

It augurs well for a person who practices the "slow but steady" motto with a long-range goal. There will be a gradual improvement in your business and financial situation. A rush or rash action will end in failure. Prudent and step-by-step efforts will lead you to attain your goal. It is favorable to travel. A poor health condition will be slow to improve. An expectant mother will have an easy delivery of a son.

Individual Lines: Analysis, Interpretation, and Divination Direction

Note: The "Progressive Advance" is represented in each line statement of this hexagram using the movement of a goose because of its careful and gradual approach and the regularity and orderliness of geese in their seasonal flights and flight formations.

Line 1-6: This yin line is improperly positioned at the bottom of the hexagram and has an antagonistic correlation with 4-6. Each line of this hexagram is compared to a goose, which symbolizes conjugal love in China. In the seasonal flights of the geese, each maintains its proper position in the flying formation in which the older geese fly in front and the younger ones in the rear.

The images signify that a wild goose (1-6) makes his first stop from a flight by making a gradual approach to the shore. Likewise, the young man handles his new business with restraint and deliberation, one step at a time. The young goose (1-6) is perilous and anxious as it approaches the shore because it is inexperienced and immature like the young man in his new venture. The old one (4-6), which has an antagonistic relationship with 1-6, complains about the conduct of the young goose. The young goose will incur no blame because its gradual, slow approach is appropriate to its youth and level of experience.

Divination Direction

Your inexperience is the cause of your confusion and stagnation in your progress. You must not be in a hurry but take a gradual and deliberate approach with a clear objective in mind. You will accumulate more experiences along the way. You are at the beginning of the rising wave of good fortune, and your gradual progress will result in success.

Line 2-6: This yin line is properly positioned at the center of the lower trigram, contiguous to 3-9 and correlating with 5-9.

The images signify that the wild goose has gradually advanced to the crag and enjoys eating and drinking, for it feels safe and content. Likewise, the man who practices the virtues of the Mean (2-6) is content with what he is doing, as he is certain that the ruler (5-9) will summon him to serve the state when the need arises. His contentment is not the reward for doing nothing; it is the reward for living virtuously with self-restraint. There will be good fortune.

Divination Direction

You are not yet ready for a leadership position. Make continuing efforts to accumulate experience and to prepare for the opportunity that will come to you before long.

Line 3-9: This yang line is properly positioned at the top of the lower trigram, with an antagonistic correlation with 6-9.

The images signify that the wild goose makes a gradual advance to the dry plain, which is not a suitable place for a water bird. The line statement text, "The husband who leaves but does not return" refers to the intemperate husband (3-9) who lacks the virtues of the Mean. He indulges or misplaces himself in an illicit relationship with a woman (4-6) who becomes pregnant. She will not nourish the child because she is immoral and lacks the proper *Tao* of husband and wife. There will be misfortune. It is to this man's (3-9) advantage to exercise restraint in his impulsive conduct and defend against his foe (4-6), or unsavory temptations, in order to regain his family's (1-6 and 2-6) support.

Divination Direction

Beware! Overconfidence in your ability will lead you to failures. There will be temptations that will ensnare you into problems. Guard especially against becoming greedy or engaging in any activity that will cause family disharmony.

Line 4-6: This yin line is properly positioned at the beginning of the upper trigram Wind that denotes compliance or humility.

The images signify that the wild goose advances to a tree, which is not a suitable place for the web-footed goose to land; if it can alight on a flat branch, there will be no error of falling. Likewise, if a person observes the principles of Progressive Advance in handling perilous situations in life, he will commit no serious error. He will secure a safe position, for he is in compliance with the way of humility (upper trigram).

Divination Direction

You must choose a safer direction because your current position is not suitable for you. You feel uncomfortable and anxious, and you need to reassess your situation to make sure you are not overextending yourself.

Line 5-9: This yang line is properly positioned at the center of the upper trigram, correlating with 2-6. This correlation represents the husband (5-9) and wife (2-6), whose relationship is obstructed by unfriendly people (3-9 and 4-6) who drive a wedge between the two.

The images signify that the wild goose gradually advances to the high mound, further away from the water. It is like the loving couple who has been obstructed by unfriendly people from meeting each other for three years (for a long time), and the wife cannot get pregnant. The unfriendly people cannot succeed in their obstructive efforts to the end, and the couple will get together. In the same way, the disloyal officials (3-9 and 4-6) cannot thwart the virtuous ruler (5-9) from meeting the noble man (2-6); in the end, the ruler will succeed in engaging the noble man to serve him.

Divination Direction

It augurs well. Do not get discouraged by a few hurdles you must overcome. Continue your earnest efforts to attain your goal. You will succeed.

Line 6-9: This yang line is properly positioned at the top of the Progressive Advance hexagram, correlating with no line.

The images signify that the wild goose gradually takes to the air. The orderly flight of the geese should serve as a model for man. Like the feather of a goose left behind in its flight that is used for a religious ornament, the virtuous conduct of a person remains valuable for others to model after he is gone. There will be good fortune. One should serve his sovereign in the same way with exemplary excellence and lofty ideals.

Divination Direction

It augurs well. You are at the apogee of the good auspices cycle. Everything you have been doing will consummate here for your successful goal attainment. However, you must know when or where to stop and not become greedy.

54. The Marrying Maiden 歸妹 (Kwei Mei) Hexagram

Key attributes: Marrying maiden, the symbol of marriage

Judgment

"*Kwei Mei* indicates that (under the conditions which it denotes) action will be evil, and in no wise advantageous." (James Legge, *The I Ching*, 180.)

Essence of Hexagram

This hexagram explains the principles of propriety from beginning to the end, not only for matrimonial arrangements but also for all other matters in life.

Hexagram Image(s)

Thunder above Lake stands for the images of the Marrying Maiden hexagram. The wise and noble uses the images as his guide for understanding how the beginning and the ending are interrelated, like the lake water that evaporates to cause the thunder to roar, in order that he can take appropriate actions to eliminate the cause that, if not dealt with, will ultimately result in an ill effect.

Hexagram Analysis

This hexagram consists of the lower trigram Lake that denotes the youngest daughter and joy, and the upper trigram Thunder, the eldest son and movement. The combined images portray the young girl who, enamored with an older man's movement, makes a matrimonial proposal. According to ancient Chinese mores, it is improper for a girl or woman to take such initiative; furthermore, there is a great age disparity between the two. A marriage out of such circumstances portends a bad omen. The yin (lower trigram Lake) is joyful to be influenced by the yang (upper trigram) of roaring thunder (upper trigram Thunder, movement).

The inner four lines of the hexagram are all improperly positioned. The only properly positioned yang line, 1-9, is at the bottom, and the only properly positioned yin line is at the top of the hexagram; neither 1-9 nor 6-6 has a correlative relationship. Furthermore, the soft and weak (3-6, 5-6, and 6-6) ride atop the hard and strong (yang lines), indicating the soft dominating the hard or disorderly arrangements.

3-6 and 6-6, directive, and 5-6, structural, are the lead lines of this hexagram.

Interpretation of Judgment

The marital relationship discussed in Hexagram #53 Progressive Advance describes a successful marriage that is consummated by taking proper and gradual steps. Hexagram #54 Marrying Maiden points out some pitfalls that can cause a marital relationship to fail, as well as an example of proper conduct of a bride that bodes a successful marriage. Marriage is of great importance because its principle is founded in the interaction between Heaven and Earth. Without the interaction, there will be no growth in anything. The interaction between male and female through marital relationships ensures the continuation of the human race. Marriage means the end of a girl's role as daughter and the beginning of her role as wife. This young lady is joyfully enamored with the movement of a much older man and marries him, which is improper and disadvantageous. Her immature judgment will invite misfortune. In decision making, it is important to keep in mind what consequences the decision will bring. The hexagram indicates the misfortune with the improperly positioned lines and the soft lines riding atop the hard lines (a stubborn and dominating wife).

Divination Direction

It augurs ill. A careless beginning will result in misfortunes. You will face many obstacles in pursuing your goal. Your thinking is not clear, and your activities are diffused. Guard against a romantic involvement.

Individual Lines: Analysis, Interpretation, and Divination Direction

Line 1-9: This yang line is properly positioned at the bottom of the hexagram, correlating with no line. This line represents the secondary wife. She attends to the bride, the youngest daughter in the family who becomes the proper wife of a feudal prince. In ancient China, a feudal prince could marry as many as nine women at one time; one as his proper wife and the others (half sister, cousin, etc., of the bride) as secondary wives, in order to ensure the continuation of the male family lineage.

The images signify that modesty is the virtue that leads to accomplishment. This woman, low in her status (the bottom line of the hexagram with no correlating line) but modest in her attitude (properly positioned), accompanies the youngest sister as a secondary wife. This woman carries out the husband's wishes well (tactfully) despite her inferior status, like the lame person who keeps walking. Anyone who makes sincere efforts to perform one's duties will have good fortune.

Divination Direction

You have good abilities but no opportunity to demonstrate them. Do not get discouraged over this; continue with your sincere efforts to do your best, and eventually you will be rewarded with the proper recognition.

Line 2-9: This yang line is improperly positioned at the center of the lower trigram, correlating with 5-6.

The images signify that there is no mutual support between husband and wife, because the husband (5-6), who is high in status but weak, does not accord his virtuous, able wife full recognition for her virtues and competence. He makes her feel lonely, and that she is falling short in carrying out the duties of a wife. Nonetheless, she maintains the correct virtues of a wife with modesty to the end. Her loyalty is like the one-eyed person who can still continue to function well.

Divination Direction

You feel dissatisfied with your situation and feel unfairly treated by others. However, you must persevere to the end. Your success will be modest but valuable.

Line 3-6: This yin line is improperly positioned at the top of the lower trigram Lake that denotes joy, correlating with no line. This line represents a concubine whose status is even lower than that of the secondary wife. (A secondary wife is related to the proper wife; the concubine is the ancillary wife.) A concubine is likely to indulge in lascivious joy (the top line of the trigram Lake).

The images signify that this woman with the temperament for improper pleasures (improperly positioned) was rejected as a concubine. She can hardly wait for a new opportunity, and returns home to remarry as a slave wife, which is lower in status than a concubine.

Divination Direction

If you cannot control your emotion, you will get into trouble. You must first learn to observe rules, and then pursue your goal step-by-step in an orderly way.

Line 4-9: This yang line is improperly positioned, correlating with no line.

The images signify that this woman who is wise and talented exceeded the customary time for marriage. Despite the delay, she takes her time to find the most suitable man, and the time will come when she finds the right man to marry.

Divination Direction

"Without haste; without waste" should be your action guide. Be patient and wait for the opportunity to make the move to achieve your goal.

Line 5-6: This yin line is improperly positioned at the center of the upper trigram, correlating with 2-9.

The images signify the time when King *Ti-yi*'s[43] younger daughter, 5-6, was wedded. (King *Ti-yi* was a well-respected king in ancient China. He made the rule that the imperial princesses must observe the same husband-wife accommodation in the relationship as any ordinary couple.) Her wedding dresses or sleeves were not as fine as those of the accompanying secondary wife-to-be. This honorable conduct of the bride was due to her practice of the Mean, for she would rather cultivate her inner virtues than embellish her appearance. Although fully virtuous, she would not put herself on an equal footing with her husband, like the moon, which has almost reached its fullness. There will be good fortune.

Divination Direction

Give up your grandiose dreams and move on with a realistic goal. If you are female, it means good fortune. For male, you will have difficulties in achieving your goal. Be careful not to become involved in a dispute with other people.

Line 6-6: This yin line is properly positioned at the top of the hexagram with an antagonistic correlation with 3-6. 6-6 represents a man and 3-6 a woman. A marital relationship between the two cannot be formed because they do not correlate (mismatched). In ancient China, the matrimonial rituals took place in the temple of ancestral spirits, and the bride and groom made sacrificial offerings. The groom slaughtered a sheep and offered the sheep's blood, and the bride made an offering of a bamboo basket filled with fruits and nuts that the groom had given her when they were formally engaged.

The images signify that there was little sincerity in making the offerings at the ceremony, as the woman (3-6) had an empty bamboo basket and the man (6-6) cut a sheep that did not shed any blood, as it was dead. Thus, the superficial formalities, carried out with no sincerity, bode ill for the marriage. There will be no advantage.

Divination Direction

It augurs ill. Something seriously ominous is developing in your life. Extreme caution is in order.

55. The Abundance 豐 (Fang) Hexagram

Key attributes: Abundance, the symbol of prosperity

Judgment

"*Fang* intimates progress and development. When a king has reached the point (which the name denotes) there is no occasion to be anxious (through fear of a change). Let him be the sun at noon." (James Legge, *The I Ching*, 183.)

Essence of Hexagram

This hexagram explains the principle of proper conduct in the time of abundance by restraining one's greed and sharing one's abundance with others.

Hexagram Image(s)

Thunder above and lightning below come together to form the images of the Abundance hexagram. The clarity of lightning combined with the power of thunder brings about abundance in material prosperity and human wisdom. In governing, the abundance must be used correctly and fairly. The wise and noble man uses the images as his guide in conducting legal justice with the brilliance of lightning (lower trigram) and in implementing punishment with the authority of thunder (upper trigram).

Hexagram Analysis

This hexagram consists of the lower trigram Light that denotes intelligence and the upper trigram Thunder, movement. When bright intelligence (inner trigram) accompanies a movement (outer trigram), great achievement and prosperity will result. Thunder roars loudly high above in the sky, and lightning flashes below, but the roaring and the lightning will end soon. There is no correlating line in this hexagram. "Gods and spirits" mentioned below refers to the unseen force that brings change to natural phenomena such as rain, wind, thunder, and lightning.

5-6 is the sole lead line of this hexagram.

Interpretation of Judgment

The Abundance hexagram means that great abundance is brought about when brilliant intelligence (lower trigram) accompanies action (upper trigram). The royal *Tao* is great, as it can produce prosperity for the whole nation; therefore, only the sovereign can achieve it. Great abundance will not last for long unless the ruler carries out his governance properly. The virtuous is free of worries. Like the blessings of the midday sun, his virtues will shine over the entire world as he properly carries out his virtuous conduct. He conducts his governance with the full understanding that at midday, the sun reaches its apex, and it then begins to decline. When the moon reaches fullness, it begins to wane. Everything in Heaven and Earth waxes and wanes at the proper time. This is even truer for man or for the gods and spirits that bring changes to natural phenomena like rain and wind.

Divination Direction

You are at the height of prosperity with a prospect of a declining trend. Save your resources and prepare for a hard time. Conclude your business dealings as quickly as possible. Refrain from any contentious involvement. Pay attention to your health problems. At the height of your success, you must know when to stop to seek more.

Individual Lines: Analysis, Interpretation, and Divination Direction

Line 1-9: This yang line is properly positioned at the bottom of the hexagram, correlating with no line. In the era of Abundance, 1-9 and 4-9 break the rule of antagonic correlation and collaborate with each other, like partners, to serve the sovereign well. The antagonistic correlation does not apply here because lightning and thunder go together naturally. It is a partnership of clear purpose (trigram Light) and action (trigram Thunder).

The images signify that this competent and clear-minded man of lower status (1-9) meets an equally competent and energetic man of higher status (4-9), and they become partners. They work in partnership for the ruler, and achieve much. The partnership of 1-9 and 4-9 is so well-suited that even if it takes as many as ten days (entire cycle of time) for 1-9 to meet his counterpart, he will incur no blame; however, if he procrastinates beyond ten days, it will result in misfortune.

Divination Direction

Cooperate with your friends to succeed; overconfidence in your ability to do it alone will lead you to difficulties and failures.

Line 2-6: This yin line is properly positioned at the center of the lower trigram, correlating with no line. In the era of Abundance, this virtuous man makes special efforts to help the ruler (5-6) achieve great Abundance.

The images signify that even a loyal subject with a clear vision and virtuous mind could cloud his ruler's mind, unless he can present his brilliance and sincerity in a correct way. This virtuous, competent subject (2-6) might make the ruler's mind so screened off (darkened) that the Big Dipper can be seen in the sky at midday. Under these circumstances, if he forces his way to help the ruler, he will end up reaping the ruler's suspicion and enmity. If he maintains his integrity with sincerity and works to instill trust in the ruler's mind, the ruler's mind will eventually clear, and he will view his virtuous, competent subject in the true light, resulting in good fortune.

Divination Direction

You may be wrongly accused by others or become the target of the other person's misunderstanding, jealousy, or suspicion. Maintain your integrity of trustworthiness and take every step prudently, and your situation will improve.

Line 3-9: This yang line is properly positioned at the top of the lower trigram Light and correlates with 6-6, the high government official. The high government official's mind is likened to being screened off by a thick, large banner, rendering his mind even darker than that of the ruler described in line 2-6 above.

The images signify that the high official's (6-6) dark, incompetent mind is not able to properly recognize this competent man (3-9), as if his mind is screened off by a thick, large banner, rendering it so dark that the small dim stars can be seen in the midday. Nothing great can be accomplished. This competent man is unable to make good use of his ability to serve the high official or the state, as if he broke his right arm in the darkness. It is not his fault; he will incur no blame.

Divination Direction

You are in a predicament and don't know what to do with your talent and resources. You must refrain from interfering in someone else's business; if you do, it will cause you many worries.

Line 4-9: This yang line is improperly positioned at the beginning of the upper trigram Thunder, correlating with no line. This line has a collaborative relationship with 1-9, which is an exception to the rule. This prime minister is competent but lacks in virtues (improperly positioned away from the center). He advises the ruler wrongly and keeps the ruler in the dark. In the hexagram, this line is not part of the lower trigram Light, and its movement (upper trigram Thunder) does not come with enlightenment (lower trigram Light).

The images signify that an energetic movement combined with a clear vision can correct past mistakes and will bring favorable results. This inexpedient prime minister, lacking in virtues, misleads the unwise ruler, rendering the people under the ruler unenlightened. It is as if the king and prime minister are screened off and live in such darkness that the Dipper is seen in the midday. If the prime minister invites the counterpart (1-9) who has a clear vision to help him serve the ruler, the wrong will be righted, and good fortune will follow.

Divination Direction

You are selfish and obstinate. That is the reason you experience hard luck and failures. Cultivate the virtue of humility and learn how to listen and accept good advice. You will benefit much if you cooperate with other people.

Line 5-6: This yin line is improperly positioned at the center of the upper trigram Thunder and is the lead line of the hexagram, correlating with no line. This line has a resonant relationship with 2-6, an exception to the rule of correlation; both practice the virtues of the Mean.

The images signify that the ruler is modest and leads the movement (upper trigram) to achieve Abundance. If he summons the noble man with brilliant ability (2-6) to help him bring other able subjects (1-9, 3-9, and 4-9) to serve him, there will be blessings and praise. Such collaboration between the ruler and his assistants will assure prosperity in the state; it means good fortune for everyone.

Divination Direction

It augurs well. You will be successful. Other people will be willing to help you to break through when you face an impasse.

Line 6-6: This yin line is properly positioned at the top of the Abundance hexagram and correlates with 3-9. This high official at the apogee of the Abundance era has become arrogant and indulges in extravagantly luxurious lifestyle.

The images signify that arrogance brings isolation. This injudicious and arrogant high official lives in the house so large and lofty that it appears to reach up to the limit of the sky. Such an arrogant and luxurious lifestyle will result in misfortune. With declining fortune, his family will appear to have been screened off, and he lives alone isolated, instead of providing useful services for the society. When one peeks through the door, he finds no one, only silence. The occupant (6-6) may be hiding. For three long years, no one can be seen in this house. There will be misfortune.

Divination Direction

It augurs ill. Nothing is working satisfactorily, with one failure after another. Refrain from an impulsive, ambitious undertaking. Be prudent in your conduct and prepare well before taking an action.

56. The Wanderer 旅 (Lu) Hexagram

Key attributes: Traveler, the symbol of wandering

Judgment

"*Lu* intimates that (in the condition which it denotes) there may be some little attainment and progress. If the stranger or traveler be firm and correct as he ought to be, there will be good fortune." (James Legge, *The I Ching*, 187.)

Essence of Hexagram

This hexagram explains the principle of proper conduct when traveling by being humble in attitude and maintaining one's moral integrity of uprightness and fairness.

Hexagram Image(s)

Fire on top of Mountain is the image of the Wanderer hexagram[44] and represents the traveler, like the fire that follows combustibles on a mountain. Besides the images of travel, the hexagram also presents the image of administering justice clearly and fairly; mountain represents deliberation on matters of justice. The wise and noble uses the image as his guide for the proper administration of justice. He makes clear distinctions (trigram Light) regarding the severity of crimes and administers careful (trigram Mountain) and swift judgment without prolonging a trial, and makes a prison only a short period of temporary lodging place for a criminal.

Hexagram Analysis

This hexagram consists of the lower trigram Mountain that denotes halt or being stationary, and the upper trigram Light, fire or being bright. In this hexagram, Mountain represents the home where relatives and friends live together without moving away (stationary), in contrast to fire which moves constantly, like a traveler. In ancient time, travel entailed many hardships; the traveler was a stranger in a strange land without adequate means of transportation. When traveling, one must act prudently with the attitude of humility and compliance, even to obtain any help.

5-6 is the sole lead line of this hexagram.

Interpretation of Judgment

The Wanderer hexagram represents small progress in achievement as the wanderer leaves his home (the Mountain) to attain the center position of the upper trigram Fire. (5-6 left the inner trigram Earth to switch with the center position of the upper trigram Heaven, changing the lower trigram to Mountain and the upper trigram to Fire.) This traveler is compliant with the strong (4-9 and 6-9), but he holds on to clarity in his judgment. There will be some attainment and progress as he maintains the correct *Tao* of traveling by being humble in attitude and fair and upright in his heart; there will be good fortune. What a matter of great importance it is to observe the principle of traveling properly! The same principle applies to man's journey of life.

Divination Direction

You feel unsettled, lonely, and troubled. You are in the declining cycle of fortune. You will have an opportunity to travel. Refrain from going into an ambitious project. Your advantage lies in engaging in cultural activities such as literature, art, or entertainment. Pay attention to your health.

Individual Lines: Analysis, Interpretation, and Divination Direction

Line 1-6: This yin line is improperly positioned at the bottom of the hexagram and correlates with 4-9.

The images signify that this wanderer (traveler) should be humble in attitude with strong integrity, but should not be so preoccupied with trivial matters and argue, for instance, over lodging fees and services. Otherwise, others will treat him with unfriendliness, thus inviting misfortune upon him.

Divination Direction

You tend to be self-centered and tunnel-visioned. You may succeed in trivial matters but not in attaining a great achievement. Cultivate your ability to cooperate with other people, instead of meddling with their business for trivial matters.

Line 2-6: This yin line is properly positioned at the center of the lower trigram, correlating with no line.

The images signify that this wanderer, who practices the virtues of the Mean, stays in a proper lodging. Without any worries about his travel expenses, he can afford the company of a servant. Such fortunate traveling is due to his being humble in attitude with internal integrity; he will not have any trouble during his travel.

Divination Direction

You are well prepared and feel comfortable. Your plans will work in your favor.

Line 3-9: This yang line is properly positioned at the top of the lower trigram, contiguous to 2-6, correlating with no line. The yang line at the top and away from the center represents arrogance and cruelty to the weak (his servant).

The images signify that this traveler is arrogant and stubborn and can get no place to rest, as if his lodging has burned down to his distress. His servant has left him because the traveler lost his sense of fairness in treating his servant. His stubborn, undisciplined temperament will create perils in his travels.

Divination Direction

You are overconfident in your own ability and do not listen to the ideas of other people. Such self-centered tunnel vision will lead you to a disastrous failure. You must cultivate a warm and friendly temperament.

Line 4-9: This yang line is improperly positioned at the beginning of the upper trigram and correlates with 1-6.

The images signify that the wanderer finds a place to rest (temporary shelter), but it is not a proper place (yang line in the yin position) for him to settle down permanently. It is like the competent and humble person who succeeds in acquiring some wealth, but he still feels insecure and has to be on guard all the time as a traveler in a strange land.

Divination Direction

Your contentment is temporary, and you have not attained real peace of mind. The unstable situation will last for a while. In the meantime, refrain from undertaking any major project.

Line 5-6: This yin line is improperly positioned at the center of the upper trigram Light, contiguous to 6-9, correlating with no line. It is the lead line of the hexagram as well as that of the upper trigram. The pheasant described below is a visual representation of elegance (upper trigram Light). In this hexagram, 5-6 does not represent the position of ruler, but only a position of high status.

The images signify that this bright and virtuous traveling statesman captures a pheasant using only one arrow (in a single shot), and wants to present it to the local ruler as his gift. He lost his arrow but earned his fame. His friends praise him for his skill and recommend him to the local ruler, who gives him proper recognition and appoints him to an honorable position. It is an analogy to a traveler who wants to settle down in a strange land, and he must know how to adjust himself in the new environment by utilizing the available resources that he has.

Divination Direction

Your must make your best efforts to overcome the barriers; then you will be fully rewarded for your sacrifice. You will successfully attain your goal.

Line 6-9: This yang line is improperly positioned at the top of the Wanderer hexagram, contiguous to 5-6, correlating with no line. Humility and compliance are virtues a traveler must possess in order to avoid a disaster. At the top of the hexagram, this line represents arrogance and obstinacy and an aggressive temperament (yang line in yin position).

The images signify that, being at the top, the traveler becomes arrogant and careless and forgets that he is a traveler. It is like the bird's nest that burns up due to the careless inconsideration of the bird in building it. Likewise, being arrogant and inconsiderate to the people he meets while traveling may be an amusing and laughing matter to him in the beginning. But he will end up in a dire situation and will be howling and wailing about his loss when he loses his belongings, yet no one will help him to find them. He is like the person who was so arrogant and careless that when he lost his cow[45] at the border of a field, no one would tell him where to find it; misfortune.

Divination Direction

It augurs ill. Your success will not last long. Whatever you try, your arrogance and obstinacy will bring failures. Make special efforts to cultivate your inner strength with virtues such as humility and cooperation.

57. The Mildness 巽 (Sun) Hexagram

Key attributes: Mildness, the symbol of penetration

Judgment

"*Sun* intimates that (under the conditions which it denotes) there will be some little attainment and progress. There will be advantage in movement onward in whatever direction. It will be advantageous (also) to see the great man." (James Legge, *The I Ching*, 189.)

Essence of Hexagram

This hexagram explains the principle of prevailing through gentle (mild) and persistent influence on others and of accepting the influence of a leader.

Hexagram Image(s)

The wind blowing continuously, as indicated by the repeated trigram Wind, stands for the images of the Mildness hexagram. The wise and noble uses the images as his guide in governing through repeated gentle efforts to explain his decrees so that his intention penetrates the minds of the people and promotes the people's understanding of and compliance with them.

Hexagram Analysis

This hexagram consists of the double trigram Wind that denotes compliance or mildness in attitude. Wind symbolizes both wood and eldest daughter; wood has the attribute of penetration like wind, and eldest daughter the attribute of obedience (compliance). The trigram Wind has one yin line under two yang lines, portraying the penetration of yin into the yang domain. It also symbolizes the compliance of the yin line with the yang line as shown by 1-6's compliance with 2-9, and 4-6's compliance with 5-9. The center yang line of both trigrams represents the great man. In this hexagram, the Wind symbolizes the imperial edict that affects everyone in the state, like the wind that penetrates every nook and corner of the ruler's domain. The doubling of the trigram Wind emphasizes that when the government issues an edict, it is important to promote the people's understanding of it through continuing educational efforts.

There are three lead lines, 1-6 and 4-6 as directive and 5-9 as structural.

Interpretation of Judgment

The Mildness hexagram is made up of the repeated trigram Wind to emphasize the importance of gentle and persistent efforts that the government has to make in order to educate the people about the ruler's edict following its issuance. The ruler (5-9) is virtuously compliant of the Mean in the issuance of his edict, and the people (1-6, 4-6) comply with it. The important goal of governing can be achieved through the gradual and continuous progress in the understanding the people have of the ruler's edict; it is not like the big changes accomplished through a revolution. Under such a penetrating and understanding leadership, the people (1-6, 4-6) will have great benefits by following the great man because he possesses the virtues of the Mean and competence.

Divination Direction

It augurs well for a trading business, but you must act decisively in business transactions. You will get along well with your superior. Whether you succeed or encounter difficulties depends on your attitude. A humble, compliant attitude toward a good leader will pave your way for some success, but your arrogance will lead you to misfortune. Guard against communicable diseases.

Individual Lines: Analysis, Interpretation, and Divination Direction

Line 1-6: This yin line is improperly positioned at the bottom of the hexagram, contiguous to 2-9, correlating with no line.

The images signify that this gentle but weak-willed person vacillates as to whether he should advance or retreat. He is unable to make up his mind if he should follow the person in the higher status (4-6) or the person who is more competent but lower in status (2-9). It will be to his advantage to make a decision, like the decisiveness of a warrior in a military action.

Divination Direction

You are likely to miss favorable opportunities due to your vacillation and weak determination. Seek advice and make up your mind to pursue a goal with determination.

Line 2-9: This yang line is improperly positioned at the center of the lower trigram Wind, contiguous to 1-6, correlating with no line. The Wind trigram represents wood or the bed frame. A shaman will search beneath the couch or bed for evil spirits to drive them away. An invoker sends messages (invocation) to the spirit to receive grace. The shaman sends the prayers of a seeker by singing and dancing to the spirit(s) and delivers the messages from the spirit(s) to the seeker.

The images signify that root causes of insidious influences must be eliminated by all means, including the help of spiritual invoker and shaman. This person utilizes spirit invokers and shamans (1-6) to solve his problem, which is spiritual or psychic in nature and invisible, as though evil spirits are penetrating under the bed. In this way, the communication between the grace seeker and the spirit is facilitated to understand and eliminate the causes. Because of his sincere, compliant attitude and the thoroughness in his efforts, there will be good fortune with no error.

Divination Direction

If you conduct yourself with a humble and compliant attitude, you will be successful. On the other hand, your arrogance and obstinacy will lead you to failures.

Line 3-9: This yang line is properly positioned at the top of the lower trigram, correlating with no line. This yang line, away from the virtues of the Mean, symbolizes restless, strong energy.

The images signify that this man is so restless and indecisive that he keeps changing his mind on his decisions, thus creating more doubts on his ability to carry them out. The mind of such repeated indecisions will bring regret.

Divination Direction

Frequent changes of your mind will damage your trustworthiness. First, make a prudent choice and then maintain it.

Line 4-6: This yin line is properly positioned at the beginning of the upper trigram, contiguous to 5-9, correlating with no line. This yin line is riding atop 3-9.

The images signify that the person with experience, combined with both enthusiasm and modesty in attitude, can produce great achievements. This prime minister who practices the *Tao* of Mildness (compliance) serves the ruler so meritoriously that any occasion for regret will disappear. The restless one (3-9) might challenge the prime minister's loyalty, but he is no match to the prime minister, whose meritorious achievements can be compared to catching all three categories of game in a hunt, which is considered a great success. (The ancient Chinese hunting tradition has three categories in the use of the game that is shot in hunting. In the first category, the game is shot in the heart and used as a religious sacrifice; in the second category, the game is shot in the thigh and used to feed guests; in the third category, the game is shot in the abdomen and used for household consumption.)

Divination Direction

It augurs well. You will enjoy the trust of people in achieving your goals.

Line 5-9: This yang line is properly positioned at the center of the upper trigram, contiguous to 4-6, correlating with no line. In ancient China, ten Chinese characters were used in the heavenly decimal cycle (*tiangan*) to designate the days. The seventh character, *geng*, denoted the issuance of a new edict. The character for three days before *geng* denotes prudence and three days after *geng*, discreteness. The ruler, represented by this structural lead line of the Mildness hexagram, is the embodiment of the virtues of humility and compliance.

The images signify that this virtuous ruler who practices the Mean maintains the *Tao* correctly and firmly and receives good fortune with no regret. To implement a reform in state affairs, he exercises sufficient prudence prior to issuing the edict and follows up with education and discreet evaluation. Such thoroughness can be expressed metaphorically as choosing the right timing of three days before the change (*geng*) and three days following it. When the ruler issues an edict, it may not be received well in the beginning because the people do not understand it, but in the end they gain an understanding and accept the edict. There is nothing that is disadvantageous in his activities. There will be good fortune.

Divination Direction

In pursuing your goal, be prudent and discreet in your conduct. You will experience a little difficulty in the beginning, but persistent and sincere efforts will lead you to succeed.

Line 6-9: This yang line is improperly positioned at the top of the Mildness hexagram, correlating with no line.

The images signify that, at the apogee of the Mildness era, this man goes to the extreme in his practice of humility and compliance, as if he is lying under a couch, restricted in his movement. As a consequence, he has lost his wealth and the ax (authority), the tool he used to make correct decisions. His insistence on the extreme practice of the correct virtues of humility and compliance will lead him to misfortune.

Divination Direction

It augurs ill. The conduct of excessive humility and compliance often hides one's ulterior motive. Your self-centered obstinacy derives from your greed, and it will lead you to failures. You will end up losing both money and reputation.

58. The Joy 兌 (Tui) Hexagram

Key attributes: Joy, lake, the symbol of pleasure

Judgment

"*Tui* intimates that (under its conditions) there will be progress and attainment. (But) it will be advantageous to be firm and correct." (James Legge, *The I Ching*, 192.)

Essence of Hexagram

This hexagram explains the principle of a joyful life through the development of peace and harmony in one's mind by staying on the correct course of *Tao* and continuous learning for enlightening the mind.

Hexagram Image(s)

Lake linked with another Lake is the image of the Joy hexagram. With the water from the lake below replenishing the one above, it will take a long time for the lakes to dry up. The wise and noble man uses the image as his guide in the joyous pursuit of truth, through revitalizing and stimulating discourse of knowledge with his colleagues and friends.

Hexagram Analysis

This hexagram consists of the double trigram Lake. The lower trigram represents the pleasure (joy) that comes from responding to the needs of the people. The upper trigram represents the joy of following the *Tao* of Heaven. The trigram Lake has one yin line above two yang lines, with a yang line occupying the center. It symbolizes the inner integrity of a person with the virtues of the Mean, as well as gentle, receptive conduct in relating with other people. These virtues and interrelationships with people are the source of a person's joy. The yin line of the trigram Lake represents water, and the two yang lines the basin of the lake that holds the water. The water evaporates to form clouds in the sky and returns to the earth as rain, thus becoming the continual source of harmony and joy for both heaven and earth. The two trigrams, sun and wind, of the primary nuclear hexagrams represent a clear, joyful day. Trigram Lake also represents a young girl (the youngest daughter) as the source of joy.

There are four lead lines in this hexagram: 3-6 and 6-6, directive, and 2-9 and 5-9, structural.

Interpretation of Judgment

The Joy hexagram represents true joy that comes from maintaining one's inner integrity with the virtues of the Mean and from establishing gentle and harmonious relationships with others, as when a man wins a girl's heart by being gentle in his manner and having sincere integrity of character. This is the way to progress and attain goals and is applicable in the same way in governing. Such a leader follows the correct path of *Tao* joyfully; he is obedient to Heaven and responsive to the needs of mankind. If he leads the people with such spiritual joy, they will follow him joyfully, forgetting or overlooking the hardships they experience.

When such a ruler faces a national crisis, the people will follow him at the risk of their lives to prevail over the crisis. Great is the significance of the Joy hexagram, for it represents the motivating force for the people!

Divination Direction

Though you appear to be joyful, you feel anxious inside. Be careful of what you say; for instance, don't get involved in an argument with other people. You will make some progress but will fail in attaining your major goal. A somewhat depressed financial situation will improve gradually. An expectant mother will give birth to a daughter.

Individual Lines: Analysis, Interpretation, and Divination Direction

Line 1-9: This yang line is properly positioned at the bottom of the hexagram, correlating with no line.

The images signify that this man, low in status but virtuous and competent (properly positioned yang line), is happy and content. He does not interfere in matters of other people, and he is the source of joy to others because he is in harmony with them and acts with integrity without leaving any room for suspicion. There will be good fortune.

Divination Direction

Move ahead steadfastly to achieve your goal while maintaining a harmonious relationship with other people. Avoid being sidetracked by the temptations that come from other people, and you will succeed.

Line 2-9: This yang line is improperly positioned at the center of the lower trigram, correlating with no line.

The images signify that this competent man who practices the virtues of the Mean is trustworthy, and his sincerity is the source of joy to other people. The petty man (3-6) of bad influence cannot damage his integrity. There will be good fortune with nothing to regret.

Divination Direction

You have peace of mind, as you are sincere and trustworthy. Maintain harmonious relationships with other people. Avoid being sidetracked from your goal by any temptations along the way.

Line 3-6: This yin line is improperly positioned at the top of the lower trigram, contiguous to 4-9, correlating with no line. This yin line comes from 6-6 (outer trigram) to improperly take the yang position between the two yang lines of 2-9 and 4-9.

The images signify that true joy must come from within, and the one who is empty of virtues within seeks joy from superficial pleasures through association with same kind of people who enjoy such indulgence. The Chinese *I Ching* text, "it (3-6) comes after joy," means it seeks joy by positioning itself in the wrong place to seek frivolous, superficial pleasures by attracting wrong people. There will be misfortune.

Divination Direction

If you use flattery to influence other people, you will experience failures and disgraceful predicaments. Build up your self-confidence and act with sincerity.

Line 4-9: This yang line is improperly positioned, contiguous to 3-6, correlating with no line. This competent prime minister deliberates as to whether he should continue enjoying the sycophantic pleasures of the friendly 3-6 or seek the honorable joy of serving the virtuous, competent ruler well.

The images signify that one's correct choice of true joyous source brings peace of mind. This competent prime minister deliberates as to which way to seek a joyous life. True joy comes from virtuous integrity of a person, which leads one to take the correct course of action, not from temporary, superficial indulgence. He finally decides to serve the ruler, and he feels as if he has rid himself of a skin disease (3-6). The prime minister's joy will be a blessing for everyone.

Divination Direction

It may be difficult to make up your mind. You must choose the most justifiable course of action instead of the most pleasurable one. Refrain from such temporary pleasures as excessive drinking, eating, or sex.

Line 5-9: This yang line is properly positioned at the center of the upper trigram, correlating with no line. Although this ruler is virtuous and competent, he may become arrogant and overly self-confident if he is not vigilant.

The images signify that this ruler is virtuous and competent (properly positioned). However, if he trusts the one (6-6) who could hurt him with unwholesome influences, he will be in danger. In the era of Joy, many sycophants surround the ruler to gain his favor by pleasing him. The ruler must have a discriminating ability to tell the good from the evil; otherwise, he will be in trouble.

Divination Direction

It augurs ill. You may fall into a trap by giving into the sweet, persuasive words of your friend. Accurately assess your own ability, and pursue your goal by staying within your own means and resources.

<u>Line 6-6</u>: This yin line is properly positioned at the top of the hexagram, correlating with no line.

The images signify that, at the apogee of the Joy hexagram, this man resorts to flattery for the joy of the ruler's favor in vain. Like attracts like, and he turns to his kind (3-6) for the unsavory joy. There is a danger that he will be trapped by their bad influence, as he has not yet attained clarity of mind.

Divination Direction

It augurs ill. You will fail in achieving your goal. Reflect upon yourself and cultivate your inner strength of virtues.

59. The Dissolution 渙 (Hwan) Hexagram

Key attributes: Dissolution, the symbol of dispersion

Judgment

"*Hwan* intimates that (under its conditions) there will be progress and success. The king goes to his ancestral temple; and it will be advantageous to cross the great stream. It will be advantageous to be firm and correct." (James Legge, *The I Ching*, 194.)

Essence of Hexagram

This hexagram explains the principle of dissolution (dispersal) to break up alienated minds or cluttered and congested situations by blowing away the clouds of psychological blockage or the confusion causing congestions.

Hexagram Image(s)

Wind blowing over Water stands for the images of the Dissolution hexagram, like the spring wind that dissolves winter ice. Former kings used these images as their guide for bringing together the alienated minds of the people. They attempted to dissolve the rigidity of the minds of the people by involving them in religious practice, building ancestral temples[46] and worshipping the Divine Ruler.

Hexagram Analysis

This hexagram consists of the lower trigram Water that denotes water or peril, and the upper trigram Wind, denoting wind or wood. The combined images portray wind blowing over water and dispersing the misty clouds over it to regain its clarity, or wind blowing away perils, thus solving problems. Wind symbolizes wood or boat; the lower trigram Thunder of the primary nuclear hexagram also symbolizes wood or boat. The boat represents the means of transportation that facilitates communication, promoting a connection among scattered people.

The first line of the upper trigram Heaven traded its position with the second line of the lower trigram Earth to make this hexagram.

5-9 is the sole lead line of the hexagram.

Interpretation of Judgment

When the minds of people become alienated and rigid, it is a sign of peril (lower trigram Water). In order to dissolve the perilous situation, the one with solid integrity of virtues (2-9) comes to occupy the position without any obstruction, and the one with gentle virtues (4-6) ascends to occupy the proper position of the outer trigram and serves the ruler (5-9). Therefore, the Dissolution hexagram stands for progress and success. In face of the peril, the virtuous and able ruler (5-9) goes to his ancestral temple to invoke the ancestral spirits to resolve the crisis. For the occasion, the pious minds of all the people come together in the religious ceremony, like the time when people join forces to successfully cross the great river in a boat. The advantage lies in maintaining the rectitude of *Tao*.

Divination Direction

It augurs well for a seafaring business and commercial business transactions. Guard against expenditures that might dissipate your resources. You will travel often. The problems you have had in the area of human relationships, which are making you feel distressed, will be resolved. You can solve your problems by getting help to clarify matters and restore balance in your mind. An expectant mother will give birth to a boy.

Individual Lines: Analysis, Interpretation, and Divination Direction

Line 1-6: This yin line is improperly positioned at the bottom of the hexagram, contiguous to 2-9, correlating with no line. Being at the bottom, this line symbolizes the situation in which the force of dispersion (evil force) has not yet taken hold firmly. It is too weak to deal with the crisis alone.

The images signify that the evil force of alienation must be dealt with before it takes roots. This person is too weak to prevail over such a force alone, and the virtuous and friendly 2-9 comes to the rescue with the speed and strength of a strong horse. There will be good fortune.

Divination Direction

Before it gets too late, seek the help of your superior or a friend to resolve your crisis, and you will be successful.

Line 2-9: This yang line is improperly positioned at the center of the lower trigram, contiguous to 1-6, correlating with no line. In the era of Dispersion, this line occupies the center of the trigram Water, the symbol of peril. The lower trigram Thunder (movement or feet) of the primary nuclear hexagram symbolizes the urgency to act to disperse the peril.

The images signify that helping others in need is the way to resolve one's own alienation problem. In the era of Dispersion, this virtuous, competent man faces the peril of being alienated from others (he is trapped by yin forces). When he sees that 1-6 needs his support, he runs quickly to rescue him. His problem of alienation is resolved, and his worries disappear.

Divination Direction

The best way to prepare for your rainy days is to help others when they are in need of your help. Now, without losing time, obtain the help of your superior or friend to resolve your crisis and prepare for the better days to come.

Line 3-6: This yin line is improperly positioned at the top of the lower trigram Water and correlates with 6-9 of the outer trigram, making them the only correlating lines of this hexagram.

The images signify that one must set aside self-centered barriers in order to help others from alienation. In the era of Dispersion, this person renounces his own needs and focuses on helping the one in the higher position (6-9) outside his circle, in order to surmount the peril coming from dispersion of people. He will have no regret.

Divination Direction

Your priority is to overcome the present crisis. You cannot afford to dissipate your resources for your casual interest. You must set aside other less important matters to seek the help of those who can help you to prevail in the current crisis.

Line 4-6: This yin line is properly positioned at the beginning of the upper trigram, correlating with no line. This line is out of the danger zone (lower trigram Water) and is in the zone of compliance (upper trigram Wind).

The images signify that, in the era of Dispersion, this prime minister rises above his personal interest and friendships to serve well the virtuous, competent ruler (5-9) for the welfare of the state by dispersing the dissenting cliques (1-6 and 3-6). This illustrious achievement results in great good fortune. Once the Dispersion is successfully achieved, there will be a regrouping of the people to better serve the state. The prime minister's prominence will stand out like a hill; his courage and foresight are beyond what ordinary people (1-6, 3-6) would be able to think of or do.

Divination Direction

First, set up a clear, prudent goal and then make concerted efforts to achieve it. Avoid playing into temptations; instead, make concentrated efforts to carry out your assignment, and you will be successful.

Line 5-9: This yang line is properly positioned at the center of the upper trigram Wind (Compliance), contiguous to 4-6 and correlating with no line.

The images signify that, in the era of Dispersion (Dissolution) when the state is in disarray with disunity among the people, this virtuous and competent ruler issues a rallying edict to reunify the dispersed people by sharing his accumulated resources. It is as if the perspiration from the ruler's body dissipates the fever at its crisis point. When the ruler carries out his governance properly, he will make no error.

Divination Direction

The time of good fortune is coming. It is the time for you to start achieving your goal through your cooperative efforts with others by sharing your resources with them. You will encounter some small obstacles to overcome. Do not get bogged down but push ahead forcefully to achieve your goal, and you will succeed.

Line 6-9: This yang line is improperly positioned at the top of the hexagram and correlates with 3-6. The era of Dispersion represents the time of disarray among the people, and bloody dissensions (lower trigram Water represents blood) ensue. This top line is farthest from the peril (the lower trigram Water) and tries not to become involved in the dissension by not responding to a call for help from 3-6 (the top line of the Water trigram; peril).

The images signify that this retired high official disperses the threat of bloodshed from dissensions by staying away from factional contentions to avoid harm to him and to keep his people away from the danger. He will make no error.

Divination Direction

It is the proper time to retire or rest from what you have been doing. It is the time to reassess the situation to find solutions to your problems. You may get hurt if you force yourself to continue to deal with the difficult situation you are in.

60. The Regulation 節 (Kieh or Jie) Hexagram

Key attributes: Regulation, limitation, the symbol of regulated restriction

Judgment

"*Kieh* intimates that (under its conditions) there will be progress and attainment. (But) if the regulations (which it prescribes) be severe and difficult, they can not be permanent." (James Legge, *The I Ching*, 197.)

Essence of Hexagram

This hexagram explains the principle of attaining success and progress through proper balance and regulation in life by exercising self-discipline and self-restraint.

Hexagram Image(s)

Water on top of Lake stands for the images of the Regulation hexagram. The wise and noble man uses the images as his guide in establishing measurements, scales, and moral standards for the benefit of the people, like the lake that must hold the proper amount of water within the limit of its capacity to meet the needs of the people.

Hexagram Analysis

This hexagram consists of the lower trigram Lake (yin trigram) that denotes joy and the upper trigram Water (yang trigram) that denotes the water in the lake. This division of yin and yang constitutes the basis of regulation. The hard yang lines (2-9 and 5-9) that occupy the center position of each trigram play a regulating function by exercising proper restriction that limits the power of the ruler and his subjects. The primary nuclear hexagram consists of the lower trigram Thunder (movement) and the upper trigram Mountain (halt). The movement of Thunder combined with the lower trigram Lake of the original hexagram portrays an excessive joyous movement that needs to be regulated by the halting action of the upper trigram Mountain of the nuclear hexagram. The water on the top of the lake represents the limit in the capacity of the lake for holding water. The Chinese character for Regulation depicts the joints of bamboos that regulate the length of each bamboo section (measurement).

5-9 is the sole lead line of this hexagram.

Interpretation of Judgment

The Regulation hexagram recognizes the need for limits for both the government and its people in order to bring about progress and attainment. Excessive regulation becomes oppressive and cannot be maintained permanently. The proper ruler (5-9) who practices the Mean handles perils (upper trigram Water) in the spirit of joy (lower trigram

Lake) by observing and instituting the principles of Regulation to achieve his goals. In nature, Heaven and Earth observe the principles of Regulation, as in the four seasons that fulfill their regulated function. In a similar fashion, regulation applied in a measured way will not cause injury, loss of the wealth, or harm to people. Above all, one must know one's limitations at all times and take self-limiting actions to avoid the excess, and to carry out one's duties appropriately.

Divination Direction

It is the time for moderation and disciplined living. Refrain from any abusive behavior, especially in eating, drinking, and entertaining. Prepare for a natural disaster like flooding, fire and earthquake. Establish your goal and the priorities of action, and carry them out according to the plan. You will attain small but favorable achievements in trading and business transactions. It is favorable for marriage, but unfavorable to travel.

Individual Lines: Analysis, Interpretation, and Divination Direction

Line 1-9: This yang line is properly positioned at the bottom of the hexagram and correlates with 4-6, the first line of the trigram Water. This virtuous and competent man could work with the prime minister (4-6) to serve the ruler, but he decides to limit his role and stay at home, as he has the foresight to see that his move will incur 2-9's wrath.

The images signify that understanding as to where to begin and where to end is the beginning of success. This competent man decides not to go out of his house to serve the state, for he understands the principle of proper timing or regulation as to when the correct *Tao* prevails and when it becomes obstructed. He will make no error.

Divination Direction

It is the time for preparation but not for an active pursuit of your goal. Be prudent in every move you make, as some unseen dangers lurk in your environment.

Line 2-9: This yang line is improperly positioned at the center of the lower trigram, correlating with no line. The water has reached the maximum level, but there is no overflow as it finds an outlet.

The images signify that one must not fail to seize an opportunity when it presents. This virtuous, competent man confines himself in his house without going beyond his courtyard gate when his service is needed, thus failing to seize the right opportunity. There will be misfortune.

Divination Direction

The self-restraint is different from being rigid, and now is the time for you to actively move to achieve your goal; be alert to seize the opportunity before you lose it.

Line 3-6: This yin line is improperly positioned at the top of the lower trigram, correlating with no line; it is neither centered nor properly positioned. Water has reached the top level, which calls for immediate measures to prevent flooding.

The images signify that this intemperate person fails to observe the *Tao* of Regulation. He is seen lamenting, as he belatedly realizes his mistakes. He cannot blame anyone else but himself for his excessive indulgence. He repents, and there will be no error.

Divination Direction

Excessive indulgence in pleasures and laziness will result in failures. Cultivate self-discipline and actively work to attain your goal.

Line 4-6: This yin line is properly positioned at the beginning of the upper trigram, contiguous to 5-9 and correlating with 1-9.

The images signify that the one who observes natural and sensible limitations will be successful. This virtuous prime minister practices the *Tao* of Regulation, and he follows the natural direction (5-9, not 1-9) in compliance with the ruler's expectations. There will be progress and success.

Divination Direction

It augurs well. Actively work to attain your goal. You may come across some obstacles along the way, but the prudent step-by-step approach will lead you to succeed.

Line 5-9: This yang line is properly positioned at the center of the upper trigram, contiguous to 4-6, correlating with no line.

The images signify that limitations must be implemented fairly and correctly in order to be successful. This virtuous, competent ruler practices the Mean and observes the *Tao* of Regulation sweetly in his governance. ("Sweetly" means that the ruler practices the *Tao* of Regulation himself first, and others will follow him without resentment.) The people will admire his achievement. There will be good fortune.

Divination Direction

It augurs well. Actively seek to attain your well-motivated goal, and you will succeed. Excessive greed will lead you to fail.

Line 6-6: This yin line is properly positioned at the top of the hexagram, correlating with no line. It symbolizes that the era of Regulation has reached its apogee with an excessive degree of regulations.

The images signify that limitations must be implemented with appropriate degrees of severity. This high official enacts excessive regulations. His insistence on the correctness of his way will result in misfortune, as it obstructs the practice of the Mean. However, if the excessive regulation was based on his belief that it was the proper way, it is better to have it than allow laxness. If the excessive regulations are moderated, there will be no regret.

Divination Direction

It augurs ill. You will experience hardship with no success. Reflect upon yourself as to whether you are obstinate and tunnel-visioned, lacking flexibility. Go slowly and relax a little.

61. The Central Sincerity 中孚 (Kung Fu or Zhong Fu) Hexagram

Key attributes: Central sincerity, the symbol of truth

Judgment

"*Kung Fu* (moves even) pigs and fish, and leads to good fortune. There will be advantage in crossing the great stream. There will be advantage in being firm and correct." (James Legge, *The I Ching*, 199.)

Essence of Hexagram

This hexagram explains the principle of inner sincerity or faithfulness that should prevail in one's relationship with the spirits and other human beings and creatures on earth, as well as in one's undertakings, including the administration of justice.

Hexagram Image(s)

Wind blowing over Lake stands for the images of the Central Sincerity hexagram. The wind penetrating lake water creates ripples to reveal more than the surface of lake. The wise and noble uses the images as his guide in the administration of justice. He examines every detail of the criminal's underlying motive and behavior when deliberating whether there is cause for mitigating the death penalty, like the wind that affects every ripple of the lake water.

Hexagram Analysis

This hexagram consists of the lower trigram Lake that denotes joy, and the upper trigram Wind, compliance. The combined images portray the people being joyous of the virtuous rule coming from above, and the ruler being compliant with the wishes of the governed. The Chinese character for sincerity[47] in the hexagram name "Central Sincerity" is the ideogram that depicts a bird protecting a hatching egg with maternal care and devotion (爫) to child (子). The two yin lines at the center of the hexagram symbolize the egg yolk; the two yang lines of 2-9 and 5-9 the egg white, and the two yang lines of 1-9 and 6-9 the egg shell.

Another image of the hexagram is the wind blowing over the lake, creating ripples in the water. This symbolizes the virtuous influence of a sage king that affects a multitude of people favorably. Furthermore, the image of sincerity is derived from the two yin lines at the center that represent the emptied mind, devoid of sordid thoughts or prejudice. The two yang lines, one from the centerline of each trigram, represent the integrity of the heart. The upper trigram Wind symbolizes wood and the lower trigram Lake metal; the combined images represent a boat made by cutting wood with a metallic tool. The "pigs and fish" in the judgment text refers to the people most difficult to influence with sincerity.

3-6 and 4-6, directive, and 2-9 and 5-9, structural, are the lead lines of this hexagram.

Interpretation of Judgment

The Central Sincerity hexagram presents the images of the soft (yin) occupying the innermost positions (3-6 and 4-6), and the hard (yang) occupying the center of each trigram (2-9 and 5-9). The hexagram represents love and kindness in the heart and moral integrity in conduct, which are essential for success in any human association. The ruled live joyously (lower trigram Lake) under virtuous governance, and the ruler is compliant (upper trigram Wind) with the wishes of the ruled.

This mutual sincerity and trust will transform the state. Even the men who are as difficult to influence as "pigs and fish" will be favorably moved by inner sincerity, resulting in good fortune. One who faces difficulties in life with a sincere heart will have the advantage, like the person who crosses a great river in an empty wooden boat that will not sink. One who has Central Sincerity and firmly practices the correctness of *Tao* will have every advantage, for he lives according to the precepts of Heaven.

Divination Direction

It augurs well, especially for human relationships, marriage, travel, and move to a new house. You will prevail in a pending litigation. Do everything with a sincere mind, and you will succeed. Cooperate with your friends to overcome the obstacles you meet in the course of your actions. Guard against a physical injury or a health problem.

Individual Lines: Analysis, Interpretation, and Divination Direction

Note: Each line of this hexagram represents the stage of a bird's egg being hatched by the mother bird.

Line 1-9: This yang line is properly positioned at the bottom of the hexagram and correlates with 4-6. This is the beginning stage of the hatching process, with the mother bird brooding over the egg with her concentrated effort and sincere desire for success.

The images signify that, in the era of Sincerity, one has to maintain the integrity of inner sincerity with good objectives (4-6). If he becomes unfaithful with an ulterior motive, he will lose inner peace and his good fortune.

Divination Direction

Concentrate all your efforts for the pursuit of your main goal. The one who chases after two rabbits will get neither one.

Line 2-9: This yang line is improperly positioned on the yin line as the center of the lower trigram. This line represents the second stage of the hatching process with the embryonic life form taking place inside the eggshell.

2-9 also represents the crane (a lake bird) standing in the shadowy side of the lake (yin position stands for shadow), which is the south end of the lake and north of the mountain. The inner trigram Thunder of the primary nuclear hexagram symbolizes both sound and the eldest; in this hexagram it symbolizes the parent crane. The outer trigram Mountain of the primary nuclear hexagram symbolizes the youngest offspring of the crane. Although 2-9 and 5-9 do not correlate, they are related; 2-9 symbolizes the parent crane and 5-9 the youngest male offspring. The lower trigram Lake denotes mouth and tongue, and when combined with the inner trigram Thunder of the primary nuclear hexagram, it portrays their mutual call and response. The parent crane calls out to its offspring who responds to the call. This line symbolizes communicating one's desire to share what one has with others; it reaches far and wide when it is done with inner sincerity.

The images signify that the one who has sincerity in his heart, which is expressed in speech and deed, creates such invulnerable power that it can transmit his influence far and wide. It is likened to the parent crane calling to its offspring[48] from the thicket in the lake, saying, "I have a goblet of good spirits that I want to share with you." The offspring responds with a sincere yearning, saying he will partake of the spirits with his parent.

Divination Direction

It augurs well. You will achieve your goal. You cooperate and get along harmoniously with other people, and you and others will enjoy the successful results together. You will be amply rewarded for the efforts you make to help other people.

Line 3-6: This yin line is improperly positioned at the top of the lower trigram and correlates with 6-9. This line and 4-6 are the directive lead lines of this hexagram and are referred to as "enemy," since both are yin lines. The "mate" or "comrade" of 3-6 is 6-9; the improperly positioned 3-6 denotes its ambitious and suspicious nature.

This line represents the third stage of the hatching process, which is the crucial but uncertain stage of the embryo's success in hatching.

The images signify that one who lacks in the central core of sincerity cannot maintain the peace of his mind. This ambitious and suspicious man who occupies the position improperly lacks a central core of sincerity as his base to feel and act. He is dependent on his comrade (6-9), who is strong and of higher status. However, his comrade is also improperly positioned and lacks central sincerity. He cannot be relied upon to be consistent and is not a reliable partner in time of need. When one (3-6) lacks central sincerity and relies on others (6-9) for his lot, his fate (mood) will be tossed around. It is as if he beats the drum to attack an enemy (4-6) and then stops; he weeps when he fears a counterattack and sings with joy when the enemy does not come. In reality, 4-6 is not his enemy; in his distorted mind, 3-6 perceives 4-6 to be his enemy.

Divination Direction

You are in a difficult situation and yet do not know whom to turn to for help because you lack inner resources to depend on. You do not have the sincerity to trust other people fully to attain a goal cooperatively. You must cultivate your moral integrity to foster mutual trust and cooperation with other people. Refrain from a rash action or judgment.

Line 4-6: This yin line is properly positioned at the beginning of the upper trigram Wind that denotes compliance and correlates with 1-9. This line represents the position of the prime minister, which is metaphorically compared to the "moon nearly full," and it will wane when it stands before the "sun" or the ruler (moon receives its light from the sun).

This line represents the fourth stage of the hatching process, which is the imminence of hatching; this requires devoted efforts for success.

The images signify that one must turn to a virtuous leader (sun) to receive enlightenment, like this virtuous prime minister serving the ruler (5-9) with sincerity and devotion. 4-6 and 1-9 are likened to two horses pulling a chariot ahead without side-glances. The prime minister is faced with the need to serve his ruler with total devotion or continue his relationship with his kind (1-9). He cuts off his relationship with 1-9 to serve the larger goal (choosing devotion for a righteous cause over selfish benefits). His modest and reverent conduct is like the "moon nearly full." The moon does not contend with the sun, the source of its light. There will be no error.

Divination Direction

It is the time to reconsider your relationships with the people who do not promote your goal. You must act with an open mind and sincerity. You can attain your goal if you seek it with persistence and sincerity.

Line 5-9: This yang line is properly positioned at the center of the upper trigram, contiguous to 4-6, and accepts 2-9 as a virtuous subject, not as his opponent.

This line represents the fifth stage of the hatching process; the egg has hatched successfully.

The images signify that this virtuous, sage ruler is so sincere that his mutually trustful relationship with his subjects (2-9, 4-6) is as secure as if they were tethered, and the ruler occupies the proper position. There will be no error.

Divination Direction

Because you are sincere and trustworthy, people will trust and respect you. Cooperative efforts with other people will be successful.

Line 6-9: This yang line is improperly positioned at the top of the hexagram and correlates with 3-6. At the apogee of the era, he becomes overconfident about his competence, positioning himself above the ruler.

This line represents the baby bird learning to fly.

The images signify the heightened ambition of this high official who lacks the inner virtues of sincerity. He is already at the highest position (top position of the hexagram) and cannot go any higher, although he wants to. He is like a cock that cannot fly to heaven, and so it flaps its wings and crows (brags) in an attempt to be heard in heaven. Such unreasonable ambition will bring misfortune before long.

Divination Direction

It augurs ill. Lower your unrealistic expectations. Even if you succeed in getting what you want, it will be temporary, as you are ill prepared for the position.

62. The Small Excess 小過 (Hsiao Kwo) Hexagram

Key attributes: Small excess, the symbol of minor preponderance

Judgment

"*Hsiao Kwo* indicates that (in the circumstances, which it implies) there will be progress and attainment. But it will be advantageous to be firm and correct. (What the name denotes) may be done in small affairs, but not in great affairs. (It is like) the notes that come down from a bird on the wind; to descend is better than to ascend. There will (in this way) be great good fortune." (James Legge, *The I Ching*, 201.)

Essence of Hexagram

This hexagram explains the principle of maintaining a balance in life through self-knowledge, foresight, and temperance.

Hexagram Image(s)

Thunder above Mountain stands for the images of the Small Excess hexagram. The wise and noble man uses the images as his guide for when to appropriately exercise little excesses (preponderance) with care and temperance in such nonessential or ceremonial matters as being reverent, grieving for the deceased, and being thrifty in spending. The small excess of a thunderous sound when heard high on the mountains is temporary and cannot change the constant (lower trigram Mountain) principles.

Hexagram Analysis

Hexagram #28 The Large Excess has four yang lines within, and a yin line at the bottom and the top of the hexagram. The Small Excess hexagram has only two yang lines in the center of the hexagram and two yin lines at the bottom and two at the top of the hexagram. This characterizes the small excess of the yang lines in this hexagram as compared to the Large Excess hexagram with four. The two yang lines of this hexagram, supported by yin lines, are strong but inadequate, as none of the two occupies any center position of the trigrams.

The Small Excess hexagram consists of the lower trigram Mountain and the upper trigram Thunder, presenting an image of a relatively small thunder extending its roaring sound over the big mountains (the sound becomes a little louder when heard on a mountain, as it is closer to the thunder), from which the hexagram name "Small Excess" is derived. The yin line symbolizes small, the yang, big. The excess of yin (small) lines also denotes the Small Excess. The yin lines occupy the centers of both the lower and upper trigrams (2-6 and 5-6), and the yang line (4-9) is away from the center in the improper position, as even lines belong to yin.

The hexagram portrays the image of a bird; the two yang lines in the middle represent the body and the two yin lines on both sides of the yang lines, the wings of the bird. The yin line riding atop the yang line (5-6 above 4-9) symbolizes the bird flying against the air current into the storm, or the insubordination of the underling. The yin line below the yang line (2-6 below 3-9) symbolizes the bird descending, or the underling being obedient to the one above. In ascending or descending, a bird leaves behind its sound, indicating that the bird is either flying against Heaven (insubordination) or toward Earth (obedience).

2-6 and 5-6 are the lead lines of this hexagram.

Interpretation of Judgment

The Small Excess hexagram represents the time when temperance in Small Excess brings progress and attainment. When the excess represents the strong yet inadequate, it conforms to the correct *Tao* to pertain itself to small personal matters and carry them out with care and temperance. Because the soft (yin line) obtains the center positions (2-6 and 5-6), the proper handling of small personal or family matters will result in good fortune. Since the hard (yang line, 4-9) has lost both the proper position and the center, it is not appropriate to deal with great or large matters such as national affairs. If one lacks in the virtues and proper qualifications, he should be content with a position that deals with small matters and should not be so ambitious as to handle such a great responsibility as governing the state. The principle of this hexagram can be read from its images of a bird flying up against the sun or into a storm and leaving a trailing sound. These images indicate that the bird's ascent will be an ill fortune (insubordination), while a bird descending in flight toward the safety of its nest indicates great good fortune (obedience). Any acceptable excess in dealing with small matters (like the bird's faint trailing sound) must be done only when necessary and within one's ability.

Divination Direction

It augurs ill. Refrain from undertaking any major project, especially if you tend to be greedy or overambitious. Start modestly and build up step-by-step. Financial investments are on a declining trend. You must try to preserve what you already have and get ready for the better time to come. You will experience difficulties in human relationships. Pay close attention to your health, as it will tend to get worse once you become ill.

Individual Lines: Analysis, Interpretation, and Divination Direction

Line 1-6: This yin line is improperly positioned at the bottom of the hexagram and correlates with 4-9. It is neither centered nor properly positioned, meaning that this man has the lowest status. As the beginning line of the lower trigram Mountain that denotes halt, he should stay where he is, but he has a friend with high status (4-9, the first line of the upper trigram Thunder, movement) who urges him to move.

The images signify that, like the fledgling bird that flies too high and gets caught in a disaster, this incompetent but ambitious man, wanting to be promoted to a higher position, makes the move when he is not yet ready for the position. There will be misfortune.

Divination Direction

Do not undertake anything that is beyond your capability, and act prudently based on a realistic assessment of your ability and resources.

Line 2-6: This yin line is properly positioned at the center of the lower trigram, correlating with no line. For the family, this hexagram represents the following: 3-9 the father, 4-9 the grandfather or ancestor, and 5-6 the grandmother or ancestress. In terms of social status, 3-9 represents the minister, 4-9 the prime minister, and 5-6 the ruler.

The images signify that in the family worship ceremony this genial woman bypasses her ancestor (4-9) to pay respect to the spirit of her ancestress (5-6). This may seem like a "Small Excess" or somewhat excessive in conduct. However, she will incur no blame for her conduct, as it is done out of her affinity toward her late grandmother. However, it is a different matter in the king's court. There, one (2-6) should not commit even small excess in his quest to meet the ruler; instead, he should meet with the minister (3-6) first, which will incur no error.

Divination Direction

Stay within your capability and resources, and you will succeed in your quest. Keep your mind open and accept the advice of the more experienced.

Line 3-9: This yang line is properly positioned at the top of the lower trigram, contiguous to 2-6, and correlates with 6-6. The four yin lines of this hexagram exert a constraining effect on the yang lines. This yang line has the potential to be aggressive because it is yang and away from the center.

The images signify that this man is overconfident and self-righteous; he is disdainful of others who look weak or unfriendly toward him. To the extent of paying a little too excessive attention, he should be careful about whom he follows. There may be someone coming to assail him, causing him an injury or death. There will be misfortune.

Divination Direction

It augurs ill. Be modest in your conduct. Beware of unsavory companions. Be careful with your speech and conduct that might be insulting to others or arouse jealousies in the mind of other people.

Line 4-9: This yang line is improperly positioned at the beginning of the upper trigram Thunder that denotes movement and correlates with 1-6. Being a yang line like 3-9 and being in the yin position, its movement is constrained by the yin lines.

The images signify that this competent prime minister conducts himself prudently. He does not commit the error of being intemperate in Small Excess, in spite of his improper position (yang in yin position indicates an aggressive urge). In his meeting with the ruler, he must keep in mind that it will be perilous if he tries to venture ahead to attain his own wishes. His conduct must be humble and cautious, for the favor he receives from the ruler is only temporary and will not last long. It is proper to stay for life on the correct course of *Tao*.

Divination Direction

It augurs ill. Go slowly at a deliberate pace as the situation presents itself. You will have only a small reward for your efforts and investment. It is the time to concentrate your efforts on cultivating your inner strength, rather than trying for an enterprising achievement.

Line 5-6: This yin line is improperly positioned at the center of the upper trigram, correlating with no line. The "western suburbs" below refers to the traditional observation that rain falls when clouds gather in the northeast, but it does not rain when they gather in the southwest (refers to a great leader waiting for a right time to bring about great achievements). Rain is formed when yin and yang interact harmoniously. In the era of the yin dominance when petty officials dominate, the virtuous but weak ruler cannot achieve his greatness by bringing together all the different talents of his subjects.

The images signify that in the era of Small Excess, the ruler cannot achieve greatness because yin has predominance over yang, and there is no harmony between the two. Although the ruler anticipates rain from the dense clouds gathering in the western suburbs, there is no rain. The dense clouds in the west symbolize that the opportunity to achieve order in the country is near. The ruler needs to bring his wise subjects (3-9, 4-9) who are in hiding or withdrawn from the state affairs into his regime to help him achieve greatness in the era of Small Excess. This will be as difficult as the ruler shooting arrows into a cave in an attempt to capture birds. The time is not yet ripe for a major undertaking.

Divination Direction

It is a hard time. You will have a tantalizing experience because you have come close and yet fallen a little short of reaching a successful conclusion. Be patient and proceed deliberately, as important achievement cannot be obtained in a hurry. Get the help of those with experience for your endeavor.

Line 6-6: This yin line is properly positioned at the top of the hexagram and correlates with 3-9. As the top line of the upper trigram Thunder, which denotes movement, it over-reaches its limit in movement in the era of Small Excess.

The images signify that this incompetent man (6-6) occupying the high office is unrestrained in his arrogance, and he does not have the sincerity to meet with the competent man (3-9) to handle the needs of the time properly. This is excessive arrogance, like the bird that keeps flying beyond its nest until it gets snared in a net, resulting in misfortune. It is a case of calamity and self-inflicted ruin.

Divination Direction

It augurs ill. Your arrogance will lead you to a calamitous failure. Cultivate your inner strength of self-discipline to control your excessive ambition and greed.

63. The Completion 既濟 (Ki Zi) Hexagram

Key attributes: Completion, consummation, the symbol of accomplishment

Judgment

"*Ki Zi* intimates progress and success in small matters. There will be advantage in being firm and correct. There has been good fortune in the beginning; there may be disorder in the end." (James Legge, *The I Ching*, 204.)

Essence of Hexagram

This hexagram explains the principle of maintaining what has been completed, which requires constant vigilance in tying up loose ends and taking measures to continue the progress.

Hexagram Image(s)

Water over Fire stands for the images of the Completion hexagram. When water that is being heated spills over the fire, it is a calamity, for the fire is extinguished (the image of completion). The wise and noble man uses the images as his guide to assess the danger of calamity and to take preventive measures. (On the other hand, when water and fire are properly arranged with care to carry out their respective functions, the task is satisfactorily completed.)

Hexagram Analysis

The Completion hexagram consists of the lower trigram Fire, which burns upward, and the upper trigram Water that flows downward. The upper trigram Water symbolizes internal strength with the yang line inside and two yin lines outside. The lower trigram Fire symbolizes external strength with yin line inside and two yang lines outside. The combined images indicate the opposite natures of the two elements. They can destroy each other when there is no harmonious relationship established, while their collaborative, harmonious relationship can bring beneficial achievements when they carry out their respective functions, as in cooking. Two Chinese characters are used to denote the Completion hexagram. One portrays what has been completed, and the other ferrying or crossing the stream, with the secondary meaning of helping and completing. The two characters together mean accomplishment or completion.

This is the most perfectly formed hexagram of the sixty-four hexagrams, and it denotes the concept of Completion. Each line of this hexagram is properly positioned in perfect alignment, with each yin line in the yin position and each yang line in the yang position. Moreover, each line of the hexagram has a correlating line. In this hexagram, the major goal has been achieved (reached the apex) and, as with everything, decline follows. Therefore, after the main goal is accomplished, the inevitable small details or loose ends that remain must be addressed, which, when neglected, will result in decay and deterioration. This hexagram refers to the historical episode in the experience of King *Wan*, who founded his feudal state and finally attained peace after years of perilous disorders by successfully ferrying the ship of state across the dangerous water. When peace was achieved, there remained smaller tasks that needed to be addressed, requiring constant vigilance and management skills.

2-6 is the sole lead line of this hexagram.

Interpretation of Judgment

"Hexagram Completion intimates progress and success" in the judgment text means that when constant and judicious attention is given to everything, even to the small and petty (yin line), there is progress and success. Because this hexagram has both the hard (yang) and the soft (yin) lines that are all properly positioned, it is to one's advantage to observe the correct principles of *Tao*, irrespective of how small the matter might be. The soft (yin) occupying the center (2-6) of the lower trigram means "good fortune in the beginning" for the successful completion of important tasks by the virtuous who practices the Mean. In the era of the Completion hexagram, people become so complacent with their achievement that they may cease making continuing efforts to handle daily tasks properly, or to deal with the new situations in ways that are in accord with the correct principles of *Tao*. There will be "disorder in the end," and chaos will ensue, because the practice of *Tao* became blocked.

Divination Direction

At present, you are enjoying peace of mind at the apex of your good fortune. However, your fortune will start to decline sooner or later. This calls for making preparations to delay or minimize it. You may experience distress and sickness from unexpected difficulties. Be alert and prepared for any contingencies in your life. It is favorable to conclude a marital arrangement or to travel.

Individual Lines: Analysis, Interpretation, and Divination Direction

Line 1-9: This yang line is properly positioned at the bottom of the lower trigram Fire and correlates with 4-6. In the line text, this line is compared to a fox, and "wet his tail" refers to the fox's habit of raising his tail above water when it wades across a stream. Fire burns upward, and as the first line of the trigram Fire, this line exhibits a strong urge to move upward to collaborate with 4-6. This urge must be restrained to avoid misfortune.

The images signify that, in the era of Completion, the great goal has been achieved and everything is moving forward. But, there is danger in continuing to move ahead without paying attention to minor details that need to be worked on or without maintaining a clear vision on the direction. It is the time to proceed deliberately and carefully, like applying the brakes to slow down the cart. A rushed action will result in a misfortune, like the fox that gets its tail wet. There will be no error.

Divination Direction

It is respite time for you; go slowly at best, even with minor matters that can cause you unexpected difficulties. An aggressive movement without careful planning will put you in a difficult predicament.

Line 2-6: This yin line is properly positioned at the center of the lower trigram, contiguous to 3-9 and correlating with 5-9. This line emphasizes that, in the era of Completion, major objectives have been achieved but there are still minor evil acts that need to be addressed, and the moral integrity and the rectitude of *Tao* must prevail over them as well. The line text reference "in seven days" refers to the line cycle of a hexagram, in which a line returns to its original position on the seventh move.

The images signify that this virtuous loyal man (2-6) wants to respond to the ruler's (5-9) invitation to come and serve in his court, but his departure is delayed because someone places an obstacle (upper trigram Water) in his way, and he cannot proceed. He should wait for a new opportunity that is bound to come (a person's virtuous quality will always find a good use, even if it is not in use temporarily). The situation is like the wife who cannot travel to see her husband (5-9) because the screen of her carriage that hides her from public view was lost. She should not look for it and maintain the virtues of the Mean; it will be returned in seven days when this time cycle has ended.

Divination Direction

Your problem is temporary, and you need not be overly anxious about it. A good opportunity will open up for you. Be in firm control of your emotions and prepare for the opportunity.

Line 3-9: This yang line is properly positioned at the top of the lower trigram and correlates with 6-6. This line refers to the perils of the expedition, which was conducted to secure the borders of the state following the successful stabilization of the state (Completion). The historical event of King *Kao Zung* (King *Wu Ting* of *Shang* dynasty, 1364–1324 B.C.) is used here as the analogy.

The images signify that minor or large tasks to be undertaken following the completion of a main objective must be attended to with a great deal of caution and effort, especially so when a military mobilization is required. The risk inherent in a military mobilization is evidenced in the case of King *Kao Zung*'s colonization expedition. Even such an outstanding sovereign as King *Kao Zung* who attacked the "Demon" territory (the barbarian territory northwest of the mainland) to colonize it took as many as three years to subdue it and, in the process, he exhausted both human and material resources. Such an expedition should not be assigned to a petty man.

Divination Direction

It is not the proper time to initiate a new enterprise. Pay close attention to what you are doing now. Do not neglect small details for successful completion of each task before preparing for a new opportunity.

Line 4-6: This line is properly positioned at the bottom of the upper trigram Water. The era of Completion has entered into its second half with some signs of decline, like a ferryboat in which water (upper trigram) is beginning to leak.

The images signify that there are some signs of deterioration in the stability of the state. In the complacency of peace and stability, some unexpected problems occur. In dealing with the situation, one must pay close attention and act quickly, like, in the situation of the leaking ferryboat, stopping the leaks with rags. One has to be on guard all day long, as there are always new situations that need to be addressed.

Divination Direction

It augurs ill. You have reached the stage in which accumulated problems begin to break loose. You must act quickly to deal with each situation, which will not leave much time for you to pursue a new goal.

Line 5-9: This yang line is properly positioned at the center of the upper trigram and correlates with 2-6. "Neighbor State in the east"[49] in the line text refers to 5-9, and the "Neighbor State in the west" to 2-6. This line emphasizes that one's sincerity is more important than rituals or religious offerings. In the mellowing stage of the Completion era, this line warns against materialistic indulgence and spiritual laxity.

The images signify that the strong neighboring state in the east (5-9) makes an extravagant sacrificial offering by slaughtering an ox[50] (lavish and superficial), which falls short of the meager but sincere and timely sacrificial offering made by the neighboring state in the west (2-6). The sincerity of the western state will be blessed with great good fortune.

Divination Direction

You must cultivate self-discipline and refrain from being boastful and materialistically indulgent. You will fall short of attaining your goal.

Line 6-6: This yin line is properly positioned at the top of both the hexagram and the upper trigram Water. The era of Completion has reached its apogee with signs of its decline. This high official has become so accustomed to peace and prosperity in the Completion era that he is not attentive to the emerging sign of its decline, which will result in an inevitable misfortune.

The images signify that an ending requires as much calm and effective attention as the beginning; complacency in the era of Completion will lead one to disaster. It is analogous to a ferryboat sailing smoothly that capsizes just before it lands because the person in it becomes too excited, or looks back being vainglorious of his achievement. He goes overboard, and his head gets immersed in the water. It is a dangerous time, and there will be a disaster before long.

Divination Direction

It augurs ill. You are faced with a danger that may bring all your cumulative efforts to failure. You will have the tantalizing experience of always falling a little short of success. Move at a deliberate pace and approach every step with prudence.

64. The Incomplete 未濟 (Wei Zi) Hexagram

Key attributes: Short of completion, the symbol of what is not yet accomplished

Judgment

"*Wei Zi* intimates progress and success (in the circumstances which it implies). (We see) a young fox that has nearly crossed (the stream), when its tail gets immersed. There will be no advantage in any way." (James Legge, *The I Ching*, 207.)

Essence of Hexagram

This hexagram explains the principle of completing a task successfully through constant efforts to the end, continually assessing the forces that influence the attainment of a goal.

Hexagram Image(s)

Fire above Water stands for the images of the Incomplete hexagram. In order to complete a task, proper arrangements of tools and procedural priorities must be established. The wise and noble man uses the images as his guide in classifying each thing[51] according to its nature and function so that it can carry out its proper functions effectively in completing a task.

As an example, Fire burns upward (south) and Water flows downward (north). When these two elements are placed improperly for cooking, they do not produce the heat that is needed, and the cooking cannot be completed. Fire also symbolizes clarity, and Water the efforts; clarity must always precede efforts. In the Incomplete hexagram, efforts precede clarity, which is contrary to the natural sequence to achieve progress toward completion.

Hexagram Analysis

This hexagram consists of the lower trigram Water, which flows downward, and the upper trigram Fire that burns upward. The combined images indicate that there is no interplay between the two elements to complete their collaborative functions, creating the image of Incomplete. None of the six lines is in its proper position, denoting incompletion. However, every line has its proper correlation, denoting the potential for favorable auspices. Hexagram #63 Completion represents autumn, after which winter follows; this hexagram represents spring that comes out of the freezing winter and leads into prolific summer.

This hexagram portrays the hopeful but difficult task of bringing the disordered state out of its stagnation to an orderly and productive state. Such a task requires one to be constantly cautious, like the fox walking over ice.

The Incomplete hexagram is the last of the sixty-four hexagrams and follows the Complete hexagram. Thus, it embodies the central concept in *I Ching* that everything is in a state of constant change, that nothing ever attains a state of perfection that will not entail further change. This is the basis of *"I"* in *I Ching*, representing changes in the *Book of Changes*. With an ending, there is always a new beginning.

The good auspices of this hexagram derive from the yin line occupying the center of the upper trigram (5-6) and its correlative relationship with 2-9. It symbolizes that the virtuous ruler works effectively with the loyal subject (2-9) for the benefit of the people. The "young fox" in the judgment text refers to 1-6, denoting one who is immature and inexperienced and mired in danger (lower trigram Water), due to his impulsive venture to cross a deep stream, like the fox that is forced to get its tail wet.

5-6 is the sole lead line of this hexagram.

Interpretation of Judgment

The Incomplete hexagram stands for the images of progress and success, as the soft (yin, 5-6) occupies the center as the virtuous ruler. In the era of Incomplete, it is as improper for an immature or inexperienced person to venture into an activity imprudently as it is for a young fox (1-6) to venture forth to cross a deep stream. The fox gets exhausted toward the end and is unable to reach the shore; it ends up getting its tail wet in the water during its struggle to survive. There is no advantage in undertaking an important venture unprepared and without prudence, as it will not come to a successful end. On the other hand, the auspices of this hexagram are not all unfavorable; the yin and yang lines correlate with each other, even though they are not properly positioned. The cooperation between the correlating lines will bring good fortune.

Divination Direction

Although you are still confused and do not know what to do, you see a light at the end of the tunnel. Your situation cannot get worse than it is now and will get better gradually. Be patient and prepare for opportunities that will come before long. Calm down and assess the situation accurately before you act. You will find help if you seek it.

Individual Lines: Analysis, Interpretation, and Divination Direction

Line 1-6: This yin line is improperly positioned at the bottom of the hexagram Incomplete and correlates with 4-9. In the unsettling era of Incomplete, one has to be prudent in every action. Otherwise, one will experience a regrettable result. The lower trigram Water denotes peril, and the immature and inexperienced (1-6) should not commit the folly of undertaking an ambitious venture just because he has a friend high up in the government (4-9) or he relies on another person's whims.

The images signify that this immature and inexperienced man ventures forth to seek an important office without understanding the limit of his ability, like a young fox that ventures forth to cross a big stream and ends up getting its tail wet from exhaustion. He will have regret.

Divination Direction

It is still premature to actively pursue your goal. Your rash action will result in failure. Assess the situation and your ability accurately to prevent a wrong move and wait for a better opportunity to act.

Line 2-9: This yang line is improperly positioned at the center of the lower trigram Water and correlates with 5-6. This competent man practices the Mean, and his conduct is moderate.

The images signify that many important tasks need to be worked on to bring order to the state, and this virtuous, competent man has strong confidence in the virtuous ruler (5-6) to bring order. He maintains his proper conduct, waiting to serve the virtuous ruler when he is invited to come and help. The era of Incomplete has numerous unseen pitfalls (lower trigram Water). In such a time, while waiting patiently, this man steadfastly maintains the correct principles of *Tao* and conducts himself properly without deviating from the virtues of the Mean. It is like braking the wheels of his carriage (slowing down) to measure the prudence of his conduct each step of the way. He will have good fortune.

Divination Direction

The time is not yet ripe to actively pursue your goal. Do more preparations and await a better opportunity.

Line 3-6: This yin line is improperly positioned at the top of the lower trigram Water and correlates with 6-9. Being at the top, it is about to get out of its perilous situation and move into the enlightenment stage (upper trigram Light). The upper trigram Water of the primary nuclear hexagram indicates that another perilous stage is lurking before the enlightenment stage arrives. Another perilous stage prevents this line from taking advantage of its correlative relationship with 6-9, forcing it to be extremely careful in its movement.

The images signify that, in the era of Incomplete, this man, who has an improper position for which he is not qualified, should not undertake an ambitious venture to advance, as it will result in misfortune. Even if he gets outside assistance for the undertaking, it will be to his advantage to conduct himself as cautiously as if he were crossing a great stream.

Divination Direction

You are still mired in a difficult situation, but your hardship will end soon, and a new opportunity will open up for you before long. Be patient and prepare yourself for the opportunity.

Line 4-9: This yang line is improperly positioned at the beginning of the upper trigram Light, denoting the beginning of the era of enlightenment; it correlates with 1-9. The correct *Tao* for this competent prime minister is to concentrate his full energy to assist the virtuous and gentle ruler to govern the state and not diffuse his energy to look after the inexperienced office seeker (1-9).

The images signify that, in the era of Incomplete, concentrated efforts must be made in order to achieve the difficult task of putting the state in order. This competent prime minister lives up to the correct principles of *Tao* and carries out his ardent intent to serve the ruler well, and his concerns about his suitability for the task disappear. Encouraged, he sets out to conquer the "Demon" barbarian territory, or the degenerative forces (quell the rebels who oppose the new order). It took as long as three years to complete the conquest, after which his ruler of the great kingdom honored him with awards.

Divination Direction

It augurs well. Shake off your worries and petty concerns and actively pursue to achieve your goal, but take every step prudently without taking a rash action for a quick reward.

Line 5-6: This yin line is improperly positioned at the center of the upper trigram Light that denotes enlightenment, correlating with 2-9. This is the lead line and symbolizes the glory of the enlightened governance of the ruler (upper trigram Light) that is extended to everyone in the state. This virtuous and gentle ruler practices the virtues of the Mean and has the services of talented people (2-9 and 4-9) who help him govern the state and subdue the invaders (rebels).

The images signify that this virtuous ruler who abides by the correct principles of *Tao* has won the battle over evil forces to bring order and makes any concern about his shortcomings (yin line in yang position) disappear. His glorious virtues reach the people as if he has a halo, and his sincerity will bring good fortune.

Divination Direction

It augurs well. Your goal will be attained. Seek the cooperation of those with ability and experience to help you achieve your goal.

Line 6-9: This yang line is improperly positioned at the top of the hexagram, denoting that the era of Incomplete is nearing its end with a new era approaching. The ruler (5-6) has achieved peace and stability in his state, and this well-respected retiree (6-9) deserves to relax and enjoy his life; no one will blame him.

The images signify that this sincere and confident man, after having completed his tasks to help stabilize the state, now spends his days engaging in drinking wine and feasting. He will incur no blame for it. However, if he does not temper himself but keeps drinking until he is immersed in wine to his head, he is in violation of the Mean and will end up losing his sincerity and confidence. It is important to maintain sincerity and confidence in order to adapt in the ensuing era.

Divination Direction

Be careful of becoming arrogant and overconfident over your success. If you have achieved your goal, celebrate it, but with temperance in feasting or material luxuries.

I Ching **establishes the principle of perpetual cycle, with change as a constant. Hexagram #64 Incomplete follows Hexagram #63 Completion, in order to attain the major accomplishment before the new cycle begins with Hexagram #1 Heaven to bring forth creation.**

Notes

PREFACE

¹ ***Tao*** is a metaphysical concept relating to the creation and functioning of the universe. Everything in the universe originates in *Tao* and works on the principles of *Tao*. *Tao* nourishes everything but does not dictate. According to *Han Fei Tzu*, Chinese scholar in early third century, *Tao* is the state or condition in which all principles agree. Each thing has its own principle, and when all the things are carried out in accordance with each and every principle, *Tao* has been attained. *Tao* is commonly referred to as nature's way and "the constancy." Constancy is the concept of *Tao* as one constant truth, and each operational principle of *Tao* represented in nature is also referred to as *Tao*.

² ***The Book of Changes*** is called *Chou I* or *Book of Changes of the Chou Dynasty*. Two earlier books on divination did not survive.

³ **Binary system** The sixty-four hexagrams of *I Ching* are composed of only two numbers, yin as 0 and yang as 1. Each hexagram numerically stands for a number from 0 through 63, expressed in the binary system that corresponds to a power of 2.

⁴ **Ancient Chinese sages** Four sages most often mentioned as the sage kings in *I Ching* are *Fu Hsi, King Yu* of *Hsia, King Tang* of *Shang (Yin),* and *King Wan* of *Chou. Fu Hsi* is the first of the five legendary sage rulers in the Neolithic period. *King Yu* became king following his successful control of a great flood, and he established the *Hsia* dynasty (2207–1766 B.C.), which had fourteen rulers. *Tang* overthrew *King Jie*, a tyrant and last king of *Hsia. Tang* established his own *Shang* or *Yin* dynasty. This dynasty lasted through thirty-three rulers until the self-indulgent *King Zhou* was overthrown by *Wu* of *Chou*, a son of *King Wan (King Wu* elevated his father to king posthumously).

PART I THE OVERVIEW OF I CHING

CHAPTER 1   INTRODUCTION TO *I CHING*

[5] ***Shi I* (*Ten Wings*)** The ten appendices to the original *I Ching* texts by Confucius are as follows:

1-2: treatise on individual hexagrams with interpretation of its judgment (*Tuan* or *Thwan*)

3-4: treatise on the symbolism of hexagrams and hexagram lines

5-6: the "Great Commentary" or "Great Appendix," interpreting the trigrams and hexagrams in the cultural and historic contexts

7: explanations of the first hexagram, Heaven, and the second hexagram, Earth, on their attributes in connection with man

8: structural analysis of hexagrams and discourse on trigrams

9: treatise on the sequence of the hexagrams

10: miscellaneous comments on the structurally contrasting hexagrams

[6] **Five Confucian Classics** *I Ching, Shu Ching* (*Book of History*), *Shih Ching* (*Book of Odes*), *Li Chi* or (*Book of Rituals*), and *Ch'un Ch'iu* (*Spring and Autumn Annals*).

CHAPTER 2   THE ORIGIN OF YIN AND YANG

[7] ***Lao Tzu*** Father of Taoism and author of *Tao Teh Ching*, in which he advocated *"Wu wei"* or "doing nothing." "Doing nothing" is to follow nature's way without any artificial manipulation of nature. His followers criticized Confucius's codes of human conduct as a human contrivance that upset the natural order.

[8] **The concept of major and minor** The energy of yin and yang moves clockwise. It begins with minor and develops into major. Yin has yang element in it, and yang has yin element in it. In the diagram of *Fu Shi*'s trigram that is known as the "Sequence of Early Heaven," the trigrams on the left side—Thunder, Light, Lake, and Heaven—are yang energies, of which Light and Lake represent the yin energies in yang, and each is called *minor yin*. The trigrams on the right side—Wind, Water, Mountain, and Earth—are yin energies, of which Water and Mountain represent the yang energies in yin, and each is called *minor yang*. Note how the single line that is different from the other two in each trigram determines its energy category. (In the Heaven and Earth trigrams, all three lines of each trigram are treated as one, Heaven as major yang and Earth as major yin.)

CHAPTER 5 THE *I CHING* MAPS AND NUMBERS

[9] **King *Yu*** See note 4 on ancient Chinese sages.

PART II THE SIXTY-FOUR HEXAGRAMS

HEXAGRAM #1 HEAVEN

[10] **The great man** The great man has the attributes that are in harmony with Heaven and Earth; in his brightness, with the sun and the moon; with the four seasons in his orderliness. He conducts himself in accord with *Tao* of Heaven and Earth.

[11] **Line 6-9 Keep speeding upward** Confucius commented that 6-9 appears to be highest in status, but he has no status because the fifth line is the ruler's position. As he keeps lifting himself higher and higher, there is no one who can follow him to serve. He is so arrogant that he will be doomed.

HEXAGRAM #3 GERMINATION

[12] **1-9** The Chinese character in this hexagram (屯), portrays the dynamism of this line, a leaf of grass (−) breaking out of the earth (屯).

HEXAGRAM #4 THE INEXPERIENCE

[13] **Principles of education** In ancient China, there were six areas emphasized in education: rituals, music, archery, horseback riding, calligraphy, and mathematics.

HEXAGRAM #5 THE DELAYING

[14] **2-9** This line is close to the upper trigram Water, and sand is used as the metaphor for this line.

HEXAGRAM #6 THE CONFLICT

[15] **Major preventive measures** They are: look after one's health before one becomes sick, discipline oneself before a greedy mind takes over, and govern the state well before it becomes disorderly.

[16] **Subsists on bequest (old virtues)** The Chinese character for "virtues" in the Chinese text means government remuneration. "Old virtues" means the bequest of such government award accorded to one's ancestor(s).

[17] **In the short span of one day** "Before the breakfast" means within a very short period of time.

HEXAGRAM #7 THE HOST

[18] **The host** In the ancient Chinese military organization, the word "host" represented twenty-five hundred personnel.

[19] **Issue orders to reward** The king rewarded the most meritorious with one thousand chariots and feudal lands to rule; the less meritorious was rewarded with one hundred chariots and smaller areas of land to rule, such as the marquisette. All others received no land to rule over.

HEXAGRAM #8 THE UNION

[20] **Always provided an escape route** There is a related ancient Chinese anecdote. One day, King *Tang,* founder of the *Shang* dynasty, met a person in his field trip who was praying that all the hunting game and birds in the state be snared in his traps and nets. The king thought, "If that is to be, soon there will be no animal or bird left to catch." He ordered that if one escapes to the left to let it go, and if one escapes to the right to let it go; if fate drives one into the snare, so be it that it be caught.

HEXAGRAM #9 THE MINOR RESTRAINT

[21] **No rain coming from our borders in the west** Rain symbolizes blessings to all beings. Coming from the west, where the family of Chou was situated, suggests that the family of Chou was worthy to be the ruler of the whole state, which was under the tyrannical rule of the *Yin* dynasty king. No rain with gathering clouds indicates that the family of Chou has not yet taken over the rule of the whole state while the people of the state are eagerly waiting for it.

HEXAGRAM #11 THE PEACE

[22] **Rush plant** Also called *couch grass*, it is slender, sharp-edged grass. Its roots are interconnected. Therefore, when one plant is pulled up, the other plants come up with it.

[23] There is a historical reference here. King *Tang* of the *Shang* dynasty married his daughter off to his trusted subject, who was loyal and competent but whose social status was not high.

[24] The Chinese character for this moat indicates that it is a dry moat. A moat without water is a sign that the city is not well defended.

HEXAGRAM #13 THE COMPANIONSHIP

[25] "The wide open field" means that the fair and harmonious influence of the noble man or the ruler is extended widely to a large number of people. The Chinese people believe that an ideal society existed in ancient

China where the wealth was shared among all the people in the society. There were no private properties, and there was no need to lock the house.

HEXAGRAM #20 THE OBSERVATION

[26] Following the ritual of absolution, a small amount of fragrant herbal wine is poured over the ground to invoke the spirit to be present for the ceremony. The sacrificial offering is then presented to the spirit.

HEXAGRAM #28 THE LARGE EXCESS

[27] To invoke the spirit to be present for the ceremony, the mat is placed on soft white lawn grass on which a small amount of wine is poured. The mat is also used to place the offering containers on it. The white color of the grass symbolizes purity of mind.

HEXAGRAM #30 THE CLINGING

[28] There are two different interpretations for "very old man" (3-9): one is a person who is eighty years old and the other, seventy years old.

HEXAGRAM #31 THE INFLUENCE

[29] The *Ten Wings* interprets this line through natural phenomena as the model of mutual influences without selfish motivation. It states, "What thought or worry would the universe have? There are different routes, but all return to the same destiny; when the sun goes, the moon comes; when the moon goes, the sun comes. The sun and the moon take turns to generate the light. When cold goes, heat comes; when heat goes, cold comes. Cold and heat take turns to make a year."

HEXAGRAM #35 THE ADVANCE

[30] This hexagram describes the harmonious relationship that existed between King *Wu* of the *Chou* dynasty and his youngest brother, the Marquis of Peace. Later, the youngest brother served the king in a position equivalent to the minister of justice.

HEXAGRAM #36 THE DARKENING

[31] The tyrant King *Zhou* of the *Yin* dynasty put King *Wan* in prison in a place called *Yuri* before the kingdom of *Yin* was conquered by King *Wan's* son. Even though King *Wan's* popularity was sufficient to overthrow the tyrant king, he served the king obediently and endured prison life. It is said that he worked on the hexagrams of *I Ching* in prison.

HEXAGRAM #42 THE INCREASE

³² **Jade object** A scepter or the wand of office, made of jade, to certify the bearer's rank in the government (symbol of trust).

HEXAGRAM #46 THE RISING AND ADVANCING

³³ **Religious ceremonial rites** The king of the state held ceremonial rites to worship the spirits of Heaven and Earth, and the feudal lord held rites for the spirits of the mountains, rivers, and the feudal land under his jurisdiction.

³⁴ **Mt. *Khi*** The kingdom of *Yin* was situated east of its feudal state of *Chou*. The name Mount *Khi* comes from the twin peaks of the mountain at the western border of *Chou*.

HEXAGRAM #47 THE OPPRESSION

³⁵ **Vermilion knee cover** Ancient ceremonial attire that hangs down to cover the knees.

HEXAGRAM #48 THE WELL

³⁶ The Chinese character for the well (井) is descriptive of the well: in the center, surrounded by eight families, which share the well among them. In the political system of the state, the center symbolizes the government.

HEXAGRAM #49 THE REVOLUTION

³⁷ Trigram Lake represents Metal in the Five Elements. The lower trigram Fire can bring about a radical change to the metal by melting it.

³⁸ *Tang* overthrew the tyrant king *Jie* of *Hsia* dynasty and became the first king of *Shang (Yin)* dynasty. *Wu,* the eldest son of King *Wan,* overthrew the tyrant king *Zhou* of *Yin,* became king, and elevated his father as the first king of the *Chou* dynasty.

HEXAGRAM #50 THE CAULDRON

³⁹ **Severe punishment** was meted out not only to the official who committed the crime, but also to the family clans of both parents.

HEXAGRAM #52 THE CHECKING

⁴⁰ In ancient China, all family rituals were conducted in the family's courtyard.

⁴¹ Organ senses of ears, eyes, nose, and mouth are located in the front side of the human body, and "to not be conscious of them" means not to be greedy or self-centered.

HEXAGRAM #53 THE PROGRESSIVE ADVANCE

⁴² **Six matrimonial steps** The steps are: first, marriage proposal, usually initiated by the family of the groom through a go-between; second, the formal asking of the would-be bride's name; third, the groom's report of the matrimonial plan to his ancestral spirits; fourth, formal consent of the marriage by both families; fifth, the agreement of the bride's family on the wedding date and wedding site (usually in the bride's home); sixth, the ceremony of welcoming the bride into the groom's family.

HEXAGRAM #54 THE MARRYING MAIDEN

⁴³ *Ti-yi* was a king in the *Yin* dynasty and father of the tyrant king *Zhou*.

HEXAGRAM #56 THE WANDERER

⁴⁴ The Chinese character for this hexagram Wanderer or Traveling also means a large number of people, or a traveling army brigade of five hundred soldiers that encamps in temporary sites during a military campaign.

⁴⁵ A cow is a gentle and friendly animal, and to lose a cow symbolizes losing the virtue of being gentle and friendly.

HEXAGRAM #59 THE DISSOLUTION

⁴⁶ The ceremony conducted with sincerity would bring the spirits of ancestors together from their different locations in the spiritual world to help the offspring solve problems or overcome difficulties.

HEXAGRAM #61 THE CENTRAL SINCERITY

⁴⁷ Chinese character for sincerity is (孚), which is made up of (爫) symbolizing the nails of feet and (子) child. The combined image of the ideogram is the maternal protection of her child with love and care.

⁴⁸ **The crane calling to its offspring** The *Ten Wings* explains that when a nobleman says good words in his room, the words travel beyond his room and reach people thousands of miles away, not to speak of those living nearer to him, and the people respond to them. If he says bad words in his room, they will affect the people negatively, and they distance the people from him. This line emphasizes the importance of one's speech and conduct.

HEXAGRAM #63 THE COMPLETION

⁴⁹ **Neighbor State** The people of the feudal state of *Chou* called their state the West land, and the kingdom of *Yin* the East land. In this hexagram, 2-9 represents the western neighbor state and 5-9 the eastern Neighbor state.

⁵⁰ **Slaughtering an ox** Sacrificial offering of an ox is regarded to be a generous offering, and that of a pig or fish is regarded as meager.

HEXAGRAM #64 THE INCOMPLETE

⁵¹ **Classifying each thing** Not only in things like plants, animals, and tools, but in the areas of personnel management, the noble man and the petty man must be classified, and each must be assigned a proper role to carry out properly.

Bibliography

Chinese

Kong Yinda, ed. *Correct Meaning of the I Ching:* Taipei: Yi Wan Publishing, 1955. (Commentaries on the thirteen classics)

Wang Bi, ed. *General Comments on Chou I.* Beijing: Zhonghua Shuju, 1980.

—————. *Commentary on Chou I.* Beijing: Zhonghua Shuju, 1980.

Li Guengdi, ed. *Imperial Compilation on Interpretations of I Ching.* 1715; Taipei: Chengwen, 1975.

Zhu Xi. Enlightenment on I Ching. Hu Guang Zhuan, ed. 1414; Seoul: Myung Moon Dang, 1981.

English

Anthony, Carol K. *A Guide to the I Ching.* Massachusetts: Anthony Publishing Co., 1988.

Legge, James. *The I Ching: The Book of Changes. Ch'u Chai and Winberg Chai,* eds. New Hyde Park, New York: University Books, 1964.

—————. *The I Ching: The Book of Changes.* 1882; New York: Dover, 1965.

Lynn, Richard John. *The Classic of Changes: A New Translation of the I Ching, As Interpreted by Wang Bi.* New York: Columbia University Press, 1994.

Ni, Hua-Ching. I Ching, The Book of Changes and the Unchanging Truth. Santa Monica, Calif.: Sevenstar Communications Group, Inc., 1994.

Ponce, Charles. *The Nature of I Ching, Its Usage and Interpretation.* New York: Award Books, 1970.

Ritseman, Rudolf, and Karcher, Stephen. *I Ching, The Classic Chinese Oracle of Change: The First Complete Translation with Concordance.* New York: Barnes & Noble Books, 1994.

Wilhelm, Richard. *The I Ching or Book of Changes.* 3rd ed. Trans., Cary F. Baynes. Princeton, N.J.: Princeton University Press, 1967.

Korean (with Chinese text):

Il Bong Park. Chou I. Oriental Classic Series #12. Seoul: Yook Moon Publishing Co., 1994.

————. *The Doctrine of the Mean.* Oriental Classic Series #3. Seoul: Yook Moon Publishing Co., 1994.

————. *Tao Teh Ching.* Oriental Classic Series #9. Seoul: Yook Moon Publishing Co., 1994.

Korean *Chou I* Society. *Modern Perspectives on Chou I. Chou I Study Series* #1. Seoul: Beum Yang Publishing Co., 1992.

Index